942.07
BUS
G20937.

ST. PAUL'S SCHOOL LIBRARY WITHDRAWN
LONSDALE ROAD, SW13 9JT

BY RITE

Custom, Ceremony and Community in
England 1700–1880

D1419827

BY RITE

Custom, Ceremony and Community in England 1700–1880

Bob Bushaway

JUNCTION BOOKS   LONDON

© 1982 Bob Bushaway

First published in Great Britain by
Junction Books Ltd
15 St John's Hill
London SW11

ISBN   0 86245 072 1   (hard)
          0 86245 073 X   (paper)

All rights reserved. No part of this publication may be reproduced,
transmitted or stored in any retrieval system, in any form or by any
means, without permission in writing from the publisher.

Printed and bound in Great Britain by
Biddles Ltd, Guildford and King's Lynn

Contents

For my parents

Introduction

Victorian collectors of folk songs and customs, who forayed out of their smoky cities into the English countryside, prized their 'finds' as quaint and precious artefacts of a way of life which they perceived of as long since lost. The customs and rituals which they recovered were as unknown to them as if they had been found among African tribes or desert nomads.

Thomas Hardy believed that the rate of change in rural England had accelerated dramatically in his lifetime. He characterised the cultural difference between Tess and her mother in terms of centuries rather than a single generation:

> Between the mother, with her fast-perishing lumber of superstitions, folk-lore, dialect, and orally-transmitted ballads, and the daughter with her trained National teaching and Standard knowledge under an infinitely Revised Code, there was a gap of two hundred years as ordinarily understood. When they were together the Jacobean and the Victorian ages were juxtaposed.[1]

Yet much of the customary framework within which were conducted the social and economic relationships of the English rural community during Hardy's lifetime had been transmitted forward from the later Middle Ages and early modern period to the eighteenth and nineteenth centuries when, far from being a scattered collection of picturesque 'survivals', it remained, at least for the greater part of the Hanoverian and Victorian period, an essential context for the community, informing the lives and experiences of both the labouring poor and the rural elite alike.

This book aims to examine popular custom in rural society during the period 1700 to 1880, against the background of social and economic change, and to consider how the framework of customary practice was maintained and what forms it took. In particular, custom linked together the components of the local community calendar, and reflected, on the one hand, the symbolism of social cohesion in which the rural labourer was able to defend popular rights, and, on the other, provided models for socially disruptive behaviour and established a cultural environment for more orthodox movements of social protest. Much more than the vestigial remains of pagan belief, the function of custom and usage during this period was essentially social and economic.

The study focuses on rural communities in southern England. In general, the term 'rural community' has been taken to mean single communities such as villages and hamlets, but has occasionally been extended to include market towns and, in some instances, customary activities which took place in cities but which were important for the surrounding area have been included. Those who took part in collective rituals, whether in village or town, during the eighteenth and nineteenth centuries made reference to similar customary frameworks. The work concentrates on southern England because it is important to consider a reasonably coherent area in order to observe similarities between certain customs and rituals and their impact on different locations within that area. Much of the source material which I have used, and, in particular, the local newspapers, have been concerned with southern England. Despite the principal focus, I have occasionally extended the study to include comparisons and contrasts with other regions so that a more comprehensive analysis can be made.

The main feature of the customary framework which supported the rural community during this period was the balance between customary sanction and collective privilege. The effect on this balance of the changing social position of one section of rural society – farmers, landowners, proprietors – can be traced in the conflict which took place over the maintenance of popular customs. In response, some customs were adapted by the labouring poor to protect long-held rights. Popular customary collective behaviour sought to preserve such rights as gleaning, fuel gathering, access to recreational venues, and non-institutionalised largess collections, by binding them in ceremony and ritual often adapted from older forms or other festivals.

The book opens with an introductory chapter which

attempts to explain the context of custom by illustrating that historical continuity was seen as the principal requirement for any kind of collective action to be characterised as 'customary'. Some legal opinion in the eighteenth century strove to undermine the notion of custom and replace it with the certainties of statute law. From this it can be seen that an official culture was often in conflict with unofficial popular morality. Chapter 2 represents an endeavour to reconstruct several local customary calendars for the eighteenth and nineteenth centuries and to show that the efforts of folklorists and others have resulted in the construction of artificial regional or even national calendars of custom and usage which destroy local specificity. In fact, the local calendar was made up of several different kinds of calendar relating to the range of experience within village life, from work and leisure to parish or manor government. The relationship of one particular group within the community whose role was shaped by customary practice – the church ringers – to the local calendar is also examined.

Chapter 3 examines some aspects of the notion of legitimation and suggests that, in part, the collective action of the labouring poor which took place on certain customary dates until the mid-nineteenth century, was legitimated by reference to church and manor practice, particularly the annual state services which were celebrated in the parish church, and the structure of manorial organisation. Thus, parish perambulations during Rogation Week, Guy Fawkes night celebrations, and Oak Apple Day customs were reinforced. Chapter 4, by concentrating on an examination of harvest practices, considers the socially cohesive nature of custom and assesses its importance for the labouring poor. Chapter 5 illustrates the socially disruptive side of other customs and rituals and relates them to forms of collective action adopted during periods of more overtly political social protest, in particular the Captain Swing disturbances.

Wood gatherers whose actions had previously been legitimated by reference to custom found, during the later eighteenth century, that statute law had eroded their right and cast them in the role of wood stealer. Chapter 6 looks at the struggle between custom and law in the context of the poor's belief in a general customary right to collect wood for fuel.

3

Chapter 7 deals with the suppression of many customs in the mid-nineteenth century, and describes the change from village feast to benefit club day (which transformed one of them). The chapter concludes with an account of the deliberate attempt to remodel some customs, such as the harvest home supper, to conform with and promote more acceptable values of sobriety and good order, and to recreate a kind of deferential community orderliness, supposed by some Victorian writers and painters to recall former times.

I should like to acknowledge the Warden and Scholars of Winchester College for permission to quote from documents in their possession and to record my thanks to the staff of the British Library, the Public Record Office, and the record offices for the counties of Dorset, Hampshire, West Sussex and Wiltshire, and the library of the Wiltshire Archaelogical and Natural History Society at Devizes, for all the assistance which was given to me. My thanks are also due to John Rule whose help and encouragement have been inestimable, and to Walter Minchinton, guiding hand of the Exeter Economic History Paper series, in whose pages earlier versions of some of my work appear. Any errors which remain are, of course, my responsibility.

Others who have greatly assisted my work include Bill Jones, Brian Luffman, Fred Mather, Len Smith and William Tyler, I should like to thank Michael Mason of Junction Books for his patience and kind assistance in the production of my work, and Barbara Davies and Sally Murray for typing the book whilst coping with an exacting manuscript. Finally, I should like to thank my wife and family for all the support given me whilst the book was in gestation.

Note

1   Thomas Hardy, *Tess of the d'Urbervilles* (London, 1974), pp. 50-1.

4

1 The Context of Custom

Custom and the Past

> In a friendly manner this house we salute
> For it is an old custom, you need not dispute
> Ask not the reason from where it did spring
> For you very well know it's an old ancient thing.

Grampound Christmas
wassailers' song[1]

An appeal to the past, or at least to historical continuity ('for
it is an old custom, you need not dispute') is implicit in much
of the customary activity of the labouring poor and of local
communities in England during the eighteenth and nineteenth centuries. This appeal might be supported by reference
to documentary evidence such as manorial records or charitable bequests but was more often dependent upon the testimony of repeated performance. A 'plough bullock' informed
an observer who asked about the possibility of the intervention of agents of the law in their Plough Monday visitations
in search of largess that 'They can stand by it and no law in
the world can touch 'em, 'cause it's an old charter.'[2] He was
acting within the frame of reference of custom and not law.
The 'old charter' was not, in this case, a written document
(although such a document might well have existed at some
time in the past) but was the corpus of customary activity
within which operated the plough bullocks of late-nineteenth-
century England in the same way as their predecessors had
done a century before.

In Shropshire, at Ellesmere, in 1813 a successful attempt
was made to suppress the annual bull-baiting on Wake-
Monday. An exchange took place between Robert Clarke,
head-agent to the Earl of Bridgewater and the leader of the
bull-baiting procession, Thomas Byollin: ' "What are you

5

going to do with that bull?" asked "Captain" Clarke (as he was popularly called, from his command in the Volunteers) . . . "Goin' to bait 'im, sir," replied Tom; "We al'ays bait a bull at the Wakes – it's a rule." "Well, don't bait this one," said the Captain. "What will you take to let him go?" "I dunna know", answered Tom; " 'e mun be baited – it's a rule".[3] The insistence that the bull-baiting took place at Ellesmere because of a 'rule' was not untypical. Indeed, bulls were often donated for the use of local inhabitants in some places by manorial custom or charitable bequest.[4]

In eighteenth-century Muncaster, in Cumberland, an appeal to the past was made explicitly by the poor:

> On the eve of the New Year, the children go from house to house, singing a ditty which craves the bounty 'they were wont to have in old King Edward's days'. There is no tradition whence this custom rose; the donation is two-pence, or a pye at every house. We have to lament that so negligent are the people of the morals of youth, that great part of this annual salutation is obscure, and offensive to chaste ears. It certainly has been derived from the vile orgies of heathens.[5]

Similarly, the origins of other calendar festivals in England were popularly ascribed to the bounty of royalty or nobility, such as the hood game at Haxey in Lincolnshire, the bread and cheese dole at St Briavels in Gloucestershire, the bread dole at Tichborne in Hampshire, and many others.[6] Whether fictitious or not, the attempt to legitimate custom by reference to the past underpinned much of the labouring poor's activity.

In eighteenth-century England, custom enjoyed a wide spectrum of support, as one commentator observed: 'Shall custom be advanced as an excuse in this enlightened age? Shall custom vindicate a ridiculous and infamous action? Indeed, I fear it has too much weight, even with persons superior to the ignorant and vulgar, and though with such it cannot justify, yet we have too much reason to believe it makes many practices, scandalous in their natures, appear less shameful and less wicked . . .' This was written of the widespread Shrovetide practice of 'throwing-at-cocks' or 'cock-squoiling'.[7]

Custom, in this context, had two senses in the eighteenth century. The first is the idea of customary law as derived from established usage, in particular as it related to the practice of manorial courts or tenure. Customary law was perceived as either general or local. In its general form it formed the basis of common law, and in its local form was applied to the practices pertaining in local districts. The phrase 'from time immemorial' was often applied to custom, legal memory being fixed as not going beyond 1189. The customs of the medieval manor were set down in the custumal book and were interpreted by the manor court, and were applied to land tenure, common rights such as rights of pasture or to collect turves, and to services which the tenant owed to the lord of the manor. Secondly, by extension of meaning, custom was the term applied to activities or practices which were usual and which were annually or otherwise regularly performed. It is through the second sense that custom is related to folklore. Both senses will be explored and their inter-dependence in the popular mind shown.

The reliance upon custom was criticised by eighteenth-century jurists who insisted that, to have force, a particular custom must have been continuous, universally accepted, definite, reasonable (not in contradiction of any other laws), and held to be binding. The comforting certainties of statute law were preferred.

The greater part of customs (with which we are not to confound what are properly privileges) being unknown to the inhabitants, being transmitted to them by a tradition that carries no authority with it, being expressed in old obsolete language that is dark and ambiguous, and being sometimes directly contrary to the written laws; there must every day be difficulties arising about them; as, whether they are really such or not, whether the collections made of them by private, unauthorised persons be exact or not, whether they are not set aside by contrary usage and whether the written law, appearing in certain cases more equitable, does not deserve the preference; so that, they are so far from establishing a fixed and immutable rule, that they oftentimes serve only to furnish matter for suits, and even to perplex judges.[8]

The final criticism – that judges might be confused by the interpretation of custom – indicates the reluctance of propertied men to submit themselves to a code of social relationships within the community which could not be controlled by the use of magisterial power. This view was not held by everyone. Oliver Goldsmith argued that, far from leading to confusion, custom led to clarity: 'The simplicity, conciseness, and antiquity of custom, give an air of majesty and immutability that inspires awe and veneration; but new laws are too apt to be voluminous, perplexed, and indeterminate; whence must necessarily arise neglect, contempt, and ignorance.'[9] Law, he argued, was open to the influence of interest:

> But, let us suppose a new law to be perfectly equitable and necessary, yet, if the procurers of it have betrayed a conduct that confesses by-ends and private motives, the disgust to the circumstances disposes us, unreasonably indeed, to an irreverence of the law itself: but we are indulgently blind to the most visible imperfections of an old custom.[10]

He warned of the consequences of the overextension of law and the extinguishing of custom:

> Thus nothing can be more certain than that numerous written laws are a sign of a degenerate community, and are frequently not the consequences of vicious morals in a state, but the causes ... Laws ever increase in number and severity, until they at length are strained so tight as to break themselves. Such was the case of the latter Empire [Roman], whose laws were at length become so strict that the barbarous invaders did not bring servitude but liberty.[11]

In 1848, John Stuart Mill considered that custom could control the operation of social and economic relationships:

> Competition, in fact, has only become in any considerable degree the governing principle of contracts, at a comparatively modern period. The farther we look back into history, the more we see all transactions and engagements

under the influence of fixed customs. The reason is evident. Custom is the most powerful protector of the weak against the strong; their sole protector where there are no laws or governments adequate to the purpose. Custom is a barrier which, even in the most oppressed condition of mankind, tyranny is forced in some degree to respect . . . But though the law of the strongest decides, it is not the interest nor in general the practice of the strongest to strain the law to the utmost, and every relaxation of it has a tendency to become a custom, and every custom to become a right. Rights thus originating, and not competition in any shape, determine, in a rude state of society, the share of the produce enjoyed by those who produce it.[12]

The young Marx also recognised the role of custom in defending the economic rights of the poor. In 1842, he commented on proposals to strengthen the laws in Prussia regulating wood theft:

We unpractical people, however, demand for the poor, politically and socially propertyless many what the learned and would-be learned servility of so-called historians has discovered to be the true philosopher's stone for turning every sordid claim into the pure gold of right. We demand for the poor a customary right, and indeed one which is not of a local character but is a customary right of the poor in all countries. We go still further and maintain that a customary right by its very nature can only be a right of this lowest, propertyless and elemental mass.[13]

He continued:

If someone intentionally acts contrary to law, he is punished for his intention; if he acts by custom, this custom of his is punished as being a bad custom. At a time when universal laws prevail, rational customary right is nothing but the custom of legal right, for right has not ceased to be custom because it has been embodied in law, although it has ceased to be merely custom. For one who acts in accordance with right, right becomes his own custom, but it is enforced against one who violates it, although it is not

9

his custom. Right no longer depends on chance, on whether custom is rational or not, but custom becomes rational because right is legal, because custom has become the custom of the state.

Customary right as a separate domain alongside legal right is therefore rational only where it exists alongside and in addition to law, where custom is the anticipation of legal right.[14]

Marx suggested that customary rights arose from the indeterminate nature of some forms of property: 'These legislations were necessarily one-sided, for all customary rights of the poor were based on the fact that certain forms of property were indeterminate in character, for they were not definitely private property, but neither were they definitely common property, being a mixture of private and public right.'[15] It will be seen that this point accurately reflected the nature of some forms of property in eighteenth and early-nineteenth-century England, in particular as related to customary rights of the poor. Marx concluded: 'In these customs of the poor class, therefore, there is an instinctive sense of right; their roots are positive and legitimate.'[16]

Custom, both in its legal sense, and its extended meaning in terms of folklore, often conflicted with established concepts of law precisely because of its association with the rights of the poor. This analysis was also used by nineteenth-century folklorists. The antagonism between popular custom and orthodoxy has been pointed out by the folklorist, G.L. Gomme, when giving the definitions and scope of the concept of 'folklore':

Folklore consists of customs, rites, and beliefs belonging to individuals among the people, to groups of people, to inhabitants of districts or places; and belonging to them apart from and oftentimes in definite antagonism to the accepted customs, rites and beliefs of the State or the nation to which the people and the groups of people belong. These customs, rites, and beliefs are mostly kept alive by tradition . . . They owe their preservation partly to the fact that great masses of the people do not belong to the civilisation which towers over them and which is never of their own creation.[17]

An examination of the role of custom and of folk culture in defence of popular rights, and the context of customary activity within the community in eighteenth-century and nineteenth-century England, illuminates any understanding of social and economic relationships. A language of custom was understood by the community, which indicated action which was tolerated, censured action which was not, and acted as a vehicle for enforcing the collective will. Transgressors of this code were made to feel the force of its sanctions, whilst its supporters were permitted to enjoy the reciprocal rewards. In many cases these benefits amounted to the recognition of formal status within the established social hierarchy of the local community. It is in this way that Antonio Gramsci recommended the study of folk custom as a legitimate and indispensable means of understanding the structure of society and its tensions and conflicts. He wrote:

> We can say that to date folklore has been studied mainly as something 'picturesque' (in fact, to date, only erudite material has been gathered and the science of folklore has consisted mainly in the study of methods of collection, selection and classification of such material, that is in the study of cautious practices and empirical principles which are necessary for the fruitful development of a particular aspect of erudition, but this does not mean we should neglect the importance and historical significance of certain great scholars of folklore). We must study it, instead, as a 'view of the world and of life', in great measure implicit, of certain strata (determinate in space and time) of society, in opposition (here, too, mostly implicit, mechanical, objective) to the 'official' views of the world (or, in a wider sense, of the cultured parts of a particular society) that have occurred through history's development . . . We can only understand folklore as a reflex of the conditions of cultural life of the people, although certain folkloric concepts may last after conditions change (or seem to change) or may give way to bizarre continuations.[18]

He elaborates this view in stating that: 'It is also true there

11

exists a "popular morality", understood as a certain whole (in space and time) of maxims of practical conduct and customs which are derived from it or have produced it, ranging to real religious beliefs: there exist imperatives which are much stronger, more tenacious and more effectual than those of official "morality".'[19] He further advised the unpicking of the various strands in the fabric of popular custom:

> We must distinguish between diverse strata even in this sphere: those values which are fossilised, which reflect the conditions of past life and are thus conservative and re-actionary, and those which are a series of innovations, often creative and progressive, determined spontaneously by the forms and conditions of developing life and which contradict or are different only from the morality of the ruling strata.[20]

It is this notion of the innovative aspects of folk culture which is most useful to the social historian. Gramsci identified the conflict between what he termed 'common sense'[21] and the 'official views of the world' and pointed to the threat of popular custom to authority and the state, urging that folklore should be studied with a view to exploring this conflict. 'Folklore must not be regarded as bizarre, strange, or picturesque, but as something very serious and to be taken very seriously.'[22] The idea that the study of custom can uncover aspects of the tensions within social structures has been a fruitful one in the case studies of social anthropologists. In the words of one anthropologist, 'If folklore can provide a means of either actually or vicariously doing what the folk would like to do, then clearly it provides a unique source of information.'[23]

Custom can be both socially cohesive and socially disruptive: on the one hand providing a vehicle for the reproduction of the social structure and on the other hand giving an outlet for social protest and conflict. William Bascom writes: 'Viewed in this light, folklore is an important mechanism for maintaining the stability of culture. Here, indeed, is the basic paradox of folklore, that while it plays a vital role in transmitting and maintaining the institutions of a culture and in forcing the individual to conform to them, at the same time it provides socially approved outlets for the repressions which these same institutions impose upon him.'[24]

In late Hanoverian and Victorian England, the propertied class attempted to annex popular custom and the customary rights of the poor, partly by suppression and partly by acquisition and transformation. One defender of popular calendar festivals observed in 1849:

> The utility of festivals to nations and society in general is a question of considerable controversy: the opposing arguments are founded chiefly on the interruptions they occasion in public business, the facilities they afford to improvidence and idleness, and the abuses by which they have been too frequently disgraced among the working-classes, to the injury of both their means and morals. There is a sad truth in this last objection; but, on the other hand, it is contended that the institution of festivals is natural to humanity, and one of the distinguishing traits of our species; that they serve great moral purposes, in reviving the pious or elevating recollections connected with those events which they generally commemorate, and apt to be forgotten in the dusty bustle of business, or the dull routine of mechanical employment. It is also maintained that they contribute to the cultivation of social virtues, and refresh, with needful relaxations and amusement, the toil-worn lives of the labouring population, which without them would be 'all work and no play', with the proverbial consequence – that all human privileges and arrangements are liable to abuses, and those to which they have been subjected, are no arguments against festivals.[25]

Calendar festivals, often based upon and defended by custom, faced increasing opposition during the late-eighteenth and early-nineteenth centuries. In similar fashion, other more overtly economic customary rights such as wood gathering and gleaning were challenged. This challenge consisted both of a general attack on the nature of custom, and of direct opposition to specific local practice. In most cases, economic motivation lay behind calendar festivals, either in the form of the collection of customary doles, or in the defence of access to common social venues, or in the customary provision of food and drink, or in the reaffirmation of some other particular right such as the right to take wood for fuel.

Custom and Sources

One of the difficulties for the historian of popular custom lies in the nature of the sources. There is no single corpus of sources which can be quarried for evidence. There are no convenient files of correspondence in archives and libraries or self-contained parliamentary reports. The historian, if he is to uncover the nature of popular customs, must draw on a variety of scattered and very different sources such as local newspaper files; local histories and regional studies; lives, diaries and memoirs; the papers of scholarly antiquaries from previous centuries; the pages of local field club, natural history, archaeological or antiquary journals; the collections of early folklorists in the last century; criminal records (where they survive) for customary forms of activity which were redefined as crime; pamphlets and local ephemera; records of manor courts; ballads and songs; and, for the later period, oral evidence. The recovery of information about popular custom is therefore, disjointed, incomplete and complex. It was also, most often, provided by authorities who, at best, observed customs as outsiders, or, at worst, were hostile to it.[26]

The study of this material has been bedevilled by popular accounts aimed vaguely at the market for 'country' books and nostalgia for the rural past. With some exceptions, the taste for 'folksy' studies of English folk custom still prevails. Early works on the subject tended to consist of collections of examples, either in the form of a catalogue or dictionary, or based on the English ritual calendar. This model has a long history, beginning with the first printed collections of popular custom such as John Aubrey's *Miscellanies* or Bourne's *Antiquitates Vulgares*[27] (see Appendix 1). Indeed, the latter work was taken as the foundation of several later collections.[28] The establishment of the Folklore Society in

1878 led to the development of a more regional approach towards the collection of forms of folk custom. Many county studies appeared, and this became another standard model.[29] Indeed, the most recently published commercial exploitation of folk material in Britain adopts the same approach.[30] The General Editor to the series defended this approach:

> Once or twice since the present series was launched, I have been asked whether I had considered organising it on other than a geographical basis . . . My answer . . . is that, while it would be feasible to categorise British folklore into other analytical units, of which the occupational is perhaps the most obvious, a geographical treatment provides . . . a schematic cast which is particularly useful.[31]

The particular usefulness thus provided is not elaborated.

As Charles Phythian-Adams has pointed out,[32] folklore studies and social history in this country diverged at an early stage largely because of criticism by historians of the folklorists' failure to submit their evidence to the test of historical continuity, and their tendency to make unproven claims for the evidence on the basis of similarities and parallels in other cultures at other periods.

Since that divergence, social historians have been wary of material on custom and folklore, although some have recently used schematic casts other than the merely geographical or encyclopaedic. In his study of leisure and popular recreation, Robert Malcolmson has shown that, by using a social anthropological approach, much can be learned about the social function of certain forms of popular cultural activity during the eighteenth and nineteenth centuries.[33] Douglas Reid[34] and others have examined forms of urban and industrial custom,[35] whilst others, using oral history methods and the study of contemporary records, have studied particular aspects such as folk song,[36] or rural life.[37] E.P. Thompson, in his pioneering studies of 'rough music'[38] and of wife-sale,[39] has shown how custom and ceremony figured significantly in social relationships in the local community, which acted in Gramscian terms, as imperatives far 'more effectual than those of official "morality" '. Thompson has also shown how custom figured in determining forms of land tenure during the eighteenth century.[40]

For an earlier period and for Europe as a whole, Peter Burke has produced a perceptive and wide-ranging analysis of popular culture.[41] Popular culture in France has many historians, the work of some of whom has recently been collected.[42] Phythian-Adams, in his own work, has attempted to reunite folklore with local history.[43] His work has also influenced more recent folklore scholars such as Roy Judge and E.C. Cawte, who have provided thematic studies of particular types of popular custom.[44]

It is the difficulty of the sources themselves and of their interpretation which has perhaps deterred greater numbers of studies of popular custom. Historical accuracy and the problem of continuity remain intractable.[45] I will cite an example of this difficulty to illustrate the nature of the problem. St Briavels, in Gloucestershire, is the location for a doling custom which continues to take place. On Whit-sunday, quantities of bread and cheese are distributed, or, to be more accurate, are 'scrambled for'.[46] The custom, as with many of a similar type, is popularly supposed to date back to the reign of King John, although there is no written evidence for this supposition. However, authentic records can be found to trace the custom to at least the second half of the eighteenth century. It is recorded in 1779[47] and then, in a variety of sources, the custom is noted throughout the nineteenth century; 1807, 1816, 1836, 1860, 1884, 1890, 1893–4.[48] The last account is based on personal experience. However, the accounts of 1807 to 1890 inclusive are identical. The account which is reprinted in all of these years is as follows:

> One of the most strange customs that time has handed down to us prevails at St. Briavels, Gloucestershire. On Whit-sunday, several baskets full of bread and cheese, cut into small squares of about an inch each, are brought into the Church; and immediately after divine service is ended, the church wardens, or some other persons, take them into the galleries, from whence their contents are thrown amongst the congregation, who have a grand scamble for it in the body of the church, which occasions as great a tumult and uproar as the amusement of a village wake; the inhabitants being always extremely anxious in their

attendance at worship on this day. The custom is held for the purpose of preserving to the poor of St. Briavels at Hewelsfield the right of cutting and carrying away wood from 3,000 acres of coppice land in Hudknolls and the Meend; and for which every householder is assessed 2d, to buy the bread and cheese given away.

The only slight amendment occurs in the 1836 version when a note of disapprobation is struck by the inclusion of: 'and the tumult on these occasions is always very great; sometimes, indeed, of a character very ill suited to a sacred edifice'.

The apparent evidence of historical continuity disintegrates, as it is discovered that the same account is repeated in five separate publications at intervals over a period of almost ninety years. The antiquary's habit of building upon earlier accounts of customary activity has become, in this instance, nothing more than slavish repetition without further corroboration. I do not think that this can be taken to mean that the ceremony did not take place during that period, as the oral account recorded in 1893 states:

For many years it was customary to bring to the church on Whitsunday afternoon baskets of the stalest bread and hardest cheese cut up into small pieces the size of dice. Immediately after the service the bread and cheese were scrambled for in the church, and it was the custom to use them as pellets, the parson coming in for his share as he left the pulpit. About 1857, or perhaps a year or two later, the unseemly custom was transferred from the church to the churchyard, the bread and cheese being thrown down from the church tower. Later on it was transferred to the road outside the church gates. It now lasts but a few minutes. A few years ago all the roughs of the Forest (Dean) used to come over, and there was much drinking and fighting; but now it is very different.

This account was published only three years after the repeated and unhistorical version was reprinted by William Andrews. It was taken from the testimony of the Reverend W. Taprell Allen, Vicar of St Briavels, who was aware of the complex function of the custom, and who indicated the presence of elements of social disorder and status reversals. It has the hallmark of accuracy in that it records change as well as continuity. Allen also relates how, for reasons of propriety, the custom was moved from the body of the church, to the churchyard and, eventually, to the road outside the church. At St Briavels, popular custom was controlled in the later nineteenth century in a way which transformed the ceremony. However, without this later account, the social historian would be unaware of the complexity of the custom, and of its continuity, as the other antiquarian sources are merely repetitious.

A further difficulty with the source material is that, for much of the eighteenth and early-nineteenth centuries, there is a noticeable tendency towards under-reporting. Accounts, references and reports are not as common as they become after the middle of the nineteenth century. It is possible that this reflects the growing interest in this kind of material which to some extent both culminated in, and arose from, the foundation of the Folklore Society and the strenuous efforts of its early members.[49] It is also probable that popular custom was not regarded as respectable and was therefore unrecorded either until respectability had been imposed through the mechanism of control or until a particular custom had acquired the aspect of quaintness beloved of the antiquary. Roy Judge has demonstrated that reports of the May-day Jack-in-the-Green in Oxford occur almost annually once a respectable version of the custom was revived after 1886.[50] Before that the more boisterous and socially offensive (at least to middle-class opinion) custom was only recorded either if some particularly sensational event occurred as a result, or in a spirit of disapprobation. Thus, Judge quotes the following early account:

> 1836. On Monday last, about two o'clock, a large elm tree, growing in the church yard in Magdalen parish in the city, was by the violence of the wind torn up by the roots and blown across the street opposite the house of Mr Coleman; luckily no person was passing at the time. The horses in the Tantivy coach coming into St. Giles's soon afterwards, took fright at some sweeps in their May-day finery, and

came at full speed through the street notwithstanding the powerful exertions of Salisbury, the driver, to restrain them, until they reached that part of the road where the tree lay across it, when the leaders dashed on the pavement, and the coach was in danger of being overturned; fortunately however, by the activity of the guard and others, the accident was prevented.[51]

The only other reference, save one, to the sweeps' Mayday ceremony in Oxford recorded in the local newspaper before the revival, referred to a fine being imposed on one William Moore, for drunkenness, to which he 'pleaded the sweeps' festival in extenuation'.[52]

For much of the period, popular customs only received attention in the columns of the local press if associated with some other sensational occurrence. For example, in May 1777, in Hampshire, a carpenter was seriously injured whilst erecting a maypole at Cheriton: 'the pole gave way, and crushed him across the small of the back in such a manner that his life is despaired of'.[53] This is one of the few references to festivities concerning maypoles I have discovered for eighteenth-century Hampshire. The following case in 1785 illustrates the same point. A labourer was found dead in an out-house at Hursley, Hampshire, after having attended 'a harvest supper given by the farmer overnight, and it is supposed drank to such an excess as to occasion his death'.[54] The harvest home itself was not regarded as newsworthy, only the death of the labourer, especially as it was alleged to have resulted from alcohol abuse. At Axminster revel in the same year, a man 'who had formerly acted as a Merry Andrew' was killed whilst performing acts of bravado. He 'had the presumption to stand twice on his head on one of the battlements of the tower, to the astonishment of innumerable spectators, who having liberally rewarded him, he attempted the same a third time, but fell and was dashed to pieces'.[55] The sensational reporting of popular custom goes back to the seventeenth century, as the following account of 1656 illustrates:

At another time this (Thomas) Hurlston, wrapt up in a

19

Bull's Hide, came among the Rabble to the Meeting-House Door (in Melcombe Regis) and threw in a Horn, with which he struck off part of the Preacher's Lip. But the end of this profane man was remarkable, who being shortly after at a Bull-baiting, the Bull struck his Horn through his chin up into his Head, so that his tongue was torn out of his Mouth, and he instantly died, having but a Quarter of an Hour before told some of his companions, that he designed to be at Evershot again that day, to make sport of the Quakers. This man's exit was remarked by many as a singular instance of Divine Justice.[56]

Sensationalism remained a strong motive in reports of popular custom in the nineteenth-century press, as can be seen in the following account of Christmas wassailers from Somerset:

On Friday morning last a rick of hay on the premises of Pilton Park was discovered to be on fire, assistance was obtained and the fire was after some time extinguished, but not before a considerable quantity of hay was destroyed. It is supposed the fire was caused by the carelessness of some men who, the previous night, were keeping up the old custom of wassailing, and some of whom were smoking when they passed the rick.[57]

It is remarkable that mere accident is suspected and not the probable motive, social protest, as rick burning was the universal means of protest in rural England.

Whether common or not during the eighteenth century, it is clear that social acceptability was an important factor which conditioned whether certain customs were reported or not. Customs which were initiated by the labouring poor, or which were directed by them, were not considered suitable material as it showed the poor in an aggressive role, using ritual to threaten, albeit temporarily and within certain well-defined limits, the established social order. However, when such rituals had been annexed by bourgeois society and were ascribed acceptable attributes of the promotion of social harmony and of the image of deferential respect, custom was afforded a regular place in the pages of county newspapers and journals, where a genteel readership could delight in its quaintness and take satisfaction from the polite demonstration of true English character with its echoes of 'Merry England'.[58]

More common are the reports of popular custom which occur because of their conflict with 'official morality' as expressed in law. One Hezekia Morris, a shopkeeper of Westbury in Wiltshire, was charged, in 1821, that he 'did throw, cast or fire a squib rockett or other fireworks into the public street'. He was fined twenty shillings with nineteen shillings costs.[59] In 1793, in Durham, the ritual of stang riding, the punishment for wifebeaters, was the cause of a case of assault when 'Thomas Jameson, Matthew Marrington, George Ball, Joseph Rowntree, Simon Emmerson, Robert Parkin, and Francis Wardell' were accused of 'violently assaulting Nicholas Lowes, of Bishop Wearmouth, and carrying him on a stang'. They were all sentenced to two years' imprisonment in Durham Gaol for this customary activity.[60]

The phenomenon of under-reporting could have resulted from customary activities in the eighteenth century being so widespread and well known that they were not regarded as newsworthy. With their growing rarity in later nineteenth-century England, as legal sanction triumphed over popular custom, their very rarity gave them newsworthiness. Also, as conflicts ensued over the continuance of some customs and ceremonies, notoriety made them popular subjects for the local press.

Custom and Perspective

This study of English custom and ceremony concerns itself with the period 1700–1880, years which saw the transformation of the rural community from a small-scale system of agricultural production to the capital-intensive, large-unit farming of the mid-Victorian age of agricultural prosperity. The effect on the structure of the local community which this transition brought about can be observed through the record of popular morality. Custom and ceremony became a battleground in the struggle between the labouring poor and the increasingly wealthy landowners and proprietors,

21

over the defence of popular rights and the protection of a normative view of the structure of the community held by the labouring poor.

Social and economic relations in pre-industrialised and, to some extent, industrialising English communities in the eighteenth century, were conducted within a contractual framework which was both universally understood and held to be binding. This framework was a customary one and was often transmitted orally or by example through social replication. Within 'customary society', as it might be called, the relationship between social groups was understood to be reciprocal. The structurally superior (farmers, landowners, parish clergy, lord of the manor) accepted certain duties and responsibilities for the structurally inferior (tenants, smallholders, cottagers and squatters, wage labourers, the poor), and in return received due recognition of their structural status, and compliance or co-operation with their enterprises and decisions. This contractual relationship was not based upon deference; nor was it perceived as such by contemporaries.

Much of this framework had been transmitted forward from the late Middle Ages and from medieval social and economic structures such as the manor and the manorial system; the church and church ritual; and, in the case of towns, the borough and the customs of the corporation. Parts of this framework have been referred to as 'Folklore' by some writers. It should not be assumed that this framework had disintegrated by the beginning of the eighteenth century, or that it survived only in the form of economically and socially functionless ritual. Much of the experience of social change during the eighteenth century, particularly in the context of enclosure and agricultural change, illustrates how persistent were these older customary practices. This was not infrequently remarked on by contemporary commentators on agricultural practice who urged 'improvement'. This was usually understood as a combination of activities: enclosure; the adoption of 'scientific' farming methods; the investment of capital in the improvement of land, in machinery, and in the improvement of livestock; the cultivation of wastes and commons; and the destruction of customary ties between farmer and labourer and between proprietor and tenant.

22

Customary relationships cannot adequately be characterised as 'traditional' – a term which has become convenient shorthand with some social historians to describe rural English society before the industrial revolution and the development of capital-intensive agriculture.[61] 'Traditional' society is as misleading a notion as the conceptions of 'Merry England' once held by romantic Victorians when applied to pre-industrial England. It is a truism that all societies, beyond two generations, are traditional in the sense that one generation has transferred knowledge and experience to the next.[62] The use of the term implies immutability and is meant to contrast with the turbulence of industrial society. Indeed, it has become a general label for every manifestation of preindustrial society from hand working to harvest homes, and is applied with as little discretion as the term 'real' is to bread and beer.

A model which might more usefully be applied to eighteenth-century English rural communities is that of the *folk society*. This model, borrowed from social anthropology, was first advanced by Robert Redfield.[63] It characterises certain types of society as 'primitive . . . small, isolated, non-literate, and homogeneous, with a strong sense of group solidarity'.[64] Redfield contrasts this with modern urbanised society. Some of these characteristics can be found in certain small communities during this period, but they cannot be found all at once or generally. The ideas of group solidarity and homogeny, however, are of use to the social historian.

Customary relationships encompassed a wide experience of life in the community, not merely the narrow area of legal relationships involving tenure and common rights with regard to property. Similar customary patterns can be found in the areas of the organisation of work; the network of popular beliefs; leisure; social relationships and value systems. Certain calendar ceremonies, therefore, were customary occasions with greater importance than their mere form. The defence of customary rights through the use of ritual was common to many of them. It follows that opposition to these calendar ceremonies embodied more than an attack on disorderly or unruly behaviour. An implicit recognition of the nature of the customary claims which underpinned many calendar ceremonies can be detected. For example, at Princes

Risborough in Buckinghamshire the poor claimed a right to a Christmas distribution of food, which was examined by the Charity Commissioners:

> Up to about 1813, a bull and a boar, a sack of wheat, and a sack of malt, were given away to the poor by the lord of the manor of Princes Risborough about six o'clock every Christmas morning. This practice was then discontinued, and for about five or six years after the discontinuance, beef and mutton were distributed to the poor about Christmas, in lieu of the above articles. Mr Grubb, of the Parsonage House, the lord of the manor, whose father first discontinued the above customary distribution, produced to the Commissioners a case, which his father laid before Mr Justice Littledale when at the bar, relative to this custom, with the view of obtaining the opinion of Counsel as to whether it could be sustained as a custom at Common Law, and whether he could be subject to legal processes if he omitted to make the distribution. It appears from that document that the custom had then prevailed for a considerable number of years, that it was mentioned in the local histories, but that its origin was lost in obscurity. The practice, while it lasted, seemed to have been productive of much intoxication and riot: the poor are said to have paraded the town during the whole night preceding the distribution with an incessant clamour, effectually banishing all repose; on the following morning, they marched in crowds to Mr Grubb's house; and these assemblies often comprised many strangers from a distance, as well as parishioners.
>
> On the door being opened, they rushed to the feast prepared for them with so little decorum and forbearance, that often in their zeal for priority they inflicted wounds on one another with their knives. The whole of the remaining portion of Christmas Day is also stated to have been spent by many of them in public houses.
>
> Mr Littledale was of the opinion that this custom was not sustainable as a common-law right; and the Commissioners reported that they had received no sufficient evidence that the custom could be considered as a charitable donation, the continuance of which could be enforced.[65]

Despite evidence of historical continuity and the specificity of the dole right to the lord of the manor, the poor of Princes Risborough lost their customary distribution. In this case, the complaints about the unruly behaviour of the crowd obscure the principal motive of Mr Grubb's father, which was the extinguishing of the customary right of the poor.

Elsewhere, annual parish perambulations were discontinued after enclosure towards the end of the eighteenth century:

> The annual perambulations formerly observed here [at Scopwick, Lincolnshire] for the purpose of preserving the boundaries of the parish, have been discontinued from the period of the inclosure . . . At different points there were small holes made in the ground which were reopened on this occasion, and the boys who accompanied the procession were made to stand on their heads in these holes, as a method of assisting the memory; and several persons are now living, who, by this expedient, can distinctly remember where every hole was placed.[66]

The suppression of the parish bounds walk aimed also to suppress the memories of parisioners who could recall rights and customs associated with open fields and commons before enclosure.

Responses to social and economic changes which disrupted the mesh of customary relationships within the community were sometimes expressed within ritual contexts. The labouring poor defended their rights to 'possessionings', 'dancings', 'walkings', 'scramblings' and 'doleings' because these occasions formed part of the vision of the co-operative society in which the customary link between the poor and the gentry was preserved. Conflicts which arose over the maintenance of these seemingly insignificant rituals can illustrate deeper conflicts about the nature of relationships within the community.

The maintenance of customary rights was, in the eighteenth century, often seen as deviant behaviour and was redefined, often by statute, as crime. A well-known example quoted by the Hammonds, is that of gleaning:

Whereas I, Margaret Abree, wife of Thomas Abree, of the city of New Sarum, blacksmith, did, during the barley harvest, in the month of September last, many times wilfully and maliciously go into the fields of, and belonging to, Mr Edward Perry, at Clarendon Park, and take with me my children, and did there leaze, collect, and carry away a quantity of barley . . . Now we do hereby declare, that we are fully convinced of the illegality of such proceedings, and that no person has a right to leaze any sort of grain, or to come on any field whatsoever, without the consent of the owner; and are also truly sensible of the obligation we are under to the said Edward Perry for his leniency towards us, inasmuch as the damages given, together with the heavy cost incurred, would have been much greater than we could possibly have discharged and must have amounted to perpetual imprisonment, as even those who have least disapproved of our conduct, would certainly not have contributed so large a sum to deliver us from the legal consequences of it. And we do hereby faithfully promise never to be guilty of the same or any like offence in future. Thomas Abree, Margaret Abree, Her X mark.[67]

This was intimidation indeed. Threats of 'perpetual imprisonment' were used to cow the defenders of custom. The publication of this 'confession' of guilt, with the acknowledgement of the illegality of gleaning, was intended as much for others of Perry's own class who might be more charitable to the poor and their customary rights, as for friends and neighbours of Thomas and Margaret Abree. Indeed, from the evidence of summary jurisdiction records for Wiltshire, it would seem that there were also convictions of wood gatherers in the vicinity of Clarendon Park.[68] Wood gathering, too, was redefined as a crime during the late-seventeenth and eighteenth century. It is also interesting to note that Edward Perry induced the Abrees to recognise the illegality of any unauthorised access to fields and other property for whatever purpose.

The redefinition of custom as crime in an attempt to extinguish the rights of the labouring poor, and of small tenants, was part of the establishment of an ideology of private property and of power. The eighteenth and nineteenth centuries marked the period when both the concept of customary law and customary activities themselves were challenged in an attempt to destroy them. Oliver Goldsmith cited the dictum of John of Antioch that 'The enslaved are the fittest to be governed by laws, and free men by custom' when he published his defence of custom in 1759.[69] He wrote with eighteenth-century England in mind when he added:

> Custom partakes of the nature of parental injunction; it is kept by the people themselves, and observed with a willing obedience. The observance of it must, therefore, be a mark of freedom; and coming originally to a state from the reverenced founders of its liberty, will be an encouragement and assistance to it in the defence of that blessing: but a conquered people, a nation of slaves, must pretend to none of this freedom, or these happy distinctions; having, by degeneracy, lost all right to their brave forefathers' free institutions, their masters will in policy take the forfeiture; and the fixing a conquest must be done by giving laws, which may every moment serve to remind the people enslaved of their conquerors: nothing being more dangerous than to trust a late subdued people with old customs, that presently upbraid their degeneracy, and provoke them to revolt.[70]

Notes

1   This wassail song is still performed at Grampound in Cornwall. It is extremely long and was intended to legitimate the wassailers' request for liquor to quench their thirst. Full versions of the song can be found in: Paul Jennings, *The Living Village: A Picture of Rural Life drawn from Village Scrapbooks* (London, 1972), pp. 99–102; Roy Palmer (ed.), *Everyman's Book of English Country Songs* (London, 1979), pp. 234–7.

2   R. Chambers (ed.), *The Book of Days: A Miscellany of Popular Antiquities* (London, 1888), vol. I, p. 95.

3   Charlotte S. Burne, *Shropshire Folklore: A Sheaf of Gleanings* (London, 1883; reprinted 1973), p. 448.

4   Bulls were donated at Tutbury for the annual bull-running, by the Duke of Devonshire, until the event was suppressed in 1778. See F.W. Hackwood, *Staffordshire Customs, Superstitions and*

Folklore (Lichfield, 1924, reprinted 1974), pp. 41-3. I hope to publish shortly a full account of the Tutbury bull-running.

The bull for the Stamford bull-running was provided by the butchers of the town, and a former eighteenth-century mayor provided a special bequest towards the upkeep of the custom. See Chambers, *The Book of Days*, vol. II, p. 574.

At Wokingham the bull for the annual bull-baiting was provided by a local charity. See *Reports of the Charity Commissioners enquiry into charities in England and Wales* (1837-8), Pt. I, p. 220.

It is interesting to note that the Haxey Hood game probably arose from an earlier bull-running custom which involved the donation of a bull. See Morris Marples, *A History of Football* (London, 1954), pp. 14-15, and Venetia J. Newall, 'Throwing the Hood at Haxey: A Lincolnshire Twelfth-Night Custom', *Folklife: A Journal of Ethnological Studies*, vol. 18, 1980, pp. 7-23.

5   John Brand, *Observations on Popular Antiquities*, ed. Sir Henry Ellis (London, 1913), vol. I, p. 7.

6   For Haxey see *County Folklore. Vol. V. Examples of Printed Folklore Concerning Lincolnshire*, ed. Mrs Gutch and Mabel Peacock (London, 1908), pp. 267-74. The legend concerning the noble support for the contest is reported on p. 269. See also Newell, 'Throwing the Hood', particularly p. 20. For St Briavels see E. Sidney Hartland, 'The Whitsunday Rite at St. Briavels' in *Transactions of the Bristol and Gloucestershire Archaeological Society*, 1893-4, vol. XVIII, pp. 82-93. For Tichborne see W.G. Beddington and E.B. Christy (eds.), *It happened in Hampshire* (Winchester, 1937), p. 31.

7   *Hampshire Chronicle*, 15 February 1773.

8   *The Gentleman's Magazine*, 1750, vol. 20, p. 217.

9   *The Bee*, no. 7, 1759; Oliver Goldsmith, 'Custom and Laws Compared', reprinted in Oliver Goldsmith, *The Citizen of the World and the Bee*, ed. Austin Dobson (London, 1934), p. 415.

10   Ibid., pp. 415-16.

11   Ibid., p. 416.

12   J.S. Mill, *Principles of Political Economy* (Toronto, 1965), p. 240.

13   Karl Marx, *Collected Works*, vol. 1, 'Debates on the law and thefts of wood' (London, 1975), p. 230.

14   Ibid., p. 231.

15   Ibid., pp. 232-3.

16   Ibid., p. 234.

17   *Encyclopaedia of Religion and Ethics* (Edinburgh, 1913), entry on 'folklore' by G.L. Gomme, pp. 57-9.

18   Antonio Gramsci, 'Observations on folklore' in Alastair Davidson, *Antonio Gramsci: The man, his ideas* (Australian New Left Review Publication, 1968), p. 86.

19   Ibid., p. 87.

20   Ibid.
21   For a full discussion of Gramsci's concept of 'Common sense' see
     Antonio Gramsci, *Selections from the Prison Notebook* (London,
     1971), ed. Quinton Hoare and Geoffrey Nowell Smith, pp.
     419-25.
22   Davidson/Gramsci, *Antonio Gramsci*, p. 88.
23   Alan Dundes, 'The Functions of Folklore' in Alan Dundes, *The
     Study of Folklore* (New Jersey, 1965), p. 278.
24   William R. Bascom, 'Four functions of Folklore' in Dundes,
     The Study of Folklore, p. 298.
25   *Chamber's Edinburgh Journal*, January-June 1849, p. 222.
     Article entitled 'Festivals and Holidays'.
26   For a full discussion of this viewpoint see Peter Burke, *Popular
     Culture in Early Modern Europe* (London, 1939), pp. 65-77.
27   See Appendix 1. John Aubrey, *Miscellanies* (London, 1696);
     Henry Bourne, *Antiquitates Vulgares* (Newcastle upon Tyne,
     1725).
28   John Brand, *Observations on Popular Antiquities* (Newcastle
     upon Tyne, 1777). Republished and expanded by Sir Henry Ellis
     in his two-volume edition of 1813. The Folklore Society set itself
     the task of updating and expanding the Brand work - see *Folk-
     lore*, vol. 24, 1913, pp. 111-19, and *Folklore* vol. 26, 1915, pp.
     358-9 for statements by the Chairman of the Brand Committee,
     H.B. Wheatley. A catalogue of Brand material was subsequently
     produced by Charlotte S. Burne from 1915-18 in *Folklore*, vol.
     26, pp. 358-88; vol. 27, pp. 69-98, 193-217; vol. 28, pp. 52-86,
     164-76, 295-304, 415-31; vol. 29, pp. 66-74, 146-54.
29   See Appendix 1. Examples include: Burne, *Shropshire Folk-
     lore*; J.S. Udal, *Dorsetshire Folklore* (Hertford, 1922, reprinted
     1970); William Henderson, *Notes on the Folklore of the Northern
     Counties of England and the Borders* (London, 1879). The Folk-
     lore Society also began the systematic collecting and publication
     of printed material relating to individual counties - see:
     County Folklore Vol. 1. Printed extracts nos. 1, 2, and 3, Glou-
     cestershire, Suffolk and Leicestershire and Rutland, ed. Edwin S.
     Hartland (London, 1885).
     County Folklore Vol. 2. Printed extracts no. 4. Examples of
     printed folklore concerning the North Riding of Yorkshire,
     York and the Ainsty, ed. Mrs E. Gutch (London, 1899).
     County Folklore Vol. 3. Printed extracts no. 5. Examples of
     printed folklore concerning the Orkney and Shetland Islands,
     ed. Northcote W. Thomas (London, 1901).
     County Folklore Vol. 4. Printed extracts no. 6. Examples of
     printed folklore concerning Northumberland, ed. Northcote W.
     Thomas (London, 1903).
     County Folklore Vol. 5. Printed extracts no. 7. Examples of
     printed folklore concerning Lincolnshire, ed. Mrs E. Gutch and
     Mabel Peacock (London, 1908).
     County Folklore Vol. 6. Printed extracts no. 8. Examples of

printed folklore concerning the East Riding of Yorkshire, ed. Mrs E. Gutch (London, 1911).
County Folklore Vol. 7. Printed extracts nos. 9, 10, and 11. Examples of printed folklore concerning the counties of Fife with some notes on Clackmannon and Kinross, ed. R.C. Maclagen with an appendix by David Rorie (London, 1912).
The next major collection of English folklore material produced by the Folklore Society reverted to the calendar style; see:
British Calendar Customs, England vol. 1, 'Movable Festivals'. A.R. Wright ed. T. East Lones (London, 1936); *British Calendar Customs, England vol. II,* 'Fixed Festivals January–May', A.R. Wright ed. T. East Lones (London, 1938); *British Calendar Customs, England Vol. III,* 'Fixed Festivals June–December', A.R. Wright ed. T. East Lones (London, 1940).

30 *The Folklore of the British Isles,* general ed. Venetia J. Newall. Published by Batsford. 17 volumes so far produced, 1973–8.

31 Tony Deane and Tony Shaw, *The Folklore of Cornwall,* introduction by Venetia J. Newall (London, 1975), p. 10.

32 C. Phythian-Adams, *Local History and Folklore: A New Framework* (published for the Standing Conference for Local History 1975), pp. 7–8.

33 Robert W. Malcolmson, *Popular Recreations in English Society. 1700–1850* (Cambridge, 1973).

34 Douglas A. Reid, 'The Decline of Saint Monday. 1766–1876', *Past and Present,* no. 71, May, 1976, pp. 76–101.

35 See Roger Elbourne, *Music and Tradition in Early Industrial Lancashire. 1780–1840* (London, 1980); John Rule. *The Experience of Labour in Eighteenth-Century Industry* (London, 1981), particularly Chapter 8 on 'Custom, Culture and Consciousness'; *The Carpet Weaver's Lament: Songs and Ballads of Kidderminster in the Industrial Revolution,* introduced and edited by Len Smith (Kidderminster, 1979); Norman Sims, 'Ned Ludd's Mummers Plays' in *Folklore,* vol. 89, 1978 (ii), pp. 166–78; Alan Smith, *Discovering Folklore in Industry* (Tring, 1969).

36 See Robert Colls, *The Colliers Rant: Song and Culture in the Industrial Village* (London, 1977); A.L. Lloyd, *Folksong in England* (London, 1967); Alun Hawkins, 'The Voice of the People: the social meaning and context of country song', *Oral History,* vol. 3, pp. 50–75; Michael Pickering, *Village Song and Culture* (London, 1982); Jon Raven, *The Urban and Industrial Songs of the Black Country and Birmingham* (Wolverhampton, 1977); Reginald Nettel, *Sing a Song of England: A Social History of Traditional Song* (London, 1954); Roy Palmer (ed.), *A Touch on the Times: Songs of social change 1770–1914* (London, 1974); Palmer, *Everyman's English Country Songs.*

37 The work of George Ewart Evans is particularly useful; see: George Ewart Evans, *Ask the Fellows who Cut the Hay* (London, 1965); *The Pattern under the Plough* (London, 1966); *Where Beards Wag All: The Relevance of the Oral Tradition* (London,

1970); *The Days that We Have Seen* (London, 1975). Raphael Samuel's seminal collection of studies in *Village Life and Labour* (London, 1975) has many implications for social historians of rural life and popular culture.

38 E.P. Thompson, ' "Rough Music": Le Charivari Anglais', *Annales*, 1972, no. 2, pp. 285–312.

39 An unpublished essay to form part of E.P. Thompson's eagerly-awaited book *Customs in Common*. See also S.P. Menefee, *Wives for Sale: An Ethnographic study of British Popular Divorce* (Oxford, 1981)

40 E.P. Thompson, 'The grid of inheritance: A Comment', in *Family and Inheritance: Rural Society in Western Europe, 1200–1800*, ed. Jack Goodey, Joan Thirsk, E.P. Thompson (Cambridge, 1976).

41 Burke, *Popular Culture*.

42 *The Wolf and the Lamb: Popular Culture in France from the Old Regime to the Twentieth Century*, ed. Jacques Beauroy, Marc Bertrand, Edward T. Gargan (Stanford, 1977).

43 Phythian-Adams, *Local History and Folklore*. See also his work on Coventry which contains many insights: 'Ceremony and the Citizen: The Communal Year at Coventry 1450–1550', in: *Crisis and Order in English Towns 1500–1700: Essays in Urban History*, ed. Peter Clark and Paul Slack (London, 1972).

44 E.C. Cawte, *Ritual Animal Disguise* (London, 1978); Roy Judge, *The Jack-in-the-Green: A Mayday Custom* (London, 1979). It is interesting that both of these studies have emerged from or form part of the Index of Custom which Cawte and others have been compiling. The current trend in the work of folklorists is to depart from any analysis or conclusion beyond strictly factual ones. The accuracy of the information, itself very important, has become their principal aim. This is a deliberate and conscious veering away from the work of earlier folklorists who were not concerned with evidence (or the lack of it) of historical continuity, and who relied entirely upon similarities and parallels in form to construct grand hypotheses. Unfortunately, with one or two exceptions, English folklore studies still concerns itself with collection rather than analysis. Gramsci's comments cited earlier, still remain generally true.

45 The definitional problem can also prove difficult. See recent discussion in *People's History and Socialist Theory*, ed. Raphael Samuel (London, 1981), pp. 215–240. In particular Stuart Hall's comments (pp. 228–9) on eighteenth-century popular culture are perceptive: 'The popular traditions of the eighteenth-century labouring poor, the popular classes and the "loose and disordered sort" often, now, appear as virtually independent formations: tolerated in a state of permanently unstable equilibrium in relatively peaceful and prosperous times; subject to arbitrary excursions and expeditions in time of panic and crisis . . . They not only constantly pressed on "society"; they were

linked and connected with it, by a multitude of traditions and practices. Lines of "alliance" as well as lines of cleavage. From these cultural bases, often far removed from the dispositions of law, power and authority, "the people" threatened constantly to erupt: and, when they did so, they broke on the stage of patronage and power with a threatening din and clamour.'

46 A good description of the custom as it occurs today can be found in Homer Sykes, *Once a Year: Some Traditional British Customs* (London, 1977), p. 84.

47 S. Rudder, *A New History of Gloucestershire* (Cirencester, 1779), p. 307.

48 1807 – *Felix Farley's Bristol Journal*, 6 June 1807; 1816 – *Gentleman's Magazine*, vol. 86, Pt. II, p. 364; 1836 – *Berrow's Worcester Journal*, 2 June 1836; 1860 – *Notes and Queries*, 2nd series, vol. X, p. 184; 1884 – *Gloucestershire Notes and Queries*, vol. II, p. 266; 1890 – Ibid., vol. IV, pp. 188–9, 640; 1890 – W. Andrews, *Church Folklore* (London, 1890), p. 87; 1893–4 – *Transactions of the Bristol and Gloucestershire Archaeological Society*, vol. XVIII, pp. 82–93, 'The Whitsunday Rite at St. Briavels' by E. Sidney Hartland.

49 See R.M. Dorson, *The British Folklorists: A History* (London, 1968), and R.M. Dorson (ed.), *Peasant Customs and Savage Myths: Selections from the British Folklorists* (2 volumes, London 1968).

50 Judge, *Jack-in-the-Green*, pp. 109–12.

51 Ibid., p. 109.

52 Ibid.

53 *Hampshire Chronicle*, 5 May 1777.

54 Ibid., 6 November 1785.

55 *The Gentleman's Magazine*, vol. 55, 1785, p. 480. See also Brand, *Observations*, vol. I, pp. 68–9, 444 for accounts of a shrovetide 'throwing at cocks' and a harvest-waggon respectively, which both ended in tragedy.

56 *Somerset and Dorset Notes and Queries*, vol. III, 1893, p. 231, from Besse's *Sufferings of the Quakers* (1753), vol. I, p. 165.

57 *The Bridgewater Times*, 4 January 1850, cited in *English Dance and Song*, vol. 42, no. 2, 1980, p. 14.

58 For a full discussion of the concept of 'Merry England' in this context see Judge, *Jack-in-the-Green*, pp. 67–8.

59 Wiltshire Record Office, Records in the custody of the Clerk of the Peace for Wiltshire, Summary conviction bundles.

60 Anonymous, *Popular Pastimes, Being a Selection of Picturesque Representations of the Customs and Amusements of Great Britain, in Ancient and Modern Times Accompanied with Historical Descriptions* (London, 1816), p. 18, quoting *The Newcastle Courant*, 3 August 1793.

61 See Peter Laslett, *The World we have lost* (London, 1971), pp. 159–78.

62 See the perceptive comments made by Raymond Williams in

Keywords: A Vocabulary of Culture and Society (London, 1976), pp. 268–9, and Samuel (ed.), *People's History*, pp. 236–7, where Stuart Hall warns against 'those self-enclosed approaches to popular culture which, valuing "tradition" for its own sake, and treating it in an a-historical manner, analyse popular cultural forms as if they contained within themselves, from their moment of origin, some fixed and unchanging meaning or value.' p. 237.

63   Redfield first advanced this model in 'The Folk Society' in *The American Journal of Sociology*, vol. LII, January 1947, pp. 293–308. See also Redfield, *The Primitive World and its Transformations* (London, 1968) and in particular his chapter entitled 'Later Histories of the Folk Societies', pp. 38–63.

64   Redfield, 'The Folk Society', p. 293.

65   *Commissioners enquiring into charities*, XXVI. p. 107.

66   *The Gentleman's Magazine*, 1833, vol. 103, Pt. I, pp. 116–17.

67   J.L. Hammond and Barbara Hammond, *The Village Labourer 1760–1832: A Study in the Government of England before the Reform Bill* (London, 1913), pp. 109–10. This is taken from *The Annals of Agriculture*, ed. Arthur Young, vol. XVII, p. 293.

68   Wiltshire Record Office, Summary Conviction bundles.

69   Goldsmith, 'Custom and Law Compared', p. 414.

70   Ibid., pp. 414–5.

2 The Community and its Calendars

The Reconstruction of Local Calendars

> 'Fifty years ago 'twere all mirth and jollity . . . There was four feasts in the year for us folk. First of all there was the sowers' feast – that would be about the end of April; then came the sheep-shearers' feast – there'd be about fifteen of us as would sit down after sheep-shearing, and we'd be singing best part of the night, and plenty to eat and drink; next came the feast for the reapers, when the corn was cut about August; and, last of all, the harvest-home in September.'
>
> J. Arthur Gibbs, 1898[1]

For much of the eighteenth and nineteenth centuries, the frame of reference for conducting customary relationships within the rural community was provided by the annual calendar. The passage of events was the essential thread which connected the individual experience of the labouring poor and their families. This calendar was made up of many different types of repeated experience, that of work, of leisure, of the church, of parish or manor administration, and of the established gentry families. This calendar, comprised of many layers and forms, was perceived of as local. It is important to understand how this local calendar was constructed and how the various customary events interlocked so that an impression of its importance to the local village community can be gained.

The local customary calendar provided a frame of reference in which was expressed a perception of the social structure of the community, and also of its physical delineations. Customary rights and dues were claimed, sanction to the established hierarchy was given and maintenance of the physical form of the parish or manor as an entity was achieved. Calendar customs should not be thought of as merely a collection of social occasions which occurred in any one year, and which were found, to a greater or lesser extent, in most other places.

Gibbs's informant set out a catalogue of the most important festivals in the rural calendar of the Cotswolds in the last decade of the nineteenth century. The Elizabethan agricultural commentator, Thomas Tusser, also set down a rhymed list of the principal holidays in the country year for his time. He included Plough Monday, Shrovetide, sheep-shearing, the wake-day, harvest home, and wheat sowing. These occurred in January, February to March, June, at various times depending on local custom, late September and October to November respectively.[2] There are both differences and similarities between the calendars of Gibbs and Tusser. Both calendars include community festivals which delineate the cycle of rural labour; that is, festivals which were secular and which were perceived as festivals of the workforce or labourers' holidays. Even those festivals which were connected to or derived from church calendar ceremonies are not referred to for their significance as ecclesiastical rituals. Thus the secular term of Shrovetide is ascribed to the pre-Lent religious festival. The wake-day is not described by its more correct title of the Feast of Dedication of the Parish Church.

The differences between the two calendars arise partly from the nature of local usage and partly from changes in the economic basis of the calendar itself, and the degree to which certain calendar festivals received the full sanction of the whole community. Thus, Plough Monday does not figure in the Cotswold work calendar because of the more predominantly pasture economy of the region. Shrovetide had disappeared from the customary calendar by the end of the nineteenth century and local wakes receive no mention at all in the later calendar.[3]

The calendar of customs was finely intermeshed with the specific structure of the local economy and society in the eighteenth and nineteenth centuries. The practice of the antiquary and the folklorist of collecting material from widely scattered locations has destroyed its local basis, by implying a wider, more national, or, at least, regional calendar than was the case.

As Charles Phythian-Adams has suggested, it is likely that the most common unit for the observance of a customary calendar was the parish, although larger calendar events such as fairs, markets and mops might draw together people from a wider locality. Customary calendars which were based upon similar economic and social contexts clearly had similarities and parallels as the labouring poor of one parish would have a knowledge of more general calendar customs which were derived from a wider geographical context.

Other territorial boundaries were important, particularly the manorial boundaries. Indeed, confusion which might arise from the conjunction of manorial and parish boundaries was cited as a reason for their rationalisation. As one writer pointed out at the beginning of the nineteenth century:

> the civil division of *manors*, though frequently confined to the whole or part of a parish, comprehends, in some instances, part of two parishes, and has within it parts of different townships; and the jurisdiction of court leets are not always confined to the hundred they are situated in. Thus difficult is it to speak of the divisions of a county, from the want of coincidence in boundaries and jurisdictions; many of them appearing independent of each other, rather than separate but component parts, of one and the same scheme.[4]

The memory of the existence of manorial boundaries was often preserved in the popular mind by the continued existence of customary rights to local inhabitants, and by such annual ceremonials as the ritual perambulation of the boundaries in Rogation week.

By reconstructing some local customary calendars, their impact for the community can be seen. The reconstruction of such calendars is not an easy task. Material is usually fragmentary and, in many cases, one particular custom assumes a greater significance in the sources than others and becomes predominantly associated with that particular locality. Five reconstructions, aided by the nature of the sources, will be attempted. One local customary calendar can be reconstructed for mid-eighteenth-century Bletchley from the diary of the Reverend William Cole. This local calendar includes the Rogation week Parish Perambulation described in May 1766: 'I went to meet my Parishioners who had been the rounds of the parish in procession, at the corner of Rickley Wood . . . it being so windy and the roads so bad for a chaise I did not care to go the whole way.'[5] On Whit-Monday, Morris dancing featured as the main event, accompanied by other Whitide pastimes: 'Woburn Abbey Morrice dancers here. Tom went to the Alehouse with the young people of the parish.' A Whitide fair took place on the following Whit-Thursday at nearby Buckingham which Tom and his friends also visited.[6]

Cole records a form of hay harvest ceremony which occurred at Bletchley:

> Gloomy day, however I got in all my hay, 6 loads more, in all about 18 jags from the Clay Pit Close . . . They [his labourers] made a sort of procession, with a fiddle and a German flute, Jem dressed out with ribbands and Tom Hearne dancing before the last cart, I giving a good supper to all my hay makers and helpers, being above thirty persons in the kitchen, who staid 'till One . . . I gave Will Grace for helping me a Quarter of a Guinea and Tom Watts as much more. They were both well pleased. Will Grace mowed for me almost all the time. I gave John Holdom my last year's hat.[7]

Here the elements of ceremonial and commensality – the sharing of food and drink in a harmonious relationship – are combined to reinforce an important event in the community's year, as the success of the harvest determined the likelihood of the survival of the livestock during the winter months.

Later in the year, in September, a harvest home took place at 'Master Holdoms'[8] and then followed the local parish feasts and wakes. Bletchley's feast Sunday was held on 14 September (Holy Cross Day)[9] and the ubiquitous Tom also attended neighbouring Newton-Longville's feast on 19 October.[10] On 5 November, Guy Fawkes day was celebrated with 'Bonfires on the green', wood for which had been collected during the preceding week.[11]

In the following year, two further calendar customs are

recorded. On St Valentine's Day, parties of local children went 'hallooing under my chamber window before I was up', and on Shrove Tuesday there was 'football playing on the green'.[12] More customs associated with specific elements in the community are mentioned, including the local bell-ringers' feast (the campanologists' equivalent of the harvest home) and the custom of midnight ringing on Christmas Eve.[13] The eighteenth-century customary calendar at Bletchley was not unusual. It can be recovered from the local diary record of only two years. Its special value is its unusual completeness.

A second local calendar can be recovered for early nine-teenth-century Ashford-in-the-Water in Derbyshire, comprising Plough Monday festivities, Shrove Tuesday 'gooding' and football, Easter Sunday 'sugar-cupping', and sheep-shearing suppers.[14] Specific local practice on Shrove Tuesday at Ashford dictated that 'at eleven o'clock in the morning of that day, a bell called the "Pancake Bell" was rung in the church tower, and on the first sounding of that bell that children of the schools in the village were released from their studies, and had the rest of the day for holiday purposes – indeed it was a general holiday. The game of football was generally played during the after part of the day.'[15]

This does not mean that Shrovetide Pancake Bells and street football were confined to Ashford. Both customs were found in many other places, but in Ashford they formed part of the specific local customary calendar which was known and sanctioned there at the beginning of the nineteenth century.

For Castle Carey in Somerset during the eighteenth century, a third local customary calendar can be reconstructed from the diaries of James Woodforde. A pattern of regular visits at Christmas from parties of mummers and Christmas singers which were sanctioned by the local community illustrates the maintenance of one key date.[16] On Christmas Eve 1764 'The new singers came very late this evening and they sang a Christmas carol and an anthem and they had cyder as usual and 0.2.0. The old singers did not come at all and I have heard that they have given it over.'[17] The disappearance of the 'old singers' perhaps gives evidence of a localised conflict between opposing groups in the Castle

Carey community which affected adherence to and was conducted within the customary calendar.

In 1768, local encouragement to the new singers was recorded by James Woodforde: 'It being Christmas Eve we had the new singers of Castle Carey this evening at the Parsonage, and they having been at great expense in learning to sing, my father and myself gave them double what we used to do.'[18] On Christmas Day in 1764, 'fifteen poor old people dined here [the Parsonage] as usual being Christmas Day'.[19] Mummers (described as 'Fine') visited the Parsonage in Castle Carey in 1769. Guy Fawkes day was accompanied with the customary activity of bonfires localised by the burning of the effigy of one particular individual who had displeased the community, Justice Creed ('the whole parish are against the Justice'[20]).

When James Woodforde moved to another living in Norfolk at Weston Longeville, he accepted and adapted to a new local customary calendar which reflected the arable economy of that county, and expressed a greater emphasis on customs associated with grain harvest. He recorded in 1776 'largess given to farmers harvest men'. This was a customary dole levied by harvest labourers on the residents of the parish.[21] Two days later Woodforde notes that 'my harvest men dined here today, gave them some beer and some plum pudding and as much liquor as they would drink'.[22] Woodforde's commensality towards his men underpinned the maintenance of this custom which without his support could not have taken place.

At Weston Longeville (as at Bletchley in William Cole's day) it was customary for small amounts of money to be given to children who visited the parsonage on St Valentine's morning. Woodforde accepted this custom and recorded in 1777: 'to 36 children being Valentine's day and what is customary for them to go about in these parts this day gave 0.3.0 being one penny apiece to each of them'.[23] This particular custom did not figure in Castle Carey's calendar, yet, having satisfied himself of its authenticity and local usage, Woodforde accepted its force and submitted himself, at some expense, to his customary duty as local clergyman. In 1780, he noted that he took part in the parish procession around the boundary of Weston Longeville. He 'walked most of the way. Our bounds supposed to be about 12 miles round. We were going of them full five hours. We set off at 10.00 in the morning and got back a little after 3.00 in the afternoon.'[24]

In successive years, Woodforde continued to give largess, Christmas boxes, Valentine's money and other doles as the local customary calendar demanded. He also recorded Whitmonday sports, St Thomas's day 'doleing', and local benefit club processions and feast days. In 1788: 'merry doings at the Heart today being Whitmonday plowing for a pair of breeches, running for a shift, raffling for a gown etc'. In 1788 again: 'Yesterday being St. Thomas, the poor people came to my house for their Christmas gifts this morning. To 56 poor people of my parish at 6d each gave 1.8.0.' In 1795: 'The members of the Purse Club with a Drum and Fife made their annual perambulation. They called at my House and I gave them as usual 0.10.6.'[25] In each case Woodforde accepted the customary role which was delineated for him by Weston Longeville's customary calendar.

That there was, of course, a wider regional distribution of some of the customs in Weston's local calendar can be seen from the following description of St Valentine's Day ceremony observed at West Norton in Norfolk in 1805:

> In regard to popular customs in Norfolk, the only one almost which I find to prevail here [West Norton] is that of the children of the Parish going round together to the principal houses on Valentine's Day, making no little noise and crying out 'good morrow to you, Valentine' – when it is usual to give them cakes or money . . . This custom does not prevail in every Parish tho' apparently in the greater number; and seems to afford pleasure to the old inhabitants, and best natured people, who say it is a nice frolic for the children.[26]

A regional distribution of certain calendar customs was not uncommon, but the occasion was defined by its position within local customary calendars, and by reference to the social framework of the individual parish. In some cases, though, the calendar event was more widespread, particular local names were ascribed to it. Joseph Hunter, when referring to the St Thomas's Day 'doleing' custom noted that he could not 'remember the expression "going a gooding", but the thing I well remember. Poor people went from one farmhouse to another, begging corn, professedly to make their Furmitry at Christmas – I think St. Thomas's Day was the chief day for making their visits.'[27]

Reference to a local customary calendar was still made as late as the 1880s in Flora Thompson's Oxfordshire hamlet, although she records that this was changing and that only some of the principal occasions remained. A fourth local calendar can then be reconstructed in which national stereotypes of festivals can also be observed, and other customary occasions were less frequent: 'If one of the women was accused of hoarding her best clothes instead of wearing them, she would laugh and say: "Ah I be savin' they for high days an' holidays an' bonfire nights." If she had, they would have lasted a long time, for there were very few holidays and scarcely any which called for a specific toilet.'[28] Many of the events in the Larkrise calendar had, by this time, taken on a national significance. The fete organised to celebrate Queen Victoria's Jubilee in 1887 was one example, modelled, as it was, on older Whitide pursuits

The men and boys with shining faces and in Sunday suits had gone on before to have dinner at the farm before meeting their families at the cross-roads. They would be having cuts of great sirloins and Christmas pudding washed down with beer, just as they did at the harvest home dinner . . . There were more people in the park than the children had ever seen together, and the roundabouts, swings, and coconut-shies were doing a roaring trade. Tea was partaken of in a huge marquee in relays, one parish at a time, and the sound of the brass band, roundabout hurdy-gurdy, coconut thwacks, and showmen's shouting surged round the frail, canvas walls like a roaring sea.[29]

This was a single rather an annual event but it is interesting to note that the Jubilee celebrations took their pattern from older customary festivals. The farmer's dinner for his workmen was similar to the harvest home; the park festivities followed the model of local club feasts; and the afternoon sports, including grinning through horse collars, was patterned on the old Whitmonday sports of former times.[30]

By contrast the older festivals such as Christmas had lost any specifically local form: 'Christmas Day passed very quietly. The men had a holiday from work and the children from school and the churchgoers attended special Christmas services.'[31] The older customary forms were not common: 'There were no visits from local mummers at Christmas, although the custom occurred elsewhere in the region.'[32]

Some highspots for Larkrise remained. Feast Sunday was a communal celebration when best clothes were worn and extra food and drink was available, but this was seen as an isolated event in the local calendar, as Flora Thompson makes clear: ' "After all, 'tis the feast," they said; "an't only comes once a year." '[33] The attraction of other events in other villages drew local inhabitants to club walkings and parish feasts, as they had done in Cole's Bletchley.[34] Whilst important for the local community, these parish feasts were seen as external to their own experience.

Palm Sunday and Guy Fawkes day were celebrated at Larkrise in customary character. On the occasion of the latter:

the night before, the boys and youths of the hamlet would go round knocking at all but the poorest doors . . . The few housewives who possessed faggot sticks . . . would give them a bundle or two; others would give them hedge trimmings, or a piece of old line-post, or anything else that was handy, and, altogether they managed to collect enough wood to make a modest bonfire which they lit on one of the open spaces.[35]

Harvest was the central event in the customary calendar for Larkrise. As the harvest-labourers

approached the farm-house their song changed to:

Harvest home, Harvest home
Merry, merry, merry, harvest home
Our bottles are empty, our barrels won't run,
And we think it's a very dry harvest home.

and the farmer came out, followed by his daughters and maids with jugs and bottles and mugs, and drinks were handed round amidst general congratulations.[36]

A harvest home dinner was provided by the farmer a few days later after the completion of the harvest.

The interconnection of the popular customary calendar with the social calendar of local landed families is significant. For in a fifth example, in eighteenth-century East Hoathly in Sussex, the social calendar was perceived differently within the same community. The labouring poor claimed their customary doles. Hop-pickers visited local houses to levy largess, with different parties making their visits on different nights. On 20 September 1757, 'In the even, Mr. Porter's hoppers bought their pole-pullers nickcloth.' On 23 September it was the turn of the Halland House hoppers of whom it was noted that they were 'poor wretches, many of them insensible'.[37]

On St Thomas's Day (21 December) the poor attended the annual distribution of the Pelham Dole:

> We arose at three to perform our task, viz: some of the ancestors of the Pelham family have ordered that, on this day (for ever) there should be given to every poor man or woman that shall come to demand it, 4d; and every child, 2d; and also to each a draught of beer, and a very good piece of bread. I believe there was between seven and eight-hundred people relieved of all ages and sexes, and near £9 distributed, besides a sack of wheat made into good bread, and near a hogshead and half of very good beer.[38]

The Pelhams themselves instituted a regular commensal custom for the locality by holding a 'publick day' at Halland House, annually during the first week of August. These festivities attracted all the neighbourhood. On Sunday 7 August 1757, the event was described as follows: 'This being a publick day at Halland I spent about two or three hours there in the afternoon, in company with several of our neighbours. There was a great company of people, of all denominations, from a duke to a beggar.'[39] At East

Hoathly, the customary calendar of the labouring poor intermingled with that of the Pelham family on their country estate in a complex relationship, in which the relationship of one social group to others was conditioned by the overlapping of customary calendars.

A complete popular customary calendar was made up of festivals and rituals drawn from other calendars whose primary functions were essentially different. The most common of these was the calendar of work, which underpinned so clearly J. Arthur Gibbs's calendar cited at the opening of this chapter. The rural year began in autumn after Michaelmas when the hiring or statute fair (popularly known as the Mop) had taken place and the labour force had been secured for the coming year. The autumn and early winter saw the sowing of grain and the threshing of the harvested crop, whilst in early spring further sowing and lambing occurred. Early summer was the period for the grain harvest and for sheep-shearing. The grain harvest took place in late summer and early autumn witnessed fruit-picking. So the farming year came full circle. Each of these stages was marked by popular custom.

The harvest home marked the transition from the old to the new year in the farming calendar. On Plough Monday (the Monday following Epiphany Sunday) drama rituals, designed to solicit food and drink from local farmers and neighbours were acted as the threshold to spring sowing. The succession of 'harvests' through the summer and early autumn were accompanied by feasts at the employer's expense. These began with the hay harvest and the sheep-shearing feasts in June–July, followed by hopping suppers and gardeners' feasts, and culminated with the harvest home. The occurrence of these festivals depended upon the local customary calendar and the economic base of agriculture in each region.

In the context of trade and industry, a comparable pattern of popular custom coinciding with the principal events of the work cycle can be observed. The forms of these festivals were, indeed, very similar. The functions of customary activity were very much the same for the rustic and the townsman – tradesman and industrial worker – because, for most of the eighteenth and nineteenth centuries, their lives

44

and experiences had not become sharply divergent. For a considerable part of this period, most trades and industries continued to be organised on the scale of the small workshop or self-contained community and the regulation of workshop practices and behaviour, and the conducting of relationships between master and man, was governed by custom.[40] Calendrical rites were common to the tradesman and to the rural labourer, and these rituals arose from the context of the work calendar itself.[41] Thus, in the printing industry, for example, at the end of August, it was customary 'for all journeymen to make every year new paper windows about Bartholomews tide at which time, the master printer makes them a feast called a "way goose", to which is invited the corrector, founder, smith, ink-maker, etc. who all open their purses and give to the workmen to spend in the tavern or ale-house after the feast, from which time they begin to work by candlelight.'[42] William Hone observed, in the early nineteenth century, the disappearance of the practice of making oiled paper covers for the windows, but noted the continuation of the master's feast or way goose.[43] Here was an industrial equivalent of the rural harvest home.

In shoemaking, a similar customary event occurred.

The first Monday in March being the time when shoe-makers in the country cease from working by candlelight it used to be customary for them to meet together in the evening for the purpose of 'wetting the block'. On these occasions the master either provided a supper for his men, or made them a present of money or drink; the rest of the expense was defrayed by subscriptions among themselves, and sometimes by donations from customers. After the supper was ended, the block candlestick was placed in the midst, the shop candle was lighted, and all the glasses filled, the oldest hand in the shop poured the contents of his glass over the candlelight to extinguish it: the rest then drank the contents of theirs standing, and gave three cheers. The meeting was usually kept at a late hour.[44]

The observer of the custom was in favour of its disappearance 'as it is mostly a very drunken usage, the sooner it is sobered or becomes altogether obsolete the better'.[45] Similar criticisms

45

were levelled at equivalent rural feasts like the harvest home and Plough Monday rituals. Some workers enjoyed similar feasts at the expense of the employer; in eighteenth-century Evesham, in Worcestershire, it was 'an ancient custom at that place for the master-gardeners to give their work people a treat of baked peas, both white and grey, (and pork) every year on Holy Thursday'.[46]

At Christmas, apprentices were permitted to collect 'Christmas boxes'[47] or donations from their masters' customers in a similar way to the visits of 'mummers' and other Christmas visitors in rural areas. Town waits or musicians toured houses at Christmas time, just as wassailers and church orchestras tramped round the farms and hamlets of rural parishes during the same period.[48]

Annual processions, common to some industries and trades, were similar in form to country Whit walks or Benefit Club parades. The feast of St Blaise (3 February) was customarily celebrated by workers in the woollen industry, particularly wool combers. For example, in 1777, the following procession was reported from Bury St Edmunds:

> This day, Monday, being the anniversary of Bishop Blaize, the same was observed in this town in a manner far surpassing anything of the kind ever seen. The Cavalcade consisting of between two or three hundred woolcombers, upon Horses in Uniforms, properly decorated, Bishop Blaize, Juno, Castor and Pollux, a band of musick, drums, colours and everything necessary to render the procession suitable to the greatness of the woollen manufacturing.[49]

In southern England the Bishop did not go without his customary honours: 'a great number of wool-combers, from Romsey, and other places, met in a large body and marched the streets of this town. They were chiefly dressed in white shirts, and were attended by the Bishop dressed in character, and mounted on a horse attended by a band of music, and colours flying.'[50] The wearing of white clothes and the display of banners, accompanied by musicians, were also central to the village club celebrations and processions at Whitsun.

Similarly, St Crispin's day was celebrated by shoemakers, and St Clement's day was of great importance to blacksmiths and to dockyard workers.[51] Cornish tinners assembled to pelt a pitcher of water on St Paul's eve, after which the day was given over to festivity.[52] On St Luke's day, a sermon was 'preached before the Worshipful Company of Drapers at St. Peter's, Cornhill, to which the masters, wardens, and court of assistants, walked in procession from their Hall, a number of their poor carrying each a pair of shoes and stockings, and a suit of cloathes, being an annual legacy to the poor of that Company.'[53] Mayday and Shrove Tuesday were celebrated in town and country alike. Mayday was marked, in the printing trade, by a procession to Stationers' Hall by masters and workers.[54] In the later eighteenth and nineteenth centuries, chimney sweeps celebrated Mayday by appearing in the streets with a Jack-in-the-Green, soliciting money from passers-by.[55] Shrovetide football was played by Midlands workers at Atherstone, Bedworth and Nuneaton,[56] and also, in a ritual form, by the Purbeck Marblers Company at their annual court in Corfe, Dorset.[57] The dichotomy between town and country did not apply to popular custom. The customary calendar of work provided a potent legitimation for urban and rural labourers alike.

A further customary calendar derived from Christian ritual. Christian ceremonies were relatively less important as religious occasions for the labouring poor than they were as social events. A.W. Smith has pointed to the need to study further the social role of church festivities for the labouring community during the eighteenth century.[58] The principal Christian festivals of Easter, Christmas, Whitsun and the local feast of dedication were matched by secular customary activities in the village. Some of the industrial holidays occurring on the festivals of saints have already been noted, and other Saints' days surviving from the pre-Reformation church calendar, took on a secular significance. These included St Thomas's Day when, throughout much of England, charitable doles were collected by the poor.[59]

Beneath the Christian ceremonial calendar some folklorists have pointed to the survival, in popular memory, of an older, pagan calendar.[60] It has been suggested that much of the form and symbolism of popular custom during this period can be traced to pre-Christian times. A good deal of this analysis is not helpful to the study of popular custom in the eighteenth and nineteenth centuries, when the social and economic functions of folk custom were of greater significance to the labouring poor than were memories of past religious systems.

The overlay of these various types of calendar, and the incidence of local or regional customary events, produced the many local customary calendars for different villages and towns, as was noted of southern England in the nineteenth century:

> The elder men, nevertheless, yet reckon by the feast-day; it is a fixed point in the calendar, which they construct every year, of local events. Such and such fair is calculated to fall so many days after the first full moon in a particular month; and another fair falls so long after that. An old man will thus tell you the dates of every fair and feast in all the villages and little towns ten or fifteen miles round about. He quite ignores the modern system of reckoning time, going by the ancient ecclesiastical calendar and the moon.[61]

Local Customary Groups: The Case of Church Ringers

> The poor man, Dawson, who died on Tuesday, was buried this evening, and a merry peal succeeded, as in the preceding case. I understand that £2 are ordered to the ringers, as Dilly, the Butler (at the Manor House) asked me how I should recommend it being paid. I said, if possible, one half to be spent in beer, the other half to be divided among them; but I feared this could not be done. I shall be heartily glad when this scene of drunkeness and uproar is at an end.
>
> Reverend John Skinner, *Diary*
> Thursday, 11 July 1822.[62]

Some groups within the parish derived their roles from their relationship to the local customary calendar. One such group was that of the church ringers. Their relationship to the inhabitants of the parish was a customary one. The church ringers were an important customary group in the local community, legitimating certain secular activities, reinforcing adherence to the so-called state services, signalling local rites of passage and claiming, as their due, customary largess. They operated within a local customary calendar and resisted attempts to control their activities.

The church, since the Reformation, had set out rules governing the use of bells in churches and had prohibited their use to herald Saints' days or other holy days or for ecclesiastical purposes. It was stated in the Canon against the profanation of churches that 'neither the bells to be rung superstitiously upon Holy-days or Eves abrogated by the Book of Common Prayer, nor at any other times, without good cause to be allowed by the Minister of the place, and by themselves'.[63] The latter referred to the churchwardens and their assistants. Bells were, however, rung to celebrate secular occasions such as military victories, and national anniversaries including Royal Oak Day. They were also rung to herald certain secular calendar events such as Shrove Tuesday and the commencement of gleaning at the end of harvest.

As Arthur Warne has pointed out, the eighteenth century saw 'great progress in the art and popularity of ringing',[64] indeed, England was known proverbially as the 'ringing Island'.[65] Yet there remained a certain ambivalence towards bell ringing for the Church authorities. The Canon made it clear that ringing 'superstitiously' was not permitted. It did not, however, define the nature of the 'good cause' for which bell ringing might be allowed nor in whom lay the authority to allow it. It implied that the power to authorise ringing lay both with the local clergyman and with the churchwardens. Indeed, the ringing of the church bells was an important symbol of legitimation to the community.

At Waddington, Lincolnshire, in 1706, the churchwardens recorded the payment of 1 shilling and 4 pence 'on Plow-day, the 7 January paid to the Ringers and Minstrels'. The Plough Monday custom of taking round the plough for largess was accompanied, in this case, by the ringing of bells.[66] The Wolverhampton churchwardens' accounts indicate that sums were paid to the ringers during Rogation week. They received 15 shillings in 1729, £1 10 shillings in 1740, 19 shillings in 1746, and 15 shillings in 1750.[67] The number of occasions for which the ringing of the church bells was required by custom, and for which payment of beer to the ringers was required, was seen as too numerous in Minehead during the early eighteenth century. At the church vestry meeting on 11 April 1732 'it was decided, as the cost of ringing had become so excessive, that the number of anniversaries on which the bells should be rung should be reduced to five, of which May 29th and November 5th were two, and in 1765–66 it was decided that the ringers should be paid "for ringing on 5th of November and 29th May yearly and on no other day at the expense of the parish".'[68] It is interesting to note that, at Minehead, these two celebrations which were authorised in the Book of Common Prayer continued to be heralded by the ringing of church bells. This customary activity was legitimated by the church services ordained by State authority, and also reinforced them publicly within the community. This practice was also customary at North Curry in Somerset, where the bells were annually rung on the anniversaries of the Gunpowder Plot and the Restoration. At Stoke St Gregory the ringers received on 5 November 15 shillings and 3 pence in cider and expenses in 1744. In 1746, they received 11 shillings and 7 pence in 'half-hogshead of cider and bread and backey'. In 1772 they received bread, meat and cheese in addition.[69]

As well as the anniversaries commemorated by the state services, church bell ringing announced other secular calendar customs. In Cambridgeshire, until the end of the nineteenth century, gleaning could not begin until the gleaning bell had been rung. This was sometimes a handbell but in some places the church bells were used. At Little Shelford the gleaning bell was rung at 8 o'clock. Any woman who commenced gleaning before the bell was set upon by the other gleaners and had her gleanings scattered around the field.[70] In 1876 the gleaning bell was still rung at Waltham-on-the-Wolds and Wymondham in Leicestershire,[71] and in 1880 it was still rung or had only recently been discontinued in no fewer than twenty parishes in Rutland.[72] It has been pointed out recently that the gleaning or leasing bell was a widespread practice throughout nineteenth-century England.[73]

As David Morgan has written, 'from the parish church itself came a formal recognition – even celebration – of this annual suspension of property rights'.[74] The gleaning bell was an important example of the legitimation given to certain secular festivals by the church. The ringing played a significant role in the defence of this customary activity.

On Shrove Tuesday, the 'pancake bell' was rung in many places in England. This bell, in pre-Reformation times, summoned parishioners to church for pre-Lent confession. It was often called the shroving or shreeving bell. After the Reformation, the bell was rung to herald the making of pancakes for the annual visit of the shrovers or lent crockers. In Leicestershire, in 1876, in no fewer than fifty-five parishes was the custom recorded as continuing or as having only recently being discontinued.[75] In 1880 in Rutland, the shroving bell was rung or had only recently ceased in nineteen parishes.[76] Significantly, eleven of the Rutland parishes are recorded for both gleaning and shroving ringing. At Belgrave, the oldest apprentice rang the shroving bell.[77] These secular festivals were defended by their public recognition by the church. The ringing of the church bells was an important symbol of legitimation.

The ringers themselves formed a distinct and independent group within the parish, preserving their skills and controlling their work in much the same way as other crafts or trades in the eighteenth century. One commentator wrote in the nineteenth century that 'The ringers are an independent body, rustics though they be – monopolists, not to be lightly ordered about, as many a vicar has found to his cost, having a silent belfry for his pains, and not a man to be got, either, from adjacent villages. It is about as easy to break this solid [church] tower over with a walking-stick as to change village customs'.[78]

Part of this independence rested upon the significance of ringers' earnings to their family economies. At Roade, Northamptonshire, in 1794, Richard Walker supplemented his annual income by £1 6 shillings for ringing the church bell twice daily.[79] Other accounts show that the ringers, as at Wolverhampton and in Somerset at Minehead, previously cited, were paid significant amounts for ringing at the customary times. Woodforde recorded that on 5 November 1763, at Thurloxton, Somerset, it was usual to pay the local ringers, 'to give them something to drink, it being customary, therefore I sent them, it being a custom, one shilling'.[80] He was also rung into the parish of Babcary in Somerset when he took up the curacy in January 1764: 'I was rung into the Parish by Mr John Bower's order, who gave the Ringers a pail of cider on purpose to ring me into the Parish. They gave me another ring this afternoon after service, and for which I gave them two shillings and six pence.'[81]

Another way in which church ringers supplemented their incomes was by the annual Christmas ringing. In 1766, at Bletchley, the ringers who were to ring the midnight peal on Christmas Eve went 'to sup at the ale-house, as usual, till near 12 o'clock'. It was also recorded of the Bletchley ringers that they were entertined by the local parish priest in September, and in 1767, on Easter Monday, they were further entertained, 'drinking ale in the kitchen'.[82]

The ringer's calendar required payment for customary ringing and such payment was also necessary for non-calendrical occasions. Local lore has it that, at Burwash, in Sussex, the ringers refused to celebrate the passage of George IV through the village on his return to Brighton from a visit to Sir John Lade at Etchingham. This was because, on his way to Sir John Lade's when the king had been rung through the Parish, no provision was made for beer for the ringers.[83]

At Christmas, in some cases, the ringers came round the parish, handbell ringing. One West Country farmer recalled of his boyhood in the 1870s. 'At Christmas there was again much jollity, the eve of that day being ushered in by the bells of the old parish church in the distance.' He also recalled the visits of the handbell ringers 'who so cleverly manipulated these sweet hand-bells'.[84] Richard Jeffries commented that 'if towards Christmas you should chance to say to the ringers that such and such a chime seemed rung pleasantly, be certain that you will hear it night after night coming with a throbbing joyfulness through the starlit air'.[85] He also stressed that, together with the village band, wassailers, and mummers, 'The ringers from the church came too, with their hand-bells, and ring pleasant tunes . . . standing on the crisp frozen grass of the green before the window. They are well rewarded, for bells are great favourites with all country people.'[86] In 1789, Woodforde noted that he paid one 'Willian Mason of Sparham who goes about at Christmas playing on 10 Bells' one shilling and six pence.[87] Similar largess was extended to 'a poor Kentish man who goes about the country and plays tunes on the church bells'.[88] The collection of largess, as with other customary visitants round the parish at Christmas, motivated the church ringers. It provided an opportunity for the parishioners to give either food, drink or money towards the maintenance of the church ringers, and to support their customary role in the parish in heralding many secular and ecclesiastical calendar occasions.

In some cases church bell ringing was not without its dangers. At a Christmas Eve ringing near Uppingham in 1824 a boy of fourteen 'was engaged at the church, with others, in ringing, when his bell overset, and instantly pulled him up to the ceiling with such force that one of his arms was fractured, and in descending from the ceiling he fell to the ground, and expired in a short time after.' This occasioned the writer of the report to issue 'a melancholy warning to youth of the danger and impropriety of their engaging in amusements calculated for maturer strength'.[89]

Bell ringers, in claiming their customary dues, sometimes found themselves in conflict with local clergymen. At Camerton, the Reverend John Skinner disapproved of the behaviour of his parish ringers. When the daughter of the family of the local lady of the manor, Mrs Jarrett, was married in 1822, the ringers celebrated with the customary ringing for which they received payment. On the Sunday following the week of general festivity, Skinner recorded:

> As soon as the bells began to ring I went to the Church to request that we might have no more rejoicing, as we had been surfeited with it the last week. Harris said it was not his intention to ring otherwise than to call the people to church, unless Mr. Gooch [the bridegroom in the recent wedding] sent to order it. I replied that it was a general order of mine that there should be no peal-ringing on a Sunday, and that order must be abided by: that I had no idea Mr Gooch would send any message of the kind; if he did, he [Harris] was to say what I told him.[90]

Skinner also quarrelled with his church singers. The following week, Skinner received a request from one Stephens to let the ringers give a peal, it being the King's Coronation Day, and that the people at Paulton and Midsomer Norton had been ringing the whole morning. I said I was as much attached to the King as any man in the country, yet could not see how His Majesty derived any good from people leaving their work to make a noise with the bells; with respect to the ringers, they certainly did themselves much injury by frequenting the Ale Houses in the manner they had done last week and then returning home and beating their wives to a jelly. I said, as the Parish seemed so desirous of having them rung (Mr Gooch had given them a guinea, and Weeks, the Churchwarden, 5 shillings for the purpose) I would not oppose it; but I recommended their not going to the Public House spending the money they had gained in folly, which might be much better spent on their families. They accordingly commenced their ringing, and I walked to the village to avoid the jingling of the bells.[91]

Here the tension between clergyman and churchwarden is clear, illustrating the essential difficulty which was created by Canon Law in that no absolute authority concerning the ringing of the church bells was given either to the church-wardens or to the local parish priest. Skinner did not quarrel with local custom but made it apparent that he did not support it.

In August, Skinner again faced conflict over the use of the church bells. In this case, the dispute concerned who was authorised to ring the bells. Mrs Jarrett was returning to Camerton and some of her workmen requested the key to the church from Skinner so that they could ring the bells. He refused saying that he 'declined giving permission, as some of them were Camerton people, and I had made a regulation that only those who rang the bells for church would be considered as the parish ringers'. They argued that he had no authority to refuse the key as it should be in the possession of the churchwarden. Furthermore, they stated that the churchwarden 'had a right to let them ring'. 'I told them', Skinner recorded, 'he had no right to let them ring without my consent, and I certainly should not grant it on the present occasion. They then became very insolent, and I left them.'

Later, Skinner heard one of the bells strike. He went to the

Church and found all the doors shut. He 'called out to the man in the belfry and desired him to come down and give me admission, which he declined to do, I put my foot to the door and forced it open. I found three men there, whom I desired instantly to leave the Church, which at first they seemed disposed to resist, but finally they went down the belfry stairs, and walked into the churchyard, which they absolutely refused to quit, saying they had as much right there as myself.' It was only after Mrs Jarrett's servants communicated her desire that they should leave that the men did so saying that 'they would do as Mrs Jarrett wished, but not for me'.[92]

John Skinner's incumbency at Camerton was not a tranquil one, but much of his dispute with the ringers and with ringing arose from the ambiguity as to with whom lay the authority for the church bells and their use. The involvement of the local landed family is also interesting. Their rites of passage provided opportunities for festivity to the parish and for financial gain to the ringers. In July 1823 the ringers rang for the coming-of-age of Mrs Jarrett's eldest son.

In 1830, Skinner had further difficulty with the ringers. After a dispute with the church choir he had permitted the singers to return to the church, although he did not like their music, preferring that of the band of school girls who had sung there in the interim. But he admitted that the singers induced people to come to church.[93] In February, he recorded that 'There was no ringing for church; when I spoke to White he was impudent, and when I told him I had given the ringers a Christmas-box on condition that they would ring the bells for Church regularly, and attend themselves, he said, if I minded so much about the money, they would give it me back again.' White later admitted to Skinner that he had not rung for the previous two Sundays because he had been drunk on the Saturday nights 'and had too bad a headache in the morning to bear the sound of the bells'.[94]

Skinner faced continued friction about the use of the bells. When he was requested to permit the bells to be rung to herald the arrival of Mrs Jarrett and her son to the parish, he stated that 'he would not permit the bells to be made playthings of; if the ringers did not employ them for the purpose they were intended I should not consent to any extra ringing'.[95]

To celebrate Christmas Day, the church bells were rung. 'I cannot say my sleep was disturbed, but my waking hours certainly were by the ringing of bells about seven o'clock announcing the joyous day, when half the parish at least will be drunk.'[96] The following Christmas Skinner was awakened by 'the loud peals these thoughtless people among whom I dwell chose to ring, as they suppose, in honour of the day. They had better retire within themselves, and commune with their hearts, and be still.'[97] He had been obliged to give up the key of the church to allow for the customary Christmas ringing.

At the death of King George IV in 1830, the ringers were again in conflict with Skinner.

> We had scarcely finished dinner when I heard a peal from the church strike out. This rather surprised me, as no one had asked for the key of the Church, and I had told the ringers they should not have it without my leave, since a pack of collier lads got together to ring only for the sake of drinking afterwards. On going to the Church, they said they rang for the King and had no occasion to ask my leave: that other Churches were ringing and they did not see why they should not do as the rest did . . . they had not gotten the key; they found the church open and had gone in.[98]

Skinner experienced many conflicts with his parish ringers, as he opposed their customary role. It is important to note that, in most cases, Skinner was obliged, albeit grudgingly, to submit to local customary practice.

In Skinner's troubles, there is no mention of the annual ringers' feast, except by implication in the accounts of largess given to the ringers for their services. It is probable that largess collected at Christmas, and at other times, was used by the ringers in general festivity, but, in some places, as has been seen already, they were given a specific feast, either at the expense of the local clergyman, or of the Parish.

At Hinkley, in Leicestershire, the ringers, on Oak Apple Day (29 May) placed oak boughs over the doors of the principal inhabitants and also affixed them to the tower of the church. They also rang the bells upon their own initiative.[99] In the early-twentieth century, at Upton Grey, Hampshire, the ringers rang the church bells at 6.00 a.m. on Royal Oak Day (29 May) and placed oak boughs over the church porch, the lychgate and the houses of the village.[100] At Castleton, this custom was also practiced on Oak Apple Day. The churchwarden's accounts record, for 1749, that 8 pence was paid 'for an iron rod to hang the ringers garland in'.[101] Until 1897, the ringers toured the village with the garland, performing a Morris dance and collecting money. They were accompanied by a King and a 'Queen' who was a man dressed as a woman. The garland is, today, hauled up to the top of the church tower. After 1897, local schoolchildren performed the dance.[102] The money collected by the ringers was used for their annual feast. The elaborate ritual of the Castleton ceremony, where other forms of May rituals were interwoven, has caused some folklorists to write of paganism, green magic and, indeed, sacrifice, as the character of the King wears the garland over his head and is 'beheaded' when the garland is raised to the top of the tower. This elaborate ritual, however, was developed by the local ringers to reinforce the customary ringing on Oak Apple day and their right to largess, and was drawn from earlier customs including the election of a summer lord[103] during the village Whitsun ales held in the Middle Ages and early modern period.

Notes

1   J. Arthur Gibbs, *A Cotswold Village: or Country Life and Pursuits in Gloucestershire* (London 1898; reprinted 1934), p. 289.

2   Tusser's Calendar (1557) is quoted in Lilias Rider Haggard (ed.), *I walked by night: The life of the king of the poachers* (London 1935), pp. 96–7, and Edwin S. Hartland (ed.), *County Folklore* (Folklore Society, London, 1885), vol. I, pp. 113–14.

3   Bob Copper's excellent work on the history of his family derived from the memoirs of his father and grandfather – *A Song for Every Season: A Hundred Years of a Sussex Farming Family* (London, 1971) – also details a specifically local calendar with its labourer's holidays: 'Tater Beer Night – after Potato planting; Black Ram – the sheep-shearing feast, and Hollerin' Pot – the Harvest Home' (see pp. 101–3, 121–4, 148–51 respectively).

4   For the Parish see C. Pythian-Adams, *Local History and Folklore: a new framework*, pp. 17–21. For the Manor see Joseph Plymley, *General view of the Agriculture of Shropshire* (London, 1803), p. 4, quoted in William Marshall, *The Review and Abstract of the County Reports to the Board of Agriculture: Vol. II: Western Department* (York, 1818), p. 205. Marshall recommended reform: 'Many or most of these anomalies, no doubt, have grown out of *reasonable* circumstances, which existed at the times of their taking place; but which are, now, no more. How irrational, then, under a change of circumstances to suffer their *memory* to be the cause of grievance to the most useful part of the community. As well might the crutches of a cripple be handed down from father to son, aye and worn too, in compliment to the meaning of a distant ancestor, to whom they happened to be useful' (p. 205).

5   *The Bletchley Diary of the Rev. William Cole 1765–67*, ed. Francis Griffin Stokes (London, 1931), p. 46. Entry for Monday 5 May 1766.

6   Cole, *Diary*, p. 51. Entries for Monday 19 May 1766 and Thursday 22 May 1766.

7   Cole, *Diary*, p. 75. Entry for Tuesday 22 July 1766. Compare the description of Bletchley's hay harvest ceremonies with the painting (anonymous) of eighteenth-century harvesters at Dixton, near Winchcombe in Gloucestershire, which is displayed in the Cheltenham Art Gallery and Museum. See also 'Hay Harvest' by Arthur Oswald in *Country Life*, 27 June 1947, pp. 1204–6. See illustration.

8   Cole, *Diary*, p. 114. Entry for Saturday 6 September 1766.

9   Cole, *Diary*, p. 119. Entry for Sunday 14 September 1766. This was, in some places, known as Crack-Nut Sunday, from the practice of cracking and consuming nuts during divine service on this day. E.W. Brayley records of Kingston in Surrey: 'Another ancient custom (but of the origin of which nothing has been ascertained) was carried on, even in the church itself, until a time far within the recollection of many aged parishioners – namely, that of the Congregation *cracking nuts* during the performance of divine service on the Sunday next before the Eve of St. Michael's Day. Hence the long-remembered phrase of *Crack-Nut Sunday*.' E.W. Brayley, *A Topographical History of Surrey* (London 1841–8), vol. III, p. 41. In other places, cracking nuts is a ritual occurrence on Michaelmas Eve itself. See Oliver Goldsmith, *The Vicar of Wakefield* (London, Penguin edition, 1982), p. 49.

10   Cole, *Diary*, p. 141. Entry for Sunday 19 October 1766. This was probably selected as the Sunday closest to St Luke's Feast who was possibly the saint to whom Newton-Longville's parish church was dedicated.

11   Ibid., p. 146. Entries for Monday 3 November and Wednesday 5 November 1766.

12   Ibid., p. 186. Entries for Saturday 14 February and Tuesday 3 March 1767.
13   Ibid., p. 204. Ringers' Feast on Easter Monday, 20 April 1767 and p. 168, midnight ringing on Christmas Eve 1766.
14   See Thomas Brushfield, 'A Second Notice of Customs, Notions and Practices, at Ashford-In-The-Water, Sixty Years Ago', *The Reliquary*, vol. V, 1864–5, pp. 152–5.
15   Ibid., p. 153.
16   For mummers see James Woodforde, *The Diary of a Country Parson 1758–1802*, passages selected and edited by John Beresford (London, 1972), p. 55. Entry for 2 January 1769.
17   Ibid., p. 28. Entry for 24 December 1764.
18   Ibid., p. 54. Entry for 24 December 1768.
19   Ibid., p. 28. Entry for 25 December 1764.
20   Ibid., p. 55, 53–4. Entries for 2 January 1769 and 5 November 1768.
21   Ibid., p. 124. Entry for 12 September 1776.
22   Ibid., p. 125. Entry for 14 September 1776.
23   Ibid., p. 130. Entry for 14 February 1777.
24   Ibid., p. 161. Entry for 3 May 1780.
25   Ibid., pp. 321, 340, 489–90, respectively. Entries for 12 May 1788, 21 December 1788 and 26 May 1795.
26   British Library. Additional Mss. 41313 ff. 78–9. Letter from Mr Skinner to the antiquary, John Brand, dated West Norton, Norfolk, 26 April 1805.
27   British Library. Additional Mss. 24544. Joseph Hunter's copy of John Brand, *Observations on Popular Antiquities*, ed. Henry Ellis, 1813, vol. I, p. 350, note 3.
      Furmity was a kind of porridge prepared in various parts of Britain from cree'd wheat, water, milk, fruit and eggs. It was called by various names: fermity, frummenty, frummitty, and so on. See, for example, Thomas Brushfield, 'Customs and Notions at Ashford-In-The-Water Sixty Years Ago', *The Reliquary*, p. 12. Furmity was consumed after sheep-shearing was completed. Most commonly, it was prepared at Christmas from grain collected from local farmers on St Thomas's Day (21 December).
28   Flora Thompson, *Lark Rise to Candleford* (London, 1973), p. 250.
29   Ibid., p. 267.
30   Ibid., p. 268. The Jubilee Sports also included climbing the greasy pole for a leg of mutton. Flora Thompson adds that 'Prudent wives would not allow their husbands to attempt it on account of spoiling their clothes, so the competition was left to the ragamuffins and a few experts who had had the foresight to bring with them a pair of old trousers.'
31   Ibid., p. 250.
32   Ibid., p. 251.
33   Ibid., p. 251.

34   Ibid., p. 253.
35   Ibid., pp. 254–5.
36   Ibid., p. 260.
37   *The Diary of a Georgian Shopkeeper: Thomas Turner* (Oxford, 1979), ed. R.W. Blencoe and M.A. Lomer, p. 14. The hoppers 'nickcloth' was the particular 'badge of office' of the hoppers' foreman. Other claims included shoe-money or foot-money when largess was claimed of visitors to the hopgardens in return for dusting their shoes with a hop brush. The pole-puller was responsible for preparing the poles for the pickers by cutting the bines and pulling the poles and laying them on the ground. See G. Sturt, *A Small Body in the Sixties* (Cambridge, 1927; new edition 1977), pp. 74–5; Alan Bignell, *Hopping Down in Kent* (London, 1977), p. 35.
38   *Turner*, p. 43.
39   Ibid., pp. 12–13.
40   See John G. Rule, *The Experience of Labour in Eighteenth Century Industry* (London, 1981), pp. 194–5.
41   For a discussion of the anthropology of calendrical rites see Victor Turner, *The Ritual Process: Structure and Anti-structure* (London, 1969), pp. 168–70.
42   William Hone, *The Every Day Book*, vol. I (London, 1864), p. 571. This is taken from Randle Holme, *The Academy of Amory and Blazon* (London, 1688), p. 126.
43   Hone, *The Every Day Book*, vol. I, p. 571. 'The way goose, however, is still maintained, and these feasts of London printing-houses are usually held at some tavern in the environs.'
44   Hone, *The Every Day Book*, vol. II (London, 1864), pp. 235–6.
45   Ibid.
46   John Brand, *Observations on Popular Antiquities*, vol. I (London), p. 178.
47   See British Library. T. Park's copy of John Brand, *Observations on Popular Antiquities* (810.e.4) (Newcastle upon Tyne, 1777), vol. I, title page. Interleaved newspaper cutting on Christmas boxes. 'It is the Christmas-box which leads the 'practice boy into a public house, or brothel; it is the Christmas-box which first corrupts his morals, and gradually leads him to ruin. The custom is pernicious as well as ridiculous'.
48   Ibid. Also see Thomas K. Hervey, *The Book of Christmas* (London, 1836), p. 185.
49   Christina Hole, *English Custom and Usage* (London, 1942), p. 33. See also Anonymous, 'Pageants of Weavers and Woolcombers' in *Long Ago: A Journal of Popular Antiquities* (London, 1873), vol. I, pp. 369–70.
50   *Hampshire Chronicle*, 7 February 1785.
51   Hone, *The Every Day Book*, vol. I, pp. 702–3. For shoemakers, ibid., vol. I, pp. 733–5 (p. 755 for blacksmiths and dock-workers).
52   Reverend T.F. Thiselton Dyer, *British Popular Customs: Present*

and Past (London, 1876), pp. 47–8 and *Notes and Queries* 2nd series, vol. VIII, p. 312.

53   *The Gentleman's Magazine*, vol. 21, 1751, p. 474.

54   Hone, *The Every Day Book*, vol. II, p. 314.

55   Roy Judge, *Jack-in-the Green: a Mayday Custom* (London, 1979), pp. 28–41.

56   Atherstone – the game is still played on Shrove Tuesday.
Bedworth – A.H. Lawrence, *Bedworth: A Short History* (n.d.), p. 14. I am indebted to William Tyler for this reference.
Nuneaton – Morris Marples, *A History of Football* (London, 1954), p. 101; *Notes and Queries*, 6th series, vol. III, 1881, p. 207, George Morley, *Shakespeare's Greenwood. The Customs of the Country* (London, 1900), pp. 102–3.

57   O.W. Farrer, 'The Marblers of Purbeck', *Papers Read Before the Purbeck Society*, vol. I, 1859–60, pp. 191–204.

58   A.W. Smith, 'Popular Religion', *Past and Present*, no. 40, pp. 181–6.

59   See, for example, *Long Ago: A Journal of Popular Antiquities* (London, 1874), vol. II, p. 22.

60   See Christina Hole, *A Dictionary of British Folk Customs* (London, 1978), p. 6: 'Folk custom ranges freely through countless centuries, and carried us back to our earliest recorded beinnings, and beyond. May Day retains its essentially pagan character today, as in the past, in spite of the new accretions of political processions and the like which have been imposed upon it. The people who burn the Clavie at Burghead on old New Year's Eve are doing what their Stone Age ancestors did, just as, father south and in a milder season, the inhabitants of Helston continue to bring home the summer in the Furry Dance, like their far-off forefathers before them.'

61   Richard Jefferies, *Wild Life in a Southern County* (first published London, 1879: reprinted Nelson, n.d.), p. 110.

62   Skinner, *Journal*, p. 6.

63   *The Constitutions and Canons Ecclesiastical . . . of the Church of England.* Made in the year 1603 and amended in the year 1865. Canon 88: Churches not to be profaned, p. 48.

64   Arthur Warne, *Church and Society in Eighteenth century Devon* (Newton Abbot, 1969), p. 58. See also Tom Ingram, *Bells in England* (first published 1954, reprinted London 1978).

65   Hone, *Everyday Book*, vol. II, pp. 69, 255.

66   *County Folklore*, vol. V, p. 173.

67   Hackwood, *Staffordshire Customs*, p. 25.

68   W.G. Willis Watson (ed.), *Calendar of Customs* (1920), p. 201.

69   For North Curry and Stoke St Gregory, ibid., p. 141.

70   Enid Porter, *Cambridgeshire Customs and Folklore* (London, 1969), p. 124.

71   Thomas North, *Church Bells of Leicestershire* (Leicester, 1876), p. 120 (cited in *County Folklore*, vol. I, p. 121).

72   Thomas North, *Church Bells of Rutland* (1880), pp. 118–166 (cited in *County Folklore*, vol. I, p. 121). The parishes were:

Ashwell, Bisbrooke (discontinued), Braunstone, Great Casterton, Clipsham, Cottesmore, Egleton, Empingham, Greetham, Hambleton, Langham, Lyddington, Manton (discontinued), Market Overton, Morcot, Oakham, Seaton (discontinued), Tickencote (discontinued), Whissendine, Whitwell.

73   Samuel, *Village Life*, p. 59.

74   Ibid., p. 61.

75   North, *Church Bells of Leicestershire*, pp. 134–309 (cited in *County Folklore*, vol. I, pp. 71–2). The parishes were: Ashby-de-la-Zouche, Aylestone, Barrow-on-Soar, Belgrave, Belton, Billesdon, Bottesford, Broughton Astley, Burton Overy, Church Langton, Claybrook, Cosby, Coston, Dalby Magna, Diseworth, Evington, Fleckney, Frowlesworth, Glen Magna, Hallaton, Hinckley, Hose, Houghton-on-the-Hill, Hungerton, Kegworth, Kibworth, Knipton, St Margaret's Leicester, St Mary's Leicester, St Mark's Leicester, All Saints Loughborough, Lutterworth, Market Bosworth (discontinued), Markfield, Muston, Nailstone, Oadby, Peckleton, Rearsby (discontinued), Rothley, Sapcote, Seale (over), Sharnford, Sheepshed, Sibson, Sileby, South Kilworth, Syston, Woodhouse, Wymondham.

76   North, *Church Bells of Rutland*, pp. 118–66 (cited in *County Folklore*, vol. I, p. 72). The parishes were: Ashwell, Ayston, Belton, Braunstone (discontinued), Caldecot, Empingham (discontinued), Glaston, Langham, Lyddington, Manton (discontinued), Market Overton, Morcot (discontinued), Oakham, Ryhall, Seaton (discontinued), Teigh, Thisleton, Wordley, Whissendine.

77   Ibid.

78   Jefferies, *Wild Life*, p. 87.

79   Sir Frederick Eden, *State of the Poor* (3 vols. 1797), vol. II, p. 546.

80   Woodforde, *Diary*, p. 22.

81   Ibid., p. 24.

82   Cole, *Diary*. For Christmas ringing see p. 168. For September hospitality see p. 124. For Easter see p. 204.

83   E.V. Lucas, *Highways and Byways in Sussex* (London, 1935), p. 422.

84   S.G. Kendall, *Farming Memoirs of a West Country Yeoman* (London, 1944), p. 37.

85   Jefferies, *Wild Life*, p. 87.

86   Ibid., p. 108.

87   Woodford, *Diary*, p. 366.

88   Ibid., p. 450.

89   *Salisbury and Winchester Journal*, 3 January 1825.

90   Skinner, *Journal*, pp. 7–8.

91   Ibid., pp. 14–15.

92   Ibid., p. 35.

93   Ibid., p. 235.

94   Ibid., p. 236.

95   Ibid., p. 17.

96   Ibid., p. 73.
97   Ibid., pp. 122–3.
98   Ibid., p. 249.
99   *County Folklore*, vol. I, p. 93.
100 See D.H. Moutray Reed, 'Hampshire Folklore', *Folklore*, vol. 22, 1911, p. 298.
101 G. Lester, *Castleton Garland* (Sheffield, 1977), p. 3.
102 Ibid., pp. 2–3.
103 See David Wiles, *The Early Plays of Robin Hood* (Cambridge, 1981), pp. 7–30.

3 Custom and Legitimation

The Church

> Be thou still our mighty Protector, and scatter our
> enemies that delight in blood: Infatuate and defeat their
> consuls, abate their pride, assuage their malice, and con-
> found their devices. Strengthen the hands of our gracious
> Sovereign, and all that are put in authority under him,
> with judgement and justice, to cut off all such workers
> of iniquity, as turn Religion into Rebellion, and Faith
> into Faction; that they may never prevail against us, or
> triumph in the ruin of thy church among us . . .
>
> A form of Prayer with Thanksgiving, to be used
> Yearly upon the Fifth Day of November[1]

As Edward Thompson has observed, 'It is possible to detect
in almost every eighteenth century crowd action some legitimising notion. By the notion of legitimation I mean that men
and women in the crowd were informed by the belief that
they were defending traditional rights or customs; and, in
general, that they were supported by a wider consensus of
the community.'[2] In this way, the actions of the crowd on
Guy Fawkes day and Oak Apple day were, to some extent,
legitimated by reference to specific state services – religious
services authorised by the State – in the Book of Common
Prayer.

There were four services appointed to be conducted in the
Church of England, confirmed in the Book of Common
Prayer by successive reigning monarchs. 'Our will and
pleasure is, That these four forms of Prayer and Service,
made for the Fifth of November, the Thirtieth of January,
the Twenty-ninth of May, and the Twenty-ninth of January,
be forthwith printed and published, and annexed to the Book
of Common Prayer, and Liturgy of the United Church of
England and Ireland; to be used Yearly on the said Days,

. . . in all Parish churches and Chapels within . . . England, and Ireland.'[3] This was the form of the confirmation as printed, by Royal Warrant of George IV, on 21 February 1820, and endorsed by Lord Sidmouth.

These were the so-called state services and commemorated 'the deliverance of King James I and the Three Estates of England from . . . the bloody intended massacre by Gunpowder: and the happy Arrival of His Majesty King William' (5 November); the Martyrdom of King Charles I (30 January); the Restoration of the Royal Family (29 May); and the King's Accession (in this case, relating to George IV – 29 January).[4]

Two of these dates, strengthened in significance by their place in the Prayer Book, were of great importance to the labouring poor during the eighteenth and nineteenth centuries. These were 5 November (Gunpowder Plot or Guy Fawkes Day) and 29 May (Restoration of the Monarchy or Oak Apple Day).

The anniversary of the Gunpowder Plot was celebrated in many places in England throughout the eighteenth and nineteenth centuries, the form of the celebration being in one account prosaically summed up as follows:

> The universal mode of observance through all parts of England, is the dressing-up of a scarecrow figure, in such cast-habiliments as can be procured (the head-piece, generally, a paper-cap, painted and knotted with paper strips in imitation of ribbons), parading it in a chair through the streets, and at nightfall burning it with great solemnity in a huge bonfire. The image is supposed to represent Guy Fawkes . . . The procession visits the different houses in the neighbourhood in succession.[5]

These ceremonies followed both the state service in the parish church and the reading, from the pulpit, of 'An Act for a public Thanksgiving to Almighty God every Year, on the 5th of November' which concluded with the following words:

> And because all and every person may be put in mind of this duty, and be better prepared to the said holy service,

65

be it enacted by authority aforesaid, that every minister shall give warning to his parishioners publicly in the church at morning prayer, the Sunday before every such 5th day of November, for the due observation of the said day. And that after morning prayer or preaching on the said 5th day of November, they read distinctly and plainly this present text.[6]

In other words, by announcing the service of commemoration on the previous Sunday, a specific period of days was deliberately delineated, culminating in the celebration itself on 5 November. This was a powerful form of legitimation combining as it did the authority of Church sanction with the power of the State. The annual burning of the Guy re-affirmed the intent of the Act and of the Service of Thanksgiving, so that, in the words of Bishop Sanderson, 'God grant that we nor ours ever live to see November the fifth forgotten, or the solemnity of it silenced.'[7]

In fact, the political and religious intentions of the celebration of Guy Fawkes Day were founded upon older popular custom. The lighting of what folklorists refer to as need-fires in November had been a widespread practice, particularly in southern England and this pre-dated the state service. An example of this form of the custom continued until the late nineteenth century in Dorset where bonfires were lit at this time on the Isle of Portland. Once the bonfire was alight the following took place: 'A man taking up one of the children in his arms gave the signal, and then all the others followed him in single file round the fire, over which he leaped with the child in his arms. When the fire began to burn low the children also jumped over it. The following doggerel was sung:

Wood and straw do burn likewise,
Take care the blankers don't dout your eyes.'[8]

It is probable that this custom had its origins in the activity of lighting bonfires at midsummer, which still occurred in some places in England during the eighteenth and nineteenth centuries. In this case, the ritual was drawn out of its appointed place in Portland's customary calendar by the powerful attraction of the new Guy Fawkes commemoration with its more secure state and ecclesiastical sanction.

Elsewhere in Dorset, and particularly at Dorchester, the celebrations were accompanied with bonfires and fireworks. The Dorset dialect poet, William Barnes, noted in 1886 that 'The 5th of November still gathers in some parishes of Dorset its fire-wielding youths to celebrate Guy Fawkes night by flaring bonfires and flying fire-works, far more fun than Faux, and rather as fire-worshippers than politicians.'[9] It was reported of the 1870s that 'on more than one occasion disturbances have taken place because the populace has considered that its ancient privileges had been interfered with or its looked-for amusement on this night curtailed. I well remember on one occasion . . . in Dorchester when the military had to be called out in order to assist the civic authorities in quelling the riots.'[10] It was not uncommon for conflicts on Guy Fawkes day to arise between the celebrants and the authorities. One reason for the crowd's confident assertion, in the face of strident opposition, was that they perhaps believed that their actions were reinforced by reference to church and state sanction in the form of the state services.

In Southampton, in the late eighteenth century, one such conflict took place. The assertion of the popular right to celebrate the event was greatly supported by the fact that 1788 was the centenary of the Glorious Revolution, which was commemorated by the same state service. More formal thanksgivings were observed at Chichester on the fifth of November of that year, where

> there was a truly respectable meeting of the principal gentlemen of this neighbourhood . . . to dine at the Dolphin Inn; a great number of constitutional sentiments were drunk, and the day spent in the utmost conviviality. In the evening there was likewise held at the Swan Inn, the annual meeting on the above occasion, which was very respectably attended; an elegant collation was provided for the company, who, on this day, never fail to engage in mirth.[11]

In Southampton, meanwhile, events took a less respectable turn on the occasion of the celebration of the same day.

Indeed:

> a terrible affray happened . . . between the peace officers
> and the populace. The mayor had previously forbidden the
> throwing of squibs, or lighting of bonfires in the public
> streets; but to testify his approbation of commemorating
> the fifth of November in the customary way, he made a
> present of one hundred faggots to the populace, upon con-
> dition that the bonfire should be made in the Marsh. This
> was complied with; but after this great fire was out, they
> assembled in the town, collected a number of fresh fag-
> gots, and made a bonfire in spite of the orders issued by
> the Mayor, and the admonitions of the peace officers.
> A violent conflict ensued, in which many of the officers,
> and even the Mayor himself, was very roughly treated; but
> the rioters were at last overpowered, and the ringleaders
> taken into custody, and are committed to the town
> gaol.[12]

The following May it was reported that 'Two of the young
men confined since 5th of November last, have made their
escape from the airing ground, in the new prison, by means
of a rope thrown over the wall by some of their confede-
rates.'[13] On the occasion of the custom in that year celebrations took place as usual in Southampton, and 'A number of
boys . . . have been informed against, for making bonfires
and throwing squibs . . . in consequence of the magistrates
having offered a reward of ten guineas for apprehending any
one of the offenders.'[14]

Prosecutions for letting off fireworks in public were
frequent during the early nineteenth century as the authorities in many towns and parishes attempted to rid the Guy
Fawkes celebrations of their rowdy and disruptive elements.
In 1814 one Mr Long of Mere in Wiltshire was punished with
one month's imprisonment and a fine of twenty pounds for
letting off fireworks. The severity of the punishment reflected the attitudes of magistrates to the use of fireworks
in public places. This attitude was maintained in Wiltshire,
for seven years later similar offences were still being
punished. Hezekiah Morris of Westbury and Jacob Stiles of
Trowbridge were accused that they 'did throw, cast or fire

a squib rockett or other fireworks into the public street'.
Long was a linen draper, Morris was a shopkeeper and Stiles
was a labourer, which indicates that this form of celebration
was not restricted to one social group in the community.[15]

In 1827, in Salisbury, the Mayor became the object of
physical abuse when he attempted to dissuade one of the
celebrants from throwing fireworks:

> The riotous outrages annually perpetuated in Salisbury
> under pretence of celebrating the fifth of November, had
> likely to have been terminated in a more serious manner
> than usual . . . as J. Cobb esq, the Mayor, was endeavour-
> ing to prevent a miscreant from flinging a serpent in the
> midst of some post horses, was struck a violent blow on
> the temple, with a short stick, by some wretch, who
> instantly let fall his weapon and fled. A reward of 50
> guineas has been offered, but hitherto without success.[16]

Occurrences of this sort led to attempts to suppress the
custom through the association of the more respectable
members of the community, and in some parts of Hampshire
during the early nineteenth century this was successful:

> The observed custom of making bon-fires, and throwing
> fireworks in the public streets, on the anniversary of the
> gunpowder plot, to the frequent endangering of life and
> property, has, by the spirited and efficient measures of
> some of the principal inhabitants of Lymington, been
> almost totally abolished in that town. For these three
> years the practice has been gradually losing ground, and
> on the evening of Monday last, the streets were as quiet
> and free from fires and serpents as if Guy Fawkes had
> never been known.[17]

Other towns were urged to adopt similar methods to suppress
the celebration of the gunpowder plot. Yet despite these
attempts to restrict the activities of the crowd, the custom
continued, reinforced as it was by the state service.

In Wiltshire, prosecutions continued during the nineteenth century. In 1830 at Salisbury Petty Sessions, one
George Harms, a clerk, was convicted 'before a full bench of

magistrates' of throwing a lighted firework into the street. The bench 'regretted that any respectable person should be found so ignorant of propriety as to persist in the commission of an offence so generally reprobated by the public'.[18] The same year, in Bridport, despite this public reprobation, 'Extraordinary exertions were made . . . to give effect to the celebrations of the Gunpowder Plot, and before the amusements were ended, the warehouse of Mr. Joseph Hounsell, in East Street, was set on fire by a rocket. Nearly the whole was destroyed, together with a large quantity of flax, hemp, etc. Another place was burnt down at the back of the town.'[19] Later in the month other fires were to be lit in Dorset by the followers of Captain Swing, and it is possible that Mr Hounsell was the target for popular censure, enacted, in this instance, under cover of the customary occasion. If the burning of his warehouse was mere coincidence, it is clear that the anniversary caused great disruption in the lives of small towns and it is not surprising that, in other places, the celebrations did not continue unopposed.

One correspondent, writing in 1830 of events in Basingstoke, 'never for a moment doubted the power of the magistracy, seconded by the inhabitants, to put down effectually the Bonfire on the 5th of November; and the result of last night fully proved the accuracy of my opinion.' Nearly 300 householders in Basingstoke assembled under the leadership of the Mayor and were sworn in as constables to preserve the peace for seven days. The account relates:

> All assembled in the Town Hall at four o'clock . . and each body of constables repaired to its station, headed by a member of the body corporate, or some gentleman of the town. The divisions most actively employed were those of Back Lane and the Old Cattle Market . . . and their exertions were particularly required in disarming those who came from the Common with weapons, in order to prevent any affray which might otherwise have happened in the town. The Mayor, with his two colleagues . . . were in the Market-Place, surrounded by a very strong posse of constables. These arrangements left the rabble and their adherents without hope, and not the slightest attempt was made to make a fire; and not more than one person was

taken into custody during the night. After every thing was quiet, the constabulary force was invited to the Town Hall, where they partook of a substantial supper.[20]

The military precision of this large-scale operation is marked. These tactics were to be used only a few days later in Hampshire against parties of farm labourers during the Captain Swing disturbances. The correspondent was clear that the model provided in Basingstoke should be widely adopted.

I hand you this account . . . to convince every town in our large and wealthy county that the rabble can really do nothing when the advocates of lawful authority and good order are determined to keep the peace; and I confidently hope that the proceedings of last night have for ever put an end to a fire in the Market-Place on the fifth of November. Our worthy magistrates have acted as they ought to act, and they deserve and will possess the confidence of those over whom they officially preside.[21]

The customary proceedings of Guy Fawkes day continued in at least one town in southern England – and, indeed, continue to this day. In 1785 'the greatest riot that perhaps ever was known at Lewes, happened on School-Hill, where an immense quantity of wood was collected, in order to be set on fire, in commenoration of the Anniversary of the powder plot, which so terrified the inhabitants that they made a formal request to the Magistrates, praying their assistance'. Having prevented the fire by the expedient of removing the wood, the magistrates were obliged to read the Riot Act at six o'clock as the crowd refused to disperse. Instead the crowd 'increased to a very high degree' and

one of the magistrates, in endeavouring to appease the tumult and to take one of the ringleaders into custody, was himself knocked down, and rolled in the Kennel, (narrowly escaping with his life) as were likewise several others, who gave their assistance. In this rebellious state, accompanied with the firing of rockets, squibs, grenades, etc. the town continued till near twelve o'clock, when at last, by the spirited exertions of the Justices, Peace

Officers, and others, nine of the ringleaders being sent to the House of Correction, and several others paying the penalty of 20s each, according to Act of Parliament, for firing rockets, the people were dispersed, and all was made quiet. Many persons, who were on the above evening taken into custody . . . broke away, and were rescued before they could be properly secured.[22]

Lewes's bonfire-night celebrations were partly legitimated by reference to the state service. One of the principal features of the custom was the burning of the Pope in effigy, after perambulating the town. That it remained a source of conflict throughout the nineteenth century will be seen later.

In Hampshire and Surrey, at Farnham and Alton 'All windows facing the streets had to be barricaded' and 'the utmost rowdyism went on'.[23] Local account says a prominent townsman was set upon and killed at Alton one Guy Fawkes night, which led to the discontinuance of the custom there. Although such extremes of violence were uncommon, personal vilification was a regular feature of the custom in rural areas. At Bovey Tracey in Devon in 1852 'The Lustleigh folks had a bonfire on the 5th, and burnt the Pope in a white surplice: therefore the old women say it was intended for the Rector.'[24] The local rector was accused of preaching 'rank popery'[25] which was the reason for his humiliation. At Castle Carey in 1768 the motive of the expression of community displeasure impelled the effigy-burning on 5 November of a local unpopular magistrate. 'The effigy of Justice Creed was led through the streets . . . this evening upon the [fire] engine and then led into the Park and burnt in a bonfire immediately before the Justice's house, for his putting the churchwardens of Carey into Wells Court, for not presenting James Clark for making a riot in the Gallery at Carey Church some few Sunday's back . . . they intend to assist the Churchwardens in carrying on the cause at Wells.'[26] In this case, a local dispute before the Episcopal Consistorial Court at Wells was the reason for the effigy burning, yet this was common practice elsewhere in England. The behaviour of the crowd was particularly reinforced by the continuation of the state service. There is no reference to proceedings being brought against the effigy burners themselves.

In the present century, organised and large-scale celebrations equal to those at Lewes also occurred at Bridgewater. It is probable that the reasons for the continuation of these robust forms at Lewes and Bridgewater, with their marked anti-Roman Catholic elements, were political. During the Marian restoration of Roman Catholicism in the sixteenth century, seventeen protestants, were executed by burning at Lewes. After the failure of Monmouth's rebellion in 1685, the visitations of Judge Jeffreys and the sentences handed down at the Bloody Assizes were enough to preserve, in the popular consciousness, a strong sense of the need to commemorate fervently the anniversary of the gunpowder plot at Bridgewater.[27] The rolling of blazing tar barrels along the streets was a particular feature of the nineteenth-century celebrations at Lewes. This also occurred at Burford where 'The town was entirely given over to the rough element. A large fire was lighted opposite the Tolsey. About Midnight, two tar barrels in flames were rolled down the hill, pushed up with long sticks and so on. The old doctor . . . objected to the noise, so they rolled a barrel against his door, shouting all the while.'[28]

At Purton in Wiltshire in the 1820s 'several weeks before, the boys of the village, go to every house begging faggots . . . They were once refused by a farmer (who was very much disliked by the poor for his severity and unkindness) and accordingly they determined to make him repent. He kept a sharp look out over his faggot pile, but forgot that something else might be stolen. The boys got into his backyard and extracted a new pump . . . and bore it off in triumph to the green, where it was burnt amidst the loud acclamations . . . generally.'[29]

Memories such as this entered the folklore of villages like Purton. Indeed, this particular Wiltshire village had a history of opposition to all attempts to enclose or divide the green where celebrations, like those which took place on Guy Fawkes night, were held.[30] Censure of individuals, through the humiliation of being 'guyed' or by general chaffing or rough handling, was common practice on Guy Fawkes day, on occasion, to some extent, legitimated by the reading of the state service. Opposition to the actions of the crowd would

73

have been interpreted as opposition to the observance of the day itself.

The second state service which legitimated a day associated with customary behaviour was the thanksgiving for the Restoration of the Royal Family held on 29 May. This was known as Oak Apple Day from its association with Charles II, who never ceased to delight in retelling the story of his escape, after the Battle of Worcester, by hiding in the branches of an oak tree. The anniversary was also variously called, in the popular tongue, 'shig-shag', 'sick-sack', 'zig-zag' or 'shick-shack' day – a term which caused some considerable confusion and much debate among folklorists and popular antiquaries in the past. It has been connected to the term 'shag' which, in the printing trade, is used to denote 'a disgraceful dirty duty, a ragged or drunken compositor' or to a rough, cheap wool cloth woven especially in the Banbury area.[31] It was also suggested that the name derived from an ancient King of Egypt, Shishack, who took treasures from Jerusalem, and who was identified with Oliver Cromwell.[32] In Hampshire, in the mid-nineteenth century, men rose early on Oak Apple Day and decorated the doors of their wealthier neighbours with oak galls. After breakfast they went round for beer. If they did not receive anything they chanted:

> Shig-shag, penny a rag,
> Bang his head in Cromwell's bag,
> All up in a bundle.[33]

It is probable, however, that the term 'shig-shag' originated in the slang name 'shit-sack' which was a term of abuse specifically applied to protestant dissenters in the late seventeenth century.[34] A rhyme chanted in mid-nineteenth century southwest England illustrates the particular religious significance of the celebration of Oak Apple Day:

> Shit-sack, lousey-back,
> Go and tell the Lord of it.[35]

It was common for oak leaves to be worn on 29 May in token of support for the Monarchy. Those republican protestants who were not in favour of the restoration refused to do so, or wore plane tree leaves instead. A verse which was chanted on Oak Apple Day as late as 1910 in Somerset illustrates this division of view expressed in terms of arboreal symbols:

> Royal Oak
> The Whigs to provoke,
> Plane tree leaves,
> The church folk are thieves.[36]

Those who did not wear oak leaves were subjected to oral abuse or were sometimes beaten with nettles. As with prank-playing on April Fools Day, this punishment could only be administered until midday, whereafter anyone continuing to wear oak leaves became the object of the nettle-attackers.

As with Guy Fawkes day, the religious and political overtones associated with Oak Apple day were powerful, and legitimated behaviour in the popular view. The commencement of the day with the state service was an important stimulus for popular activity. Woodforde records in his diary, for 29th May 1769: 'I read prayers this morning at Castle Carey being 29th of May, the Restoration of the King Charles II from Popish Tyranny.'[37] Woodforde read the state service dutifully, although the entry implies a confusion with Guy Fawkes in its reference to 'Popish Tyranny', a term usually applied in the state service for 5th November.

In the early years of the eighteenth century, the incoming House of Hanover was particularly sensitive to public behaviour on Oak Apple day, redolent as it was of Jacobitism. In 1716, one year after the first Jacobite rebellion, 'two soldiers were whipped almost to death, and turned out of service, for wearing boughs in their hats on 29th May'.[38] The following year it was reported that 'Being the anniversary of the Restoration of King Charles the Second, the same was also observed in a very particular manner and abundance of people wearing oak boughs or leaves, in commemoration of the king being wonderfully preserved . . . in the Royal Oak; a practice kept off for fifty years past, but now taken up again to show their affection for the Pretender. Many of them were deservedly beaten by the soldiers, posted in several places, divers wounded, and even . . . one said to be killed.'[39] The antiquary, Joseph Hunter, added a note to this account stating: 'This shows (1) that the practice did not continue from the Restoration, (2) that it was revived when the question of Whig and Tory ran high and was intended as a compliment to the Pretender, and a strengthening of his party.'[40]

In the previous century, there is some evidence to indicate that 1686 marked the transition away from the formal celebration of Oak Apple Day. It always remained, however, a state service in the Book of Common Prayer throughout the seventeenth and eighteenth centuries. John Evelyn recorded in his diary for 29 May 1661 that 'This was the first anniversary appointed by Act of Parliament to be observed as a day of General Thanksgiving for the Miraculous Restoration of his Majesty: our vicar preaching on 118 Psalm 24 requiring us to be thankful and rejoice, as indeed we have cause.'[41] By 1686, after the accession of the Catholic James II, Evelyn recorded that 'there was no sermon on this anniversary as there usually had been ever since the reign of the present king'. The previous Guy Fawkes day (1685) bonfires had been banned.[42] Six years later he wrote that 'Tho' this day was set apart expressly for celebrating the memorable birth, return and restoration of the late King Charles II, there was no notice taken of it, nor any part of the Office annext to the Common Prayer Book made use of, which I think was ill done, in regard his restoration not only redeem'd us from anarchy and confusion, but restored the Church of England, as it were miraculously.'[43] By the turn of the century, Evelyn noted the return of other royal ceremonies. In 1704, he reported that on 30 January 'The fast on the Martyrdom of King Charles I was observed with more than usual solemnity.'[44]

The resurgence of popular support for Oak Apple Day after the first Jacobite rebellion was matched, in some parts of England, with similar civil disturbances after the second Jacobite rebellion. At a Rochdale rushbearing in 1747, James Ramsbottom, Abraham Lowton and others, with sticks, stones and staves, attacked the Union Flag Inn and broke one hundred panes of glass and did other damage.[45] The custom of rushbearing was underpinned by reference to ecclesiastical ceremony, involving as it did the ritual carrying of rushes to the parish church on the anniversary

76

of its dedication on Feast Sunday. The Rochdale report continued:

> It is usual at Rochdale to have a sort of feast every year in August, called the Rushbearing, when the Fools and populace of our Township in the Parish vie with another in the strength of their Mob or Party, the shew of their garlands, and such nonsense, and since the Rebellion they've distinguished themselves, by the Aid and Genius of a certain Justice of the Peace in the neighbourhood into two parties, called Blacks and Jacks i.e. Whigs and Tories. On the 10th August 1747, the Blacks, not content with making their show in the streets only, attacked Mr. Robinson's house, pretending some of the Jacks were drinking there, and about eleven o'clock at night, several scores of 'em, assisted by some recruiting soldiers, broke open the house, and cast many stones out of the street in at the windows, and wounded several people of the house within, and, after insulting and threatening the plaintiff and his family, ransacked and plundered the house, and committed great enormities. The aid of the civil power was called in, and the mob dispersed.[46]

Other symbols were much in evidence, including a plaid handkerchief hung out of a window; garlands dressed up with orange ribbons; and the slogan 'down with the Rump' was used; a song was sung in praise of the Duke of Cumberland and stones and piss-pots were thrown from the balcony of the Union Flag on the crowd below.[47]

Similar political overtones can be discerned in the celebration of Oak Apple Day in the same period. Perhaps the most significant outbreak of anti-Hanoverian activity occurred in Staffordshire after the second Jacobite rebellion. In August 1750 several people were charged at Stafford Assizes with 'having made an image of his majesty at Walsall on May 29th, and shooting at the same'. The prisoners were bound to appear at the Court of King's Bench.[48] The trial took place on 23 June 1751 when the prisoners 'were sentenced, the ringleader to three years imprisonment and to stand twice in the pillory, the other two men to two years imprisonment, and to be twice pilloried; and the women to be confined two

years to hard labour'.[49] This sentence was carried out and
one of the prisoners was pilloried at Charing Cross before
being taken to Newgate.[50] On 26 October 1751, three more
prisoners were sentenced to three months' hard labour in
Clerkenwell Brideswell.[51] One account of events at Walsall
records that:

> On the report of a great insurrection at or near Birming-
> ham, two troops of Sir Philip Honeywood's dragoons
> quartered in this city, marched out very early . . and the
> same night another troop of the said regiment from Per-
> shore, for Walsall. The most material circumstances that
> have been current here, are, that a great number of people,
> having neither grace nor love in their hearts, nor any fear
> of the gallows before their eyes, but being instigated by an
> unaccountable spirit, set up effigies of certain great per-
> sonages, shot at them, and then cut off their heads and
> burst their bodies. – And, yesterday, it was strongly
> rumoured that a sharp skirmish had happened between the
> dragoons and the rioters, in which many of the former
> were killed, and wounded.[52]

It is probable that the account of the subsequent affray was
exaggerated, although the details of the ritual destruction of
the royal effigies on 29 May seems to have been accurate.
This was an occasion in which the continuation of the state
service perhaps partly contributed to the action of the crowd
or, at least, provided a very real reminder of the Stuart cause
in the form of the general thanksgiving for the restoration of
Charles II in 1660.

In the mid-nineteenth century, at Starcross in Devon, a
memory of the political significance of Oak Apple day
remained in the form of the custom of carrying 'May babies'
round the parish. A contemporary noted that 'A medical
friend, riding his hounds, last Oak-Apple Day, came up with
a group of women and children, one of whom was carrying
something covered with a loose cloth. At his request she
raised the cloth, and disclosed a doll dressed and lying in a
neat box. To his inquiries as to the object of it, the only
reply he could for some time get was, "May baby, sir." At
last one old woman, with a sudden burst of eloquence, said

"King Charles beheaded in the Oak, sir." Nothing further could be gathered.'[53] In the same region, a more elaborate commemoration also continued in the 1850s. 'An effigy, similar in construction to those in such favour on Guy Fawkes day, is constructed of old garments stuffed with straw, and a mask for a face. Its breast is decorated with a paper star, and a sash passes from the left shoulder under the right arm, in imitation of those worn by Knights of the Garter.

The effigy is seated amid and under branches of oak, and the whole is placed in a cart, with which its proprietor perambulates the neighbourhood, stopping at each of the better sort of houses, of course in the hope of largess.'[54]

From this description it is evident that the economic function was the most important motivation for the Oak Apple Day ritual, and, indeed, many older May Day customs were attracted from their usual position in the calendar to the state and church-sanctioned date of 29 May. The collection of green boughs to decorate houses and the construction of May garlands were, in some cases, transferred to Oak Apple day. This was so at Langport where, as late as this century, 'men would go round the town with boughs of trees with oak apples on to decorate the houses. They would knock at the doors and offer you a bough, and if you gave them six pence they would give you one to put up over your door. If you gave them a shilling they would not forget, and next year they would bring you two boughs.'[55] At Lyme Regis in Dorset in the 1820s it was still customary to place a bunch of nettles at the doors of dissenters who did not display oak boughs. 'Dissenters who in Charles II's reign did not celebrate his restoration by putting up oak boughs or pay those who had put them up during the night, were served in this manner.' This had become rare a decade later when the informant recalled: 'I have not seen any nettles at doors for several years; party feeling as to the restoration seems now extinct. None save the lower orders wear oak leaves in their hats.'[56] The labouring poor continued the ritual as a method of obtaining largess, as was the case at Stoke St Gregory in Somerset where 'young men of the village cut oak boughs and fix them to the gates of the principal residents on that morning, afterwards calling at the houses for a money tip or drink of cider.'[57]

Some village Club revels or feasts were held on Oak Apple day, no doubt with the aim of seeking the protection and support of the loyal ceremony.[58] At Norton in Somerset, on the occasion of the Oak Apple Day feast, a green bough was hauled up and fixed to the top of the parish church tower.[59] This practice also took place at Great Wishford in Wiltshire during the Oak Apple ceremony there.[60] In some places in Somerset, during the nineteenth century, a procession was made to the parish church with a boy acting as King Charles.[61]

The taking of oak boughs was a source of conflict between landowners and the labouring poor, as this often preserved, in the form of ritual, rights of access to woodland for the purpose of taking wood for fuel. It had been formerly accepted that the taking of green boughs for decorating houses on Oak Apple day was permitted as, in the words of one participant, 'Neither the owners of the woods, game-keepers, nor woodmen interfered with us, beyond a caution not to touch the young trees; for lopping a few branches off the large oaks was never considered to do them any harm, nor do we remember that ever a summons was issued for trespassing on the 29th of May.'[62] In fact, this attitude of sanctioning the custom altered by the nineteenth century as the owners of woodland increasingly sought legal protection for their trees. The following warning, for example, was given in 1819: 'Cutting oak boughs – As much injury is generally done to oak trees on 29th May, we think it right to mention that three persons at Botley, Hampshire, were lately sent to prison for six months, for cutting boughs from oak trees in that parish.'[63] In this case, even the association with a designated day of state service was not enough to prevent interference with the customary rituals of Oak Apple day.

The church, in its relationship with the local community, was locked into the customary calendar. It was not only the Prayer Book which produced a legitimising effect. Another ecclesiastical work important in this context was the Book of Homilies. This was originally compiled in 1562 so that those ministers who 'have not the gift of preaching sufficiently to instruct the people, which is committed unto them' should be provided with ready-made statements on theological and moral issues and on the important annual church festivals.[64] It is not possible to ascertain the extent of the use of the first and second Book of Homilies by clergymen during the eighteenth and nineteenth centuries. It is probable that its use was widespread, at least insofar as partial reference to the Homilies could be made by clergymen in support of their own efforts at sermon writing. Certainly, the Constitutions and Canons Ecclesiastical which were made in the year 1603 and were amended in 1865 charged that churchwardens should ensure that, together with the Book of Common Prayer, the parish church should be provided with 'the Bible of the largest volume' and 'the Books of Homilies allowed by authority'.[65] At least the appropriate homily was used during the perambulation of the parish boundary at Leicester in 1894, and it is probable that this was common in many places in England until the end of the nineteenth century.[66]

It was by reference to the Book of Homilies that the activities of the labouring poor customary during Rogation week can be best understood. Rogation week was the week following the fifth Sunday after Easter, and embraced Ascension Day or Holy Thursday. Rogation week was a fortnight before Whitsunday, the seventh Sunday after Easter, and was an important period in the church calendar, at which time the parish clergyman sought to instill in his parishioners the concept of God as the bountiful provider. This concept was embodied in the title of the homily appointed to be used during the days of Rogation week which stated 'That all good things cometh from God.'[67] The purpose of the homily was not only to emphasise the nature of God as provider of all good things, but also to illustrate that the orderings of society were divinely ordained. In the second part of the homily a passage from the first book of Samuel is cited in support of this notion: 'It is the Lord that maketh the poor, and maketh the rich: it is He that promoteth and pulleth down: he can raise a needy man from his misery, and from the dunghill he can lift up a poor personage, to sit with princes and have the seat of glory.'[68] The third part of this homily is followed by 'An Exhortation to be spoken to such parishes where they use their perambulations in Rogation week for the oversight of the bounds and limits of their towns.'[69] It was the custom of perambulating the parish which, in this way, was directly legitimated by the church. During the perambulation, the community was enjoined 'to consider the old ancient bounds and limits' so that each individual should 'be content with our own, and not contentiously strive for others, to the breach of charity, by any encroaching one upon another, or claiming one of the other further than that in ancient right and custom our forefathers have peaceably laid out unto us for our commodity and comfort.'[70] This statement was crucial and provided a very potent motivation for the crowd during the processioning of the parish.

The practice of processioning, or 'hunting the borough' as it was known in some places in Wiltshire,[71] should be seen as part of a holistic structure which, in the early modern period, embraced the administration of the open-field system and the common lands through the Courts Leet and Baron. The perambulation of the parish represented a public affirmation of the physical and social boundaries of the community. Other biblical passages, from the Old Testament books of Deuteronomy and Proverbs, were cited in the homily and illustrate this feature: 'Thou shalt not remove thy neighbour's mark, which they of old time have set in thine inheritance'; and 'Accursed be he who removeth his neighbour's doles and marks.'[72] These passages were quoted in the homily with open-field administration specifically in mind.

The homily continues: 'They do much provoke the wrath of God upon themselves, which use to grind up the doles and marks which of ancient time were laid down for division of meres and balks in the fields to bring the owners to their right.'[73] The destruction of field boundaries had the consequence that 'the Lord's records (which be the tenants' evidences,) be perverted and translated, sometime to the disinheriting of the right owner, to the oppression of the poor fatherless or the poor widow.'[74] This exhortation was clearly rooted in the late medieval system of open fields and commons in which the distortion of manorial records, through the destruction or obscuring of field boundaries, could threaten the social and economic stability of the entire manor. 'It is lamentable', the homily continued, 'to see in some places, how greedy men use to plough and grate upon their neighbour's land that lieth next them; how covetous men nowadays plough up so nigh the common balks and walks, which good men beforetime made the greater and broader . . . for the better shack in harvest time to the more comfort of his poor neighbour's cattle.'[75] Mention is also given of the right of access across land for the passage of the funeral procession to the parish church. The homily advised that 'These strange incroachments . . . should be looked upon, these should be considered, in these days of our perambulations; and afterward the parties admonished and charitably reformed'.[76]

Enclosure and the division of open fields and commons irrevocably altered the context in which this homily, and the Rogation week perambulation, were intended to be understood. Yet the practice of processioning continued and acted as a reminder to the labouring poor that specific rights in the use of land in the parish had been alienated. Parish perambulations had, therefore, both a secular and religious purpose. As was noted of a perambulation in 1818 of a Derbyshire parish:

> The very name processioning had been transmuted (and not inaptly) into possessioning. The constable, with a few labourers, and a crowd of boys, constituted the procession, if such an irregular company could be so called. An axe, a mattock, and an iron crow, were carried by the labourers, for the purpose of demolishing any building or fence which had been raised without permission on the 'waste ground' or for which 'acknowledgement' to the Lord of the Manor had not been paid.[77]

In some cases charitable bequests were made for the upkeep of the perambulation. This was true of the Parish of Edgcott where the annual sum of three pounds, issuing from the rents of a piece of ground known as the 'Gang Monday' land, was set against the expense of providing cakes and beer to the tenants who took part in the annual parish procession.[78] A similar charity existed as late as the 1830s at Oxburgh where the sum of two pounds was paid on Lady

Day and which was known as Walk Money.[79] At Whittlesford in Cambridgeshire the custom of providing ganging beer continued even after the parish was enclosed in 1812. The cost of this beer was met from a payment made in lieu of certain parish rights in a piece of land known as 'the Ganging ground'. In 1833, 458 pints of beer were distributed to the villagers although it is not clear whether the parish perambulation continued to take place. In 1850 it was agreed that £3 should be paid to the village by the owners of the land on the understanding that it was *not* given away in beer. That year 121 poor people received a dole of £9 of arrears and after 1850 the custom lapsed.[80] Ganging or gang days were other terms applied to the periods of the parish perambulation during Rogation week. Charities such as these were usually administered by the parish clergyman.

Processioning had also a further function in that it provided the community with a mental map of the parish. This could then be drawn upon if disputes occurred between parishes or individuals on the position of the boundary. This was important in determining the responsibility for maintenance of the poor which was an increasing problem in the late eighteenth century. Also the mental map could be referred to in resolving disputes about field boundaries, rights of way, and the extent of commons or wastes. This mental map was the collective memory of the community. The oldest inhabitants were required to give evidence in disputes, and they did this by drawing on their memories of parish perambulations which they had taken part in during their youth. In order that these memories should be the sharper, at points in the perambulations, boys would be bumped, or stood on their heads in holes, or thrown into streams or beds of nettles.

The church's role in the maintenance of the Rogation week perambulation was fundamental. The experience of James Woodforde, cited earlier, illustrates that, not only was the clergyman required to attend the perambulation, but he was charged with preserving a record of the boundary's location in the parish records, and testifying to its accurate perambulation. In 1780, he noted that 'where there were no trees to mark, holes were made and stones cast in'. George Wharton, who carried the hook used to mark the trees, was paid five shillings and Robin Hubbard, who carried the spade necessary for the excavation of the marker holes, received a similar sum. This expenditure was borne by the squire of the village as was the expense of the supper at the Hart after the perambulation was concluded. He also gave half a guinea to each of six old men who accompanied the procession.[81] In 1825, at Diss in Norfolk, the Reverend William Manning led thirty-nine of his parishioners accompanied by music around the parish boundary, some seventeen miles in length. Each person completing the perambulation received 'a shilling for dinner, a shilling to drink'.[82] The perambulation of 1794 was preserved in the parish chest in which it was recorded that 'In the Boot Lane or Tibenham Long Row they made a cross, bumped the boys and others asses against trees, ate cakes, drank half a barrel of beer, and made a cross dividing Tibenham from Diss.'[83] The entire parish administration of clergyman, churchwardens, overseers, constables, surveyors and the older inhabitants took part in the perambulation of Fersfield, which illustrates the significance attributed by both ecclesiastical and civil authority to the custom of processioning.[84] At Shenstone, in the late eighteenth century, it was the practice to 'go a processioning or bannering . . . once only in about seven years . . . on account of the expense'. As with Woodforde's squire, it was expected at Shenstone that the perambulation should be financed by the local lord of the manor.

Other occasions when Shenstone parish was perambulated included the change of the lord of the manor or the coming in of a new clergyman.[85] At St Cuthbert Wells in 1752, the perambulation was carried out over three days by the Reverend William Huddlestone. To impress upon the memories of the inhabitants the location of the boundaries, boys were whipped or scrambled for halfpence at various points on the route. In the record of the perambulation precise reference is made to the names of the owners of the land, the location of field and farm boundaries, and to encroachments. At Broom Close corner, 'William Lovell aged 83 years and went to the Perambulation about 60 years ago was examined says that towards this corner the Warren has been Enlarged and Mr. John Bath and William Young also asserted the same had been enlarged within their memory so that all the flats from the said stone in the Crossways to Broom Close corner aforesaid are Incroachments.'[86] Another interesting encroachment is mentioned where certain 'Bound stones sett up in the Gulley said to have been erected by One Robert Moor since deceased when he was Bayliff to the late Lord Clinton and is an Encroachment for and on behalf of Ashwick Parish and they erected a Lime Kiln but Mr. Bath asserted to Mr. Perkins and Mr. James that this encroachment was made for the sake of the Lime Kiln and the Quorr [sic], for says he one Chappell (and the partner with Moor) when I told him it should not be suffered Chappell answered don't say anything and you shall have your lime 1s per quarter.'[87] This seems to have been an attempt to bribe members of the procession in order to conceal the encroachment.

At Brightwalton in Berkshire, the bounds were formally perambulated for the last time in 1720, one year prior to the first enclosure agreement in the parish. A form of procession continued after that date but without the official status of the previous ceremony. In 1720 the procession was led by the 'Priest and the Patron of the church, together with the chief flag or holy banner, attended by other parishioners', and the report records that 'The tithe of Rowdown Bank was lost the last year, as they [the procession] went round, the cross being made at the farther Holt Gate, instead of going up to the Upper Corner of Taylor's ground.'[88] Tithe and its distribution was another motive for the close involvement of the church in Rogation week processions. In the case of Rowdown Bank, the perambulation error led to the forfeiture of the tithe for the year in which the mistake had occurred. Rowdown Bank tithe seems to have been recovered in later years.

The aim, as expressed in the homily, that a correct knowledge of the boundary derived from the annual perambulation would result in fewer conflicts, was not achieved everywhere. In late eighteenth-century Devon 'These boundaries are very tenaciously kept: in so much that I well remember my having, when a child, been present at some desperate conflicts between the commonalty of neighbouring parishes who happened to clash in their perambulations or chanced perhaps to meet on a spot that from the uncertainty to which district it belonged was regarded as debatable land.'[89] In

Devon, the parish processioning usually took place on Holy Thursday when 'Great crowds of Boys usually accompanied these processions for the sake of cakes or rolls that are thrown amongst them here and there by way of making them remember the Principal points of the Boundary.'[90] In Shropshire it was held, in one account, that 'the discontinuance of the custom [in Shrewsbury] is due to the serious nature of the fights, when the "rough" population had begun to join the bannering parties, tempted by the refreshments, which of course held an important place in the day's proceedings.'[91]

The church, in helping to legitimate the activities of the crowd during the parochial perambulation, also underpinned for the labouring poor the geographical basis of the community as a ceremonial unit. The public procession around the parish was followed, at other times in the year, by the more private circuits of other visitants such as mummers and wassailers at Christmas, dolers on St Thomas's day, soulers on All Hallows' Eve, and catters and clemmers on the feasts of St Catherine and St Clement, harvest workers collecting largess in late summer, lent-crockers on Shrove Tuesday, and plough bullocks leading their plough around the parish on Plough Monday. It is in this sense that the Rogation week procession supported the many other customary activities of the labouring poor, and provided them with a context for the maintenance of the local customary calendar.

Through the state services, and by its attitude to other festive periods such as Rogation week, the church legitimated not only the activities of the crowd but also reaffirmed an older economic and social structure. This was especially true of the parochial perambulation which, by annual public notice, recorded the changes in field boundaries, the progress of enclosure, and the destruction of commons. In 1824, during the perambulation of the parish of Wolverhampton, the Reverend Dr Oliver recorded this kind of change: 'From thence we proceeded to Goswell Bush on Essington Common, but in consequence of the inclosure of the Common, the bush is now surrounded by a little clump of trees by the roadside leading from Wolverhampton to Bloxwich and Essington Wood; here the Gospel was read a second time.'[92] At East Butterwick in Lincolnshire, the annual perambulation was discontinued after the enclosure of the parish.[93] In 1807, at Stafford Quarter Sessions, the bench found against a local Act for the inclosure of certain fields and wastes in the Parish of St Mary, on the grounds that 'there was no consent in writing from the Mayor or Burgesses of Stafford to alter the boundaries of the said borough, and therefore that so much of the said award as related to such alteration of the boundaries and liberties of the Manor of the borough of Stafford should be void.'[94] This kind of judgement was rare. With enclosure, the parochial perambulation became inconvenient, but because of the previous encouragement given to the crowd by the church in the past, the labouring poor persisted in its actions in many places well into the nineteenth century.

The Manor

It was not only the church which had previously sanctioned parochial perambulations during Rogation week. It was also usual for the courts of the Manor to lead processions round the manor boundaries. In cases where boroughs also performed the duties of the lord of the manor, this would be carried out by the corporation. These manor processions had little spiritual significance, and were intended as an administrative device to regulate use of the lord's estate by his tenants and to prevent encroachments or other abuses by squatters, or by other tenants seeking to enhance their holdings or rights.

In the late Middle Ages, bye-laws on boundaries were set down. These had not been used in the early Middle Ages, and probably arose as the location of manorial boundaries were more frequently disputed. At Great Horwood in 1552 three days were set aside for the tenants of the manor to go the rounds of the boundary of the fields setting stones and stakes as markers.[95] At Launton it was ordered 'that on Sunday next . . . all the Lord's tenants of this manor shall assemble themselves together and make a view through all the fields of this Lordship of all encroachments made by any tenant upon others' land by carrying or removing of meres, bounds, or marks'. This last phrase echoes the homily on Rogation processions.[96]

Perambulations of Royal forests in the Middle Ages were an important feature of the administration of Royal estates. As these Royal perambulations continued much later into the seventeenth and eighteenth centuries it is perhaps the case that manors in close proximity to Royal estates also continued the practice. At the manor of Ermington such a 'beating of the bounds' took place every seven years from its first notice in 1603 to 1859 on the following terms, that 'All persons who it may concern take notice, that a perambulation of Erme Plains [will take place], on which the tenants of this manor have a right of common pasture.'[97] These tenants were obliged to beat the manor boundaries. The lord of the manor claimed rights to wreck and flotsam and jetsam at the head of the River Erme. It is probable that, since the terms of the perambulation combined the confirmation of the rights of both tenant and lord by the ritual of perambulation, the continuation of the custom was ensured as late as 1859. Indeed, the perambulation was revived after a lapse of nineteen years in 1878. On that occasion 'The claimant proceeded to the headwaters [of the Erme], where a net was cast and the proclamation read. Both acts were repeated at intervals all down the stream, the proclamation being last read at Mothecombe, where the river enters the sea. The beaters were joined by a considerable company . . . Good-humoured obstruction was offered on the part of Lord Blachford, whose agent objected to fish being landed on the West side of the river; while Mr. Pearce of Thornham, locked his gates, which were speedily scaled and the net again cast.'[98] It is not reported whether this 'good-humoured' horseplay actually pointed to a more serious dispute between the tenants and the lord of the manor over fishing rights. It is not unusual for apparent good humour during the performance of customary rituals such as this to mask genuine conflicts about the rights being claimed.[99]

In Southampton, the mayor and corporation of the town annually rode 'cut-thorn', that is, they perambulated the boundaries of Southampton Common to enforce manorial regulations. This took place well into the nineteenth century.[100] The council's lavish expenditure in providing supper at a local inn for those who took part in 'cut-thorn' was criticised, and they were obliged to reduce the scale of hospitality by conducting the perambulation in the morning and providing only a cold collation.[101] This occurred in 1766. Despite this reduction of expenditure, the custom remained an important civil ritual. One description records in 1789 that:

> Sir Yelverton Peyton, our present sheriff, accompanied by the Court . . . and a number of inhabitants, perambulated the boundaries of the town, according to annual custom. As the day was fine, we do not remember so many come to join the procession, nor such cordiality and good decorum to subsist. The company set out in carriages and on horseback for the Town Hall, headed by the sheriff, Mayor, etc. and were refreshed on the Upper Common, at a place called Cut Thorn, at the expense of the sheriff, where a plentiful cold collation was provided, the glass profusely circulated, and many suitable songs and toasts given. They were joined by the Hampshire Band, at Cross House, who preceded them back to the Hall, playing 'God Save the King'.[102]

The burden of the expense of cut-thorn had, by the nineteenth century, been shifted from the sheriff to the corporation. It was no longer a matter of the personal responsibility of the sheriff, for in 1819 it was agreed by the corporation that 'Mr. le Feuvre the sheriff be allowed the sum of thirty five pounds for the Expenses attending that day' – i.e. Cut-thorn.[103] In fact, Mr. le Feuvre seems only to have incurred expenses to the total of £6.6.0, on the evidence of the account which he subsequently returned.[104] Southampton's cut-thorn custom shows the link between the custom of beating the bounds and the operation of manor courts. This connection held for Joseph Ashby's Warwickshire village of Tysoe in the late nineteenth century when he recalled that, within his memory, the parish bounds were still perambulated by 'the respectable and substantial inhabitants . . . to see that the boundary stones had not been moved'. The perambulation itself was followed by a meeting of the Court Leet of the lord of the manor and then more informal meetings at the local inn.[105]

That the customs of the manor and the meetings of manor

courts remained a widespread practice can be seen from the following report of 1809 on Leicestershire: 'Manor courts are pretty generally held, even where the copyhold tenure is extinct, and their utility is experienced on many occasions, as the settlement of boundaries and preventing of litigations, appointment of constables etc.'[106] The continuation of the manor courts, even in areas where copyhold tenure had disappeared, with reduced but well defined responsibilities, was a further source of legitimation for the labouring poor. As in the case of the church and parochial perambulations, the maintenance of manorial boundaries through regular perambulations acted as a reference for the local community long after the decline of the open-field system, the destruction of commons, and the disappearance of older forms of land tenure.

An interesting dispute arose at Watlington in 1786 where the lord of the manor had enclosed just over an acre of common land known as Broadcorners which had previously been used for grazing the cattle of the poor.[107] This had led to the destruction of the enclosure fences as the inhabitants threw open the land to common pasture. The lord decided to pay 10 shillings per annum to the poor in lieu of their rights to Broadcorners. No written evidence of this agreement survived, so that the parliamentary commissioners who visited Watlington in the early nineteenth century enquiring into local charities were obliged to refer to an old parishioner who verified that Broadcorners was formerly common land and that, after enclosure, the local inhabitants regularly pulled down the fences. Without documentary evidence the claim was lost, but it is significant that the evidence of the old parishioner, who clearly referred to his memory of the boundary perhaps derived from the experience of manorial processioning, was rejected. That form of customary defence of common right was increasingly rejected when no written confirmation could be produced.

At the manor of Stratton in Dorset a manorial perambulation took place in 1738, and was very similar in form to those of the late Middle Ages described earlier. 'We present and order that the several tenants of this Manor do appear . . . at the pound, to repair together to view the Bound stones, and strike land shires on the penalty of 6s 8d to be forfeited by each person neglecting to do the same.'[108] At the adjacent manor of Grimston which, like Stratton, was an open-field manor in the eighteenth century, similar boundary setting occurred in 1789, when it was recorded that 'the several tenants . . . do meet in the west field . . . to bound out the several lands. And after the same shall be so bounded out it is ordered that each Tenant leave a Lanchett or a furrow between his and the adjoining land.'[109] This was a basic feature of open-field farming and explains why the perambulation was so important. The court held at Portland continued through the nineteenth century in electing a reeve, bailiff, constables and inspectors. The duties of the latter were 'to see that no encroachments were made on the common lands, that the roads and ways are preserved'.[110]

A survey of the manor of Sturminster Marshall in 1819 reveals the familiar features of open-field farming, including the following use of a piece of ground known as Shapwick Marsh:

> the marsh was thrown open twice a year, first in June for three weeks and three days, – fully long enough for the consumption of all the grass growing there, – and secondly on the grand event of the neighbourhood, Woodbury Hill Fair, 18th September, and it then remained open till 14th February following, old Candlemas. These open periods were severally called First and Second Swathe. Within the former of these, when the cows had been about nine days or a fortnight feeding upon the grass, a feast of Sillabub was held. This was a joint-stock merry making, to which one person would contribute the milk of one cow, another the milk of two, and so on, according to his ability, and Dr. Heath [vicar, 1805–22] would send of bottle of wine as his contribution to the festivity. The sillabub was made in the milking pans, and drunk after milking time.[111]

With the Enclosure Award of 1845, this entire system was dismantled and the sillabub custom disappeared. It illustrated the link between manorial custom, community festivity, and also a rough conception of equal status in the distribution of the responsibility for the making of sillabub.

Other festivities connected with commons administration

can be found. At Ogbourne St George in Wiltshire a festival known as the herdsale took place annually until the parish was enclosed in 1795. Mrs Charlotte Mills recalled that 'all the people who kept cows . . . used to send them to Roundhill-bottom . . . Humphreys a cripple used to keep the cows, and he had a herd's ale every year. He used to have a barrel of beer and victuals, and people used to drink and give him what they chose. I don't know now what day it was, but I know it was when flowers were about, because they made a garland which was put on someone's head, and they danced round it, and they went to gentlemen's houses who used to give them beer.' She recollected that this was long before the enclosure and that a large cow common existed then in Ogbourne St George.[112] Other forms of midsummer ales and mead-mowing festivals associated with open-field and common land management were objected to increasingly in the eighteenth century as occasions for excess and of 'acts of foolery and buffoonery'.[113]

These festivals of the manorial farming year reinforced the rights and regulations concerning land use. William Barnes recalled that 'At the stocking of Poundbury Field near Dorchester (now inclosed) on May Day, Dorchester folk were wont in the olden time . . . to go forth to its flowering and airy sward a-maying and to drink syllybub of fresh milk.'[114] This recollection clearly relates to practices similar to those previously cited at Sturminster Marshall.

Manorial usage underpinned popular custom in many places in England during the eighteenth and nineteenth centuries, and was itself supported by annual events such as the meetings of the courts leet and baron, and by the procession round boundaries. At Tiverton, where the borough was also lord of the manor, this annual perambulation was an occasion of great civic show, but was also significant for the maintenance of the town's water supply. In 1774 it was recorded in the Court leet books that:

> The Portreeve and Free Suitors, having adjourned the Court Baron, which was this day held, proceeded from the Court or Church House in the following order: The Bailiff of the Hundred with his staff and a basket of cakes; the children of the Charity School and other boys two and

two; the two water bailiffs with white staves; music; freeholders and Free Suitors two and two; the steward; the
Portreeve with his staff; other gentlemen of the town, etc.
who attended the Portreeve on this occasion; the Common
Cryer of the Hundred Manor and Borough . . . as assistant
to the Bailiff of the Hundred with his staff . . . In this
manner they proceeded at first to the Market Cross, and
there at Coggan's Well, the Cryer with his staff in the well
made the following proclamation in the usual and ancient
form – 'oyez'! 'oyez'!! 'oyez'!!! I do hereby proclaim and
give notice that by order of the Lords of this Hundred,
Manor and Borough of Tiverton, and on behalf of the
inhabitants of this town and parish, the Portreeve and
inhabitants now here assembled, publicly proclaim this
stream of water, for the soul use and benefit of the inhabitants of the town of Tiverton.

After the perambulation the procession returned to the Vine
Tavern, where they dined and where the charity children and
other poor boys received twopence each for accompanying
the procession.[115] It would be easy to dismiss this activity
as mere ritual – if ever ritual can be described in this way –
yet the ceremony had a greater significance. It defined the
ownership of the water supply at Coggan's Well and it also
promoted a conception of community harmony ensured by
the rituals of the manor and borough. This conception was
reinforced by the procession – the rite itself – and the commensality at the conclusion of the procession and the distribution of dole to the poor boys who also attended. This
custom was observed in Tiverton up until 1830.[116]

At Shaftesbury in Dorset during the eighteenth and early-
nineteenth centuries similar rituals took place. The town
obtained most of its water from a spring at Motcombe in
the nearby manor of Gillingham. The water was conveyed
up the steep escarpment to the town in barrels until 1844
when it was piped from the spring to a conduit head where
the barrels could be filled by hosepipe. Prior to this the water
was ladled into the barrels by hand. In the mid-nineteenth
century reservoirs were built in Shaftesbury and a supply
of water was provided directly to the houses in the town.
As the spring was located in the Manor of Gillingham,

Shaftesbury had annually to acknowledge this for the continued right to use the water. In the sixteenth century this was confirmed by payment of 'a penny loffe, a gallon of ale, and a calve's head, with a pair of gloves' to the bailiff of the manor. All the inhabitants of the parish were obliged to descend the escarpment at one o'clock 'with their mynstralls and myrth of game' and dance at the spring. In 1663, the ceremony was fixed for the Monday before Ascension Day, that is within Rogation week.[117]

At some stage after 1663, the presentation of the bizant by the mayor to the bailiff was introduced in the ritual. This was a richly-adorned bezant, rather like a garland and was decorated with gold and peacock feathers.[118] The bizant was only a symbolic gift as it was returned to the mayor's safekeeping after the ceremony. It was similar in form and purpose to the pyramids of silver plate and pewter, assembled for milkmaid's May garlands of the same period.[119] The display of finery and, by implication, wealth, was an important feature of both the bizant and the milkmaid's May garland. The accounts of Shaftesbury show that the decoration of the bizant and the costumes of the attendants were carried out at considerable expense to the town.[120] That the ceremony was the occasion of more elaborate entertainment can be seen from an account of 1762. The custom was referred to as taking place in Bizant week, and plays were performed and balls were held in the evenings. The bizant was displayed on the day of the ceremony at the George Inn, and the account describes that:

> it consists of a form of eight square standing on a small post, and consists of great variety of silver and gold medals, stone buckles and garnett necklaces, and up the sides a number of diamond rings, there are four large fronts in the middle of which is four pictures in miniature viz. Queen Elizabeth, King Charles, a family picture of Mr. Merrifields, and one of a young gentleman of the town. Besides these 'tis decorated with purple ribbons and at the top a small tuft of peacocks feathers.[121]

The procession to Enmore Cross where the ceremony took place was accompanied by a band of musicians, town constables and sergeants and the lord and lady of the bizant, who were annually appointed. As with the Tiverton procession, the element of commensality was important. After the ceremonial dance at Enmore Green, the penny loaves and beer were distributed among those who had accompanied the procession from Shaftesbury.[122] The labouring poor also benefitted from the difficulty of the water supply to the town, as they provided the large labour force of water-carriers required to transport the water-barrels from the spring, up the escarpment to the town.

The custom provided an opportunity for much festivity and it was suggested that the annual performance of the ceremony was curtailed because 'it became cause of so much rioting and dissipation (the water, the original cause, being entirely forgotten in the presence of liquids much stronger) that it was done away with altogether.'[123] This occurred around the middle of the nineteenth century, at the same time that more efficient methods of providing a supply of fresh water to Shaftesbury were being established.

The use of the ritual of procession, both in the cases of Shaftesbury and Tiverton, and more generally with regard to the manor boundaries, remained a regular feature of much of the customary activity of communities during the eighteenth and nineteenth centuries. It retained an administrative importance in pauper settlement disputes between parishes. The difference between the manor boundary and that of the parish was a source of confusion. A long dispute took place in Hampshire in 1784 between the parishes of Hurstbourne Tarrant and Vernham Dean as to the location of the place of residence of one Richard Gilbert and his wife and family.[124] The question resolved itself upon the location of Cornhold farm, where Gilbert lived. Both the land tax rate and the window tax records showed the farm as within the parish of Hurstbourne Tarrant.[125] Yet much of the evidence offered at the Quarter Sessions depended upon the contending memories of several local people, drawing upon their experience of the parish perambulation. The position was complicated because some memories were based on the manor perambulation. One Bray, a labourer, recalled processing the manor bounds some thirty years previously. He had to be reminded that 'boundaries of manor and parish was two things'.[126] He did not recollect going round the parish boundaries on Holy Thursday. One witness, of seventy-two years, had lived most of his life in Vernham Dean and had heard 'by old people who lived before him and by general reputation the Kiblets is the boundary and that is 2 furlongs from Cornhold house'.[127] Mr Blandy recalled going on the manor perambulation and that 'Dole manor leys in different parishes'.[128] Thomas Rendal swore that he had known the two parishes 'as long as he had any knowledge' and that 'Kiblets are the boundaries . . . been informed by old people now dead'. Another witness related that he had had a conversation with his father and 'he did not talk about manor but parish'.[129] Charles North recollected attending the parish perambulation which was 'in the meadow through the farm yard so through the house. 'Twas at whitsuntide can't say if Parson was present – never remember more than one perambulation'.[130] This indicates that North did not recall the manor perambulation. John Smith stated that he had gone the rounds of the manor boundary some forty-two years earlier. He remembered that both the squire and the parish clergyman were in attendance. John Holdway carried the flag during the procession round the boundary of Hurstbourne Tarrant.[131] Thomas Blake 'went 3 times possessioning' and Thomas Stevens had been possessioning of both the manor and the parish. After all this contending evidence, the court found against Hurstbourne Tarrant and the order was confirmed.[132]

Manor customs often legitimated the actions of the crowd towards rights of common. In some cases, more orthodox movements of social protest arose against the background of such customs, and took their forms. A dramatic instance of this kind of development occurred in Oxfordshire in 1830, when the activities of the crowd were directly legitimated by former manorial and parochial custom. Otmoor Common near Islip in Oxfordshire contained about four thousand acres and was commonable to eight adjoining townships.[133] The right of common was not closely regulated by the beginning of the nineteenth century. One account reported that 'The abuses here (as in the case of most commons where many parishes are concerned) are very great, there being no regular stint, but each neighbouring householder turns out upon the moor what number he pleases.'[134] The moor was enclosed and drained by Act of Parliament in 1815, and the rights of common enjoyed by the townships around its edge were extinguished.[135] Yet the spirit of resentment did not disappear. In August and September 1830 groups of people gathered to pull down fences and uproot hedges on the moor in the mistaken but strongly-held belief that a judgement in favour of some small farmers (who had broken the banks of the newly-enclosed River Ray, and flooded the moor the previous June to prevent their own land from being flooded), ruled all enclosures on the moor null and void.[136]

Perhaps because of the continuous tradition of opposition, the events at Otmoor reflected a strong pattern of folk belief. Firstly it was believed that the land had originally been donated by an unknown lady, who had decreed that the people of the neighbouring townships could have, for common usage, as much land as she could ride round while an oat sheaf was burning. The name Otmoor, it was suggested, was a corruption of Oatmoor.[137] Also there was a widely-held belief that the land was the gift of Queen Elizabeth, or some other unspecified Queen, or of Charles I. Thus the history of the moor was, in the popular mind, rooted in folk legend.[138]

Many of the nightly depredations were characterised by recognisable folk forms. It was reported that 'large bodies of men in disguises' committed 'acts of outrage' on the moor. These visits occurred almost every night from 28 August to 6 September 1830. Other accounts confirmed that some of the men blackened their faces and others were in disguise.[139] On the night of 31 August the depredations increased in number and many 'came in disguise with their faces blackened and some with partly women's clothes. They began cutting some trees of about ten year's growth on the Oddington side of the moor . . . whenever a tree fell, a shout of exultation was raised with a blowing of horns, heard at the distance of two or three miles'.[140] The summoning of the rioters by blowing horns, and their continued use during their operations was common in the Otmoor disturbances. The wearing of female attire was favoured by several members of the crowd. Such ritual forms, which can be found in much

folk activity, were significant to the rioters in their demonstration of strength and solidarity. They were reopening the
moor, and saw themselves as restoring past patterns of
communal life which had had legal support, and, for this
reason, made clear their intentions to the wealthy proprietors
of Otmoor by ritual action.

On 6 September, Otmoor was formally repossessed by the
townships. The model for this action was the annual parish
perambulation described earlier. The crowd decided to
'perambulate the whole circumsphere of Otmoor, in the
manner which they state it was customary for them in former
times to do, and that abandoning their nocturnal sallies they
would in open daylight go possessing and demolishing every
fence which obstructed their course.'[141] In their progress
round the moor, they destroyed fences, hedges and every
obstacle in their path, in a thorough and systematic way.
The cry of 'Otmoor for ever' was the only answer given by
the crowd to questioning by the sheriff and the yeomanry.
About 1,000 people took part and one farmer who witnessed
the procession, reported: 'the zeal and perseverance of the
women and children as well as the men, and the ease and
composure with which they walked through depths of mud
and water overcame every obstacle in the march'. The same
observer said that 'he did not hear any threatening expressions against any person or his property, and he does not
believe any individuals present entertained any feeling or
wish beyond the assertion of what they conceived (whether
correctly or erroneously) to be their prescriptive and in-
alienable right'.[142] One correspondent to the Home Office
took the part of the Otmoor rioters:

These Oxfordshire squires I fear are leading you right
honourable gentlemen soundly astray. There has never
been any necessity for Military. They can do nothing but
provoke bloodshed – The dispute cannot be settled by
swords and bayonets. The people of the Otmoor towns
complain of being wronged. They have all the country
on their side – not a voice is heard but in their favour.
If you wish to preserve peace and quiet only let commissioners be appointed to inquire into their grievances.
There are times when public opinion must be listened to

. . . beware lest *Otmoor for ever* become a war cry beyond the county.[143]

At Charlton-on-Otmoor, there existed into the mid-nineteenth century a custom of perambulating the village with a May garland on 1 May, accompanied by Morris dancers, and concluding with the garland, known as 'Our Lady', being affixed to the screen in the parish church.[144] A similar custom occurred at Oddington.[145] May Day garland rituals were often nineteenth-century remnants of more robust perambulation customs.[146] The possessioning of Otmoor by the inhabitants of the surrounding towns and villages in 1830 is probably the most dramatic instance of manorial custom legitimating the activities of the crowd during this period.

Notes

1   *Book of Common Prayer* (London, 1821 edition), p. 337.
2   E.P. Thompson, 'The Moral Economy of the English Crowd in the Eighteenth Century', *Past and Present*, no. 50, February 1971, p. 78.
3   *Book of Common Prayer*, p. 351.
4   Ibid., pp. 335–51.
5   R. Chambers (ed.), *The Book of Days: A Miscellany of Popular Antiquities* (London, 1888), vol. II, pp. 549–50.
6   Contained in the Act of Parliament as quoted in: John Foxe, *The Acts and Monuments of the Church: containing the History and Sufferings of the Martyrs . . .* edited by Rev. M. Hobert Seymour (London, 1838), p. 1025.
7   John Brand, *Observations on Popular Antiquities*, ed. Sir Henry Ellis (London, 1813), vol. II, p. 313. Bishop Robert Sanderson became Bishop of Lincoln in 1660 and was the author of the preface to the revised Book of Common Prayer.
8   Account from a MS notebook of Rev. W.K. Kendall, quoted in J.S. Udal, *Dorsetshire Folklore* (Hertford, 1922; reprinted 1970), p. 49. 'Blankers' meant cinders or sparks.
9   Udal, *Dorsetshire Folklore*, p. 48.
10   Ibid., p. 5.
11   *Hampshire Chronicle*, 10 November 1788.
12   Ibid.
13   *Hampshire Chronicle*, 11 May 1789.
14   Ibid., 16 November 1789.
15   Long was convicted at the Easter Assizes in Salisbury in 1814,

100

see William Dowding, *Fisherton Gaol: Statistics of Crime from 1801-1850* (Salisbury, 1855). Morris and Stiles were convicted by summary jurisdiction before magistrates on 8 November and 30 November 1821 respectively. See the summary conviction bundles in Wiltshire Record Office.

16 *Hampshire Advertiser and Salisbury Guardian*, 20 November 1827.

17 Ibid., 17 November 1827.

18 *Salisbury Journal*, 18 November 1830.

19 Ibid.

20 *Hampshire Advertiser*, 13 November 1830.

21 Ibid.

22 *Hampshire Chronicle*, 14 November 1785.

23 J. Alfred Eggar, *Remembrances of Life and Customs in Gilbert White's Cobbett's and Charles Kingsley's Country* (London, n.d.), p. 75.

24 Cecil Torr, *Small Talk at Wreyland* (Oxford, 1979), p. 17.

25 Ibid.

26 James Woodforde, *The Diary of a Country Parson 1758-1802*, ed. John Beresford (London, 1972), pp. 53-4. Parson Woodforde records in his diary for 5 November 1768 that he 'read Prayers this morning at Cary being the 5th of November the day on which the Papists had contrived a hellish plot in the reign of King James the first, but by the Divine hand of Providence was fortunately discovered'.

27 A full account of Lewes bonfire celebrations in the early twentieth century can be found in Arthur Beckett, 'Gunpowder Plot Celebrations', *The Sussex County Magazine*, 1928, pp. 486-95. For Bridgewater, see George Long, *The Folklore Calendar* (London, 1930), pp. 205-6.

28 M. Groves, *The History of Shipton-under-Wychwood* (London, 1934), p. 60. I wish to thank Roy Judge for drawing my notice to this reference.

29 William Hone, *The Every Day Book* (London, 1864), vol. II, p. 690.

30 Ibid., p. 604. See also the account of the dispute over Purton Green contained in Ethel M. Richardson, *The story of Purton: A collection of Notes and Hearsay* (Bristol, 1919), pp. 116-17.

31 See S.J. Coleman, *Lore and Legend of Hampshire* (Treasury of Folklore, no. 37, 1954), p. 1. for 'shag' and the printing trade. I wish to thank John G. Rule for the information about 'shag' as a form of cloth.

32 Ibid. The reference to 'Shishack' can be found in I Kings xiv, 25-6.

33 See G.F. Northall, *English Folk-Rhymes* (London, 1892), p. 243, which quotes *Notes and Queries*, First Series, vol. XII, p. 100.

34 See Francis Grose, *The Dictionary of the Vulgar Tongue* (London, 1811). Entry 'sh-t sack' - 'A dastardly fellow: also a nonconformist.' Grose gives a detailed and fanciful etymology of

the term, applying specifically to non-conformists.

35   *Somerset and Dorset Notes and Queries*, 1890, vol. I, p. 124. A further etymology is suggested on p. 176.

36   R.L. Tongue, *Somerset folklore: County folklore. Vol VIII* (London 1965), p. 163.

37   Woodforde, *Diary*, p. 58. 29 May 1769.

38   Brand, *Observations*, vol. I, p. 225.

39   Brand, *Observations*, copy owned by Joseph Hunter. British Library Additional manuscripts 24544 and 24545, vol. I, interleaved note p. 224. Joseph Hunter wrote in his copy of Brand: 'This large-paper copy I bought for the purpose of annotation. August 11. 1834. Joseph Hunter F.A.S.' The account is taken from John Pointer, *A Chronological History of England . . . to the end of Queen Anne's reign. (A Chronological History of Great Britain . . . being a Supplement to Mr Pointer's Chronological History, by Mr Brockwell.)* (London, 1714-21), p. 1003.

40   Hunter's copy of Brand, *Observations*, interleaved note p. 224.

41   John Evelyn, *The Diary of John Evelyn from 1641 to 1705-6*, ed. William Bray (London, 1899), p. 276. Entry for 29 May 1661.

42   Ibid., pp. 500, 493. Entries for 29 May 1686 and 5 November 1685.

43   Ibid., p. 550. Entry for 29 May 1692.

44   Ibid., p. 558 Entry for 30 January 1704.

45   Alfred Burton, *Rush-Bearing: An account of the old Custom . . .* (Manchester, 1891), p. 65.

46   Ibid., pp. 66-7.

47   Ibid.

48   *The Gentleman's Magazine*, vol. 20, 1750, p. 378.

49   Ibid., vol. 21, 1751, p. 283.

50   Ibid., vol. 21, 1751, p. 329.

51   Ibid., vol. 21, 1751, p. 474.

52   Extract from a letter dated Worcester, July 19 in *The Gentleman's Magazine*, vol. 20, 1750, p. 331.

53   *Notes and Queries*, 2nd Series, vol. II, 1856, p. 405.

54   Ibid.

55   Tongue, *Somerset Folklore*, p. 164.

56   Udal, *Dorset Folklore*, p. 43.

57   W.G. Willis Watson (ed.), *Calendar of Customs, superstitions, Weather-lore, popular sayings and Important events connected with the County of Somerset*, (1920), p. 200.

58   The Reverend Skinner recorded in his diary that Camerton Club day was held on 29 May in 1828 - see *Journal of a Somerset Rector*, ed. Howard Coombs and Reverend A.N. Bax (London, 1930), p. 159. See also Willis Watson, *Calendar of Customs*, p. 200.

59   Willis Watson, *Calendar of Customs*, p. 203.

60   See R.W. Bushaway, 'Grovely, Grovely, Grovely, and all Grovely: Custom, Crime and Conflict in the English woodland', *History*

Today, vol. 31, May 1981, pp. 40–1.
61   Willis Watson, *Calendar of Customs*, p. 206.
62   Chambers, *The Book of Days*, vol. I, p. 697.
63   *Berrow's Worcester Journal*, 27 May 1819. I should like to record my thanks to Len Smith for bringing this reference to my notice.
64   *Certain Sermons or Homilies appointed to be read in Churches* (London, 1890 edition), p. vi.
65   *The Constitution and Canons Ecclesistical* (London, 1890 edition), no. 80, pp. 44–5.
66   Edwin S. Hartland (ed.), *County Folklore* (London, 1885), vol. I, p. 91.
67   *Certain Sermons or Homilies*, p. 502.
68   Ibid., p. 513.
69   Ibid., p. 527.
70   Ibid., pp. 527–8.
71   The parish perambulation was called 'hunting the borough' at Calne in Wiltshire, see 'Wiltshire and General: folklore and tales. Notes on beacons, gibbets and Holy Wells', in the manuscript collection of Cecil V. Goddard at the headquarters of the Wiltshire Archaeological and Natural History Society at Devizes. F. 106.
72   *Certain Sermons or Homilies*, p. 529. Deuteronomy, xix, 14; Proverbs, xxii, 28; Deuteronomy, xxvii, 17.
73   Ibid.
74   Ibid., p. 530.
75   Ibid., p. 531.
76   Ibid., p. 532.
77   Chambers, *The Book of Days*, vol. I, p. 584.
78   Charity Commissioners Reports, 27 Report, vol. XXI, p. 71.
79   Ibid., 32nd Report, vol. XXV, pt. 1, p. 628.
80   See Judith Allen, 'It is the Custom in this Village', *Folklore*, vol. 92 (1), 1981, pp. 71–2.
81   Woodforde, *Diary*, pp. 161–2. Entry for 3 May 1780.
82   Eric Pursehouse, *Waveney Valley Studies: Gleanings from Local History* (Diss, n.d.), p. 137.
83   Ibid.
84   Ibid.
85   Frederick W. Hackwood, *Staffordshire Customs, Superstitions and Folklore* (Lichfield, 1924; reprinted 1974), pp. 21–2.
86   The St Cuthbert Wells perambulation is printed in *Somerset and Dorset Notes and Queries*, 1901, vol. VII, pp. 268–71, pp. 297–8. The encroachments at Broom Close Corner are reported too on p. 297.
87   Ibid., p. 297.
88   For the Brightwalton perambulation see G.C. Peachey, 'Beating the Bounds of Brightwalton', *Berkshire, Buckinghamshire and Oxfordshire Archaeological Journal*, vol. I, no. 3, October 1904, pp. 75–81. The reference to Rowdown Bank can be found on pp. 76–7.

89   Letter from Robert Studley Vidal to John Brand, dated 31 July
      1805 from Cornborough. British Library Additional manuscripts
      41313 FF. 83–4.
90   Ibid.
91   Charlotte S. Burne, *Shropshire Folklore: a Sheaf of Gleanings*
      (London, 1883: reprinted 1973), pp. 345–6.
92   Hackwood, *Staffordshire Customs*, p. 23.
93   Mrs E. Gutch and Mabel Peacock (eds.), *County Folklore*, vol. V
      (London, 1908), p. 296.
94   Hackwood, *Staffordshire Customs*, pp. 22–4.
95   See W.O. Ault, *Open-Field Farming in Medieval England* (Lon-
      don, 1972), p. 53.
96   Ibid.
97   J.L.W. Page, *An Exploration of Dartmoor and Its Antiquities*
      (London, 1892), p. 301.
98   Ibid. The account is taken from *Western Morning News*, 9 Sep-
      tember 1878.
99   This is so of Great Wishford's wood rights. See Bushaway, 'Grovely,
      Grovely, Grovely'.
100   See entries in *Hampshire Chronicle* for 15 May 1775, 25 April
      1785, 15 May 1786, 11 May 1789, 23 May 1791, 29 April
      1793, 19 May 1794.
101   A. Temple Patterson, *A History of Southampton: 1700–1914:
      Vol. I. An Oligarchy in Decline: 1700–1835* (Southampton,
      1966), p. 68.
102   *Hampshire Chronicle*, 11 May 1789.
103   A. Temple Patterson (ed.), *A selection from the Southampton
      Corporation Journals, 1813–35 and Borough Council Minutes,
      1835–47* (Southampton, 1965), p. 23.
104   Ibid., p. 24.
105   M.K. Ashby, *Joseph Ashby of Tysoe 1859–1919* (London,
      1974), p. 9.
106   William Marshall, *The Review and Abstract of the County Re-
      ports to the Board of Agriculture: Vol. IV, Midlands Depart-
      ment* (York, 1818), p. 215, which quotes William Pitt, *A general
      view of the Agriculture . . . of Leicester* (1809), p. 17.
107   Eric Pursehouse, *Waveney Valley Studies*, p. 242.
108   Alfred Pope, 'Some Ancient Customs of the Manors of Stratton
      and Grimston, County Dorset', *Proceedings of the Dorset Natural
      History and Antiquarian Field Club*, vol. XXX, 1909, p. 92.
109   Ibid., p. 94.
110   Capt. J.E. Acland, 'The Portland reeve staff and Court Leet',
      *Proceedings of the Dorset Natural History and Antiquarian
      Field Club*, vol. XXXVIII, 1918, p. 54.
111   *Notes and Queries for Somerset and Dorset*, vol. II, 1891, 'Stur-
      minster Marshall, 1819', p. 44.
112   F.A. Carrington, 'Ancient Ales in the County of Wilts, and in the
      Diocese of Sarum', *Wiltshire Archaeological and Natural History
      Magazine*, vol. II, 1855, p. 201.

113   Brand, *Observations*, vol. I, p. 227, which cites *A serious Dissuasive against Whitsun Ales* . . . by A minister to his parishioners in the Deanery of Stow Gloucestershire, 1736, p. 8.

114   Udal, *Dorsetshire Folklore*, p. 5.

115   F.J. Snell, *The Customs of Old England* (London, 1919), pp. 207-8.

116   Ibid.

117   Lady Theodora Grosvenor, *Motcombe, Past and Present* (Shaftesbury, 1873), pp. 50-3.

118   *Notes and Queries for Somerset and Dorset*, 1890, vol. II, pp. 235-6 which quotes an account in *The Mirror* 28 May 1831.

119   For a composition see the accounts of milkmaid's garlands in Roy Judge, *The Jack-in-the-Green: a Mayday Custom* (London, 1979), pp. 3-8.

120   *Notes and Queries for Somerset and Dorset*, vol. II, p. 236. For a description of the bizant, see *Notes and Queries for Somerset and Dorset*, vol. III, 1893, pp. 296-8.

121   *Notes and Queries for Somerset and Dorset*, vol. IV, 1895, p. 35.

122   See an account of 1790 in *The Western County Magazine*, vol. IV, 1790, p. 266.

123   Lady Theodora Grosvenor, *Motcombe*, pp. 51-2.

124   Hampshire Record Office. Quarter Sessions Records. QMP/2. Minutes of Proceedings, Michaelmas 1782-Easter 1784. Epiphany sessions 1784. FF. 171-9.

125   Ibid., F. 171.

126   Ibid., F. 172.

127   Ibid.

128   Ibid., F. 175.

129   Ibid., F. 176.

130   Ibid., F. 177.

131   Ibid., F. 178.

132   Ibid., F. 179.

133   Marshall, *Review and Abstract, Midland Department*, vol. IV, p. 449.

134   Ibid.

135   Home Office Papers. Public Record Office. HO 52 (9), correspondence relating to Oxfordshire. A full report of the history of disturbances relates the following: 'seven or eight townships, comprehended within four parishes, enjoyed a right of common upon it [i.e. Otmoor], namely Beckley with the two hamlets or townships of Horton and Studley, Noke, Oddington, and Charlton with the two hamlets of Fencott and Moorcott. The Earl of Abingdon as Lord of the Manor of Beckley is Lord of the Manor of Otmoor.'

136   A full account of the Otmoor disturbances can be found in Bernard Reaney, *The class struggle in 19th Century Oxfordshire: the social and communal background to the Otmoor disturbances of 1830 to 1835*, Oxford History Workshop Pamphlets, no. 3 (1971).

137 Ibid., p. 12.
138 PRO HO 52/9. The account to the Home Office of Reverend Theophilus Cooke dated 13 September 1830. 'They had . . . an old prejudice that Otmoor belonged to the poor of the Otmoor towns, and had been given them by Queen Elizabeth . . . This is totally void of foundation and the moor is precisely upon the same footing with other commons.'
139 Cooke's account, PRO HO 52/9.
140 Ibid.
141 Reaney, *Class Struggle*, pp. 34–5.
142 *Oxford University and City Herald*, 11 September 1830, cited in J.L. Hammond and Barbara Hammond, *The Village Labourer* (London, 1913), p. 95.
143 PRO HO 52/9, letter dated 4 September 1830 from Oxford by Philip Fayette.
144 Reverend R.C. Prior, 'Dedications of Churches, with some notes as to village feasts and old customs in the Deaneries of Islip and Bicester', *Oxfordshire Archaeological Society Reports* (Oxford, 1903), pp. 22–3.
145 Ibid., p. 26.
146 See account of Abbotsbury Garland day in *Notes and Queries for Somerset and Dorset*, vol. III, 1893, p. 231.

4 Custom and Social Cohesion

Harvest and Harvest Perquisites

Come all my jolly boys and we'll together go,
Abroad with our Captain, to shear the lamb and ewe.
All in the month of June, of all times in the year,
It always comes in season the ewes and lambs to shear,
And there were must work hard, my boys, until our backs
do ache,
And our master, he will bring us beer whenever we do lack.

Sussex sheep-shearing song, nineteenth century[1]

Whatever the methods of agriculture employed, whether strip-farming in medieval open fields or the scientific operations of Victorian high farming on enclosed land, the culmination of the farming year was harvest. Equally, whatever crop was harvested, whether grain, hops, hay, fruit, or the wool harvest at sheep-shearing time, the success or failure of the harvest conditioned the success or failure of the whole year. Until large-scale mechanisation in the later nineteenth century, and until the use of combined reapers and binders in this century, harvest remained labour-intensive. Not only local labour but itinerant labour – in the nineteenth century Irish and gypsy labour – was necessary to gather in the harvest with despatch. Indeed, urban and industrial labour was also drawn upon. The participation of East Enders in the hop harvest in the Weald was a late example of this supplementation of the existing rural workforce. William Bush recalled the impact of Irish harvest workers on the local community of Calne in Wiltshire in the mid-nineteenth century. 'I remember the Irishmen, they came through Calne in droves, some a foot some on donkeys or with horses, they carried rip-hooks and boilers and all the tools they wanted just like gypsies – a rough lot – we was frightened of 'em.'[2]

107

By Rite

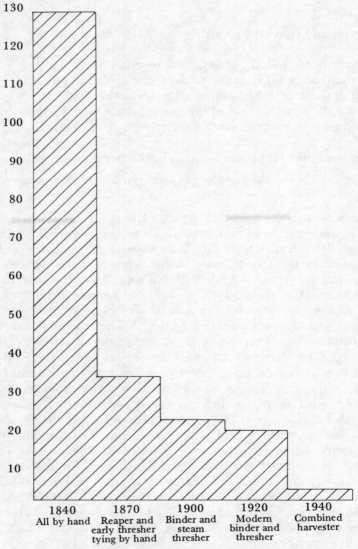

Figure 1   Labour Required for Various Operations
During Harvest

(Based on the harvesting and threshing of a 6-quarter crop of wheat
at the rate of 10 acres per day)

Source (Figs. 1–5): S.J. Wright, 'Mechanical Engineering and Agriculture', *Journal and Proceedings of the Institution of Mechanical Engineers*, vol. 156, 1947, no. 1, p. 21.

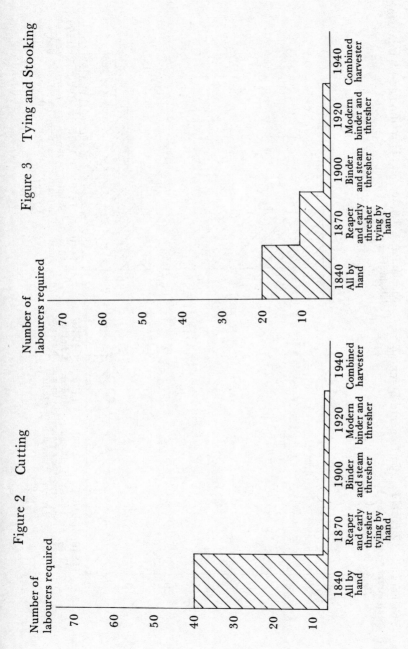

Figure 2 Cutting

Figure 3 Tying and Stooking

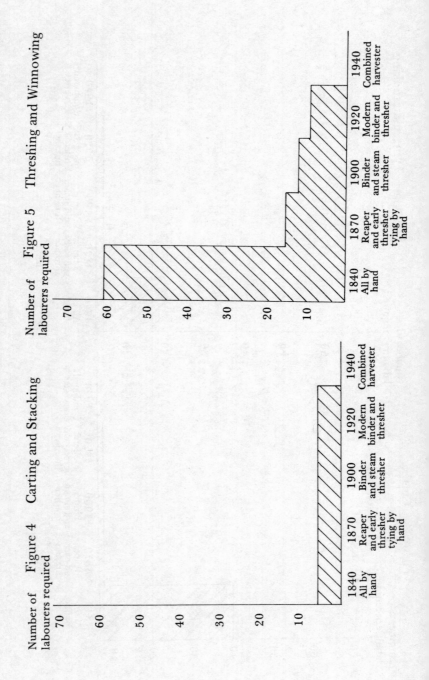

Number of   Figure 4   Carting and Stacking
labourers required

Number of   Figure 5   Threshing and Winnowing
labourers required

Figures 1–5 illustrate the decline in numbers of labourers required during the operation of harvest during the nineteenth and early-twentieth centuries, and show that the workforce continued to be sizeable during harvest, at least until the latter decades of that period despite having been reduced considerably since the eighteenth century when harvests were gathered entirely manually.

Until the 1870s the most significant inroad of mechanisation had occurred in the post-harvest operation of threshing and winnowing. Harvest itself remained essentially manual and involved large numbers of work-people labouring together in the fields. The experience of this collective labour at harvest conditioned the maintenance of customary work relationships between labourer and labourer and between farmer and labourer. These customary relationships had their origins in the Middle Ages, in the experience of open-field farming and throughout the Hanoverian and Victorian period farmers were generally obliged to submit themselves to this customary framework.

The gathering in of the crop was woven round with a complex mesh of custom and ritual concerning both the organisation of the workforce, its payments and customary rewards, as well as the acts of cutting, binding and carrying home the last sheaf and the last load. Harvest was of crucial importance to the labouring poor who were able to enforce a pattern of responsibilities and dues which reflected the mutuality of life in the community. It was a period in which earnings were higher, and in which rights to customary dues such as gleaning, the harvest home, and harvest largess were an important supplement to the annual income.

It was customary in southern England (as elsewhere in Britain) for the harvesters to elect one from among their number to act as leader or foreman. He was known as the 'lord' and his functions were described in the 1870s thus:

> To him all the rest were required to give precedence, and to leave all transactions respecting their work. He made terms with the farmers for mowing, for reaping, and for all the rest of the harvest work; he took the lead with the scythe, with the sickle, and on the 'carrying days', he was to be first to eat, and the first to drink at all their

111

refreshments, his mandate was to be law to all the rest who were bound to address him as 'my lord', and to show him all due honour and respect. Disobedience in any of these particulars was punished by imposing fines according to a scale previously agreed on by the 'lord' and all his vassals. In some instances, if any of his men swore or told a lie in his presence, a fine was imposed.[3]

In addition, the 'lord of the harvest' ensured the quality of the harvest work, fining those labourers who were slow, ill-disciplined, or whose work was shoddy. In short, by common agreement amongst the harvest-men the lord acted as leader and as negotiator between themselves and the farmer who had hired them.

The lord was also responsible for supervising the initiation of newcomers to the harvest field. In Norfolk, in the nineteenth century, this was called shoing (i.e., shoeing). The lord of the harvest

> would have a halter and take it and put it over the head of all the new men. The lady, that is the lady of the harvest, who mowed next in the line to the lord, would then take a small hammer, lift the foot of the new hand and tap him on the sole of his foot, and he would call beer. When they were all shod then they would read the Harvest rules. That is certain rules that they must abide by, under the lord of the harvest. If a man was away for a day from his work, he was fined ten shillings, if it was because of drink, if through business or family matters he could not come five shillings, and if because of illness only two and sixpence. Every man had to keep his place in the line when he was mowing, if he lost a swathe he was fined sixpence, or else he had to go back and get it up some time or other.[4]

The lord of the harvest has its origins in medieval practice, when a man was elected as head reaper to assist the haywards or beadle in the supervision of the lord's harvesters. In the words of a recent study:

> They [haywards] were to guard against pilfering, and against the careless handling of sheaves. To help them meet

this obligation the lord of the manor sometimes gave them a small piece of land sown with demesne seed, from which they made good any defects in the harvest. In turn the beadle and hayward would have had power to extract satisfactory work from the reapers and other labourers. In this way they were helped, firstly by the obligation placed on many freeholders and customarii alike to supervise their familia or the customarii in general at the precarie; and secondly, by the ripreeve, a man hired or elected from among the tenants themselves for the duration of the harvest.[5]

It is the ripreeve who provides the source for the lord of the harvest in the eighteenth and nineteenth centuries. The ripreeve was elected by the tenants of the lord of the manor as an assistant to the hayward or beadle in the operation of the harvest. He acted as an interface between the lord's officials and his tenants and helped ensure the quality of the work, that there was no pilfering and no slackness. He was responsible to the lord of the manor through the hayward or beadle and to the tenants by his election.

A similar figure acted as leader during sheep-shearing. He was known as the captain of the shearers. The following agreement was made at the Swan Inn, Falmer, in Sussex, on Wednesday 21 May 1828, 'for the government and direction of the company of sheepshearers':

1st. That the Men must be at the place they are going to work at seven o'clock in the morning, they shall then immediately go to breakfast and be in the Barn ready to go to work at eight o'clock. To be allowed cold meat, or meat pies for their breakfast and one Quart of Ale each man.

2nd. That they shall light up twice in the forenoon and be allowed each time one pint of Ale a man.

3rd. That they have at dinner boiled Meat, Meat Puddings Pies, what small beer they like and ½ pint of Strong Beer each Man after Dinner.

4th. That they be allowed to light up twice in the afternoon, that they have a Pint of Mixed Beer half Ale and half Strong the first time, and at the other, a Pint of

Ale each man.

5th. That they be allowed cold Meat and Bread and Cheese for supper, one Quart of Ale each man, with One Pint of Strong Beer a man after Supper. That they are to be allowed one hour and ½ for Supper and to drink their Beer and that no smoking or singing be allowed.

6th. That they have 10d per score of Ewes, Lambs and Tags when the whole are shorn and 18d per score for Ewes and Tags, 14d per score for Lambs, when only a part are shorn, to have 20d per score for shearing a Wether Flock, and in case any employer wishes to limit the number of his sheep to be shorn in any one day to a less number than forty per Man, the Company to be paid for that limited number the same as if forty were shorn. To have 1/- per hundred for Winding, 3d a hundred for Black Lamb and 2/6 per day extra for the Captain and 1/- for the Tar Boy.

7th. That in case of wet weather the Men to have a Breakfast as usual, with a Quart of Ale, and wait till their employer pleases to see if there is any probability of shearing any sheep on that day.

8th. That the Captain have full power to discharge any shearers not acting up to these regulations.

9th. That the Captain do have a copy of the Resolutions which he shall give to the Master where he goes to work in the morning and a Master deviating from using of these resolutions shall forfeit 5 guineas to be paid to Mr. Ellman the Chairman of this Meeting, who shall call a Meeting of not less than five Masters who shall examine the Captain and distribute the money amongst any of the shearers who from attention to their work or from any other circumstances they may think most deserving.

Signed, John Ellman, F.P. Whitfield, Henry Rogers, John Ellman, Jnr., Geo: Ellman, Geo: Filder, Wm. Arkcole.[6]

These 'resolutions' indicate that effective control of the workforce lay with the captain. He had the power to discharge any unsatisfactory shearer. He negotiated with the employer and, if the shearing gang had any grievance through infringement of the agreement, he gave the men's account at the consequent enquiry. The agreement set out the payment for shearing and the allowances of food and drink at various intervals during the day. It is interesting to note, in resolution five, that no singing or smoking was allowed at supper. It is probable that these activities were reserved for the concluding sheep-shearing supper which the gang would hold at the end of the shearing season, or that, in this particular agreement, these distractions had been prohibited. The captain agreed the resolutions at a preliminary meeting known as White Ram night,[7] and oversaw the festive proceedings at the completion of shearing known as Black Ram night.[8] It is perhaps likely that the appointment of a captain to the shearers was maintained more regularly, and for a longer period, than was that of the lord of the harvest. This was probably due to the fact that change through mechanisation did not disturb any part of the shearing operation throughout the nineteenth century, whereas the organisation of harvest work was changing during the same period.

Quite how widespread was the practice of electing a harvest lord cannot be estimated with any degree of certainty. As with most customary behaviour, much of the evidence is not quantitative. Most sources refer to specific occurrences or to general localities, using such phrases as 'in the surrounding neighbourhood' or 'in the immediate vicinity' when speaking of the distribution of customary practices. Therefore, at least for the period under consideration, quantification is impractical. However, the practice of nominating a lord to negotiate terms and organise labour was durable enough to be recorded much later in the century in Flora Thompson's Oxfordshire.[9]

As well as acting as the spokesman for the harvestmen, the lord also undertook, as has been seen, to supervise the quality of work and to ensure the ordered behaviour of the workforce. To this end, it was common for a series of fines to be levied or other punishment to be inflicted for shoddy or slow work. Infringements of popular morality in the harvest field were punished in a similar way. These infringements included swearing or other offensive behaviour in the presence of female or child harvest workers.

The poet John Clare mentions one punishment, that of 'booting', as taking place at the harvest home:

> The 'booted hogs drove over Lunnon brig,
> Boys, who had mischief in the harvest done,
> As load o'erturn'd, and foul on posts had run.[10]

'Booting' was a common punishment ritually administered under the jurisdiction of the harvest lord. The aim of the punishment was to inflict public humiliation upon the offender, rather than actual physical harm. A mid-nineteenth-century Northamptonshire glossary gives the following description of 'booting':

> A harvest home custom. When any one has misconducted himself in the field during harvest, he is subjected to a mock trial at the harvest home feast and condemned to be booted . . . a long form is placed in the kitchen upon which the boys who have worked will sit, as a terror and disgrace to the rest, in a bent posture, with their hands laid on each other's backs forming a bridge for the hogs (as the harvest boys are called) to pass over; while a strong chap stands on each side with a boot legging, soundly strapping them as they scuffle over the bridge, which is done as fast as their ingenuity can carry them.

The account continues: 'The custom is still kept up at some of the neighbouring villages. It extends into Warwickshire.'[11] In southern England, 'booting' also occurred, as one writer noted:

> I was once present at what was termed a 'booting', which was a sort of punishment for the overthrowing of a load of corn during the harvest. At the harvest supper during the evening, the delinquent was laid face downwards on the table and one of the leaders of the festival administered some blows with one of the master's boots, while holding the boot in a peculiar manner. As a physical chastisement it was of no account; but it was probably intended as a degradation in the face of the blunderer's fellow-workers.[12]

The lord, through such rituals, ensured work discipline at a level which was beyond the master himself. Their purpose lay with the medieval origins of the office where the lord of the harvest was duty-bound to guarantee for the Lord of the Manor that harvest work would be undertaken speedily and effectively. It is significant in the account from southern England that the master's boot was used. The symbolism is clear. The lord administered the punishment on behalf of the master in a manner the master could hardly have done himself.

In Suffolk 'booting' was known as 'ten-pounding', but this term had nothing to do with the number of blows applied to the offender.[13] The origin of the term is not known but, in another application, a close similarity with the practices common in eighteenth-century and early-nineteenth-century trades, particularly in the printing shop, can be seen. Punishments for persistent infringement of chapel regulations, or non-payment of 'solaces' or money fines, involved the custom of 'ten pound in the purse'. This meant that the delinquent would receive eleven blows with a piece of board, whilst laid on his belly across the correcting board.[14] The form of punishment, the motive for the punishment, and the term itself were similar for enforcement of both printing chapel and harvest field rules of work. The father of the chapel oversaw the administration of the punishment on recalcitrant printers and the lord of the harvest supervised ten-pounding of harvest workers who were at fault. This form of punishment, designed to humiliate rather than harm, was also found, during the same period, in the Army and Navy.[15]

In other words, similar customary forms were more widely distributed throughout English society during the eighteenth and early-nineteenth centuries than is usually thought. It was not that printers took part in local harvests, or that Suffolk harvestmen worked in printing chapels, although this might have happened, but that, for much of the period, a common language of ritual form linked many different areas of the experience of work. In each case, 'ten-pounding' existed in well-defined working communities, whether temporary ones as at harvest time, or more permanent ones such as the printing chapel or the Army. This was a self-generated method of work discipline – beyond the influence of the master or farmer, yet which they depended upon at a time when their own forms of work discipline were inadequate or impotent. At harvest, from the Middle Ages to the mid-nineteenth century, the delegation of authority to the lord of the harvest or the shearer's captain was a necessary consequence of the lack of professional overseers or foremen until, by the early decades of the nineteenth century, the appointment of professional estate managers or farm bailiffs became more common. This form of self-regulation was not maintained by the workforce in order to underpin the power of the farmer or landowner, but as a means of preserving the fair and equitable distribution of work among the labourers themselves, to discourage shirking or other forms of shoddy work which created more labour for others, and to minimise the amount of internal dissension detrimental to the group.

The cry which was raised at the completion of the harvest,

> Well ploughed – well sowed,
> Well reaped – well mowed,
> Well carried and never a load overthrowed[16]

was a genuine expression of self-satisfaction in the quality of harvest-work and was a public affirmation of the skills of those involved. It also signalled that the particular harvest was completed, and was designed to deprecate the farmer whose harvest was still underway through lack of enterprise or despatch by his harvestmen.

As part of the harvest contract, the lord negotiated the terms regarding the provision of food and drink in the field. Together with their wages, the harvestmen expected to be fed at the farmer's expense, and to receive generous amounts of liquor when in the field. This was also probably a custom which had its origins in the medieval experience when food and drink were given to harvest workers by the lord of the manor. At the beginning of the thirteenth century, the following was the customary provision during harvest on the manors of St Paul's Cathedral: 'at their first meal porridge of beans or pease, two loaves, one white the other maslin, i.e. mixed of wheat and rye, a piece of meat, and beer; at their second meal a small loaf of maslin bread and some cheese; else two great loaves, porridge, six herrings, a piece of some other fish, and water.'[17] On the Wiltshire manor of Charlton in 1586 it was still customary for the bailiff of the manor farm to provide food and drink to the tenants who harvested the lord's hay. It was recorded in the custumal that 'At Broadmead to the tennaunts 2 gallons of Ale, iiij penniworth of Bread and 2lbs of cheese at the reaping of the same haye. At the bringing in of the same heye into the barne Bread Cheese and Drinke as shall suffise. At Broadham one gallon of Ale iiijd in breade and in cheese 2lb. Item. At repinge Breakfast Dinner and [? Noon] meate. Item. At summer-vallowe breakfast to be brought to ploughing. Then dinner at the farme.'[18] The continuance of the practice of giving food and drink to harvestmen at this late date helps explain the maintenance of the custom, albeit in an altered form.

Ale and food were provided at the hay harvest as well and, in Dorset in 1812, 'ale which is given to labourers in hay-time and harvest is brewed with four bushels of malt to the hogshead . . . of this ale . . . even women are allowed "three pints a day or more;" and men "seven pints".'[19] Elsewhere, ale was allowed on even more generous terms. A commentator wrote in 1794 that 'The folly of Shropshire exceeds that of the Midlands Counties, in regard to excessive quantity of beverage allowed to farm labourers. The allowance of beer . . . both winter and summer, is generally given to those who take their work, in the winter 3 quarts each, in summer 4, and in harvest from 5 to 8 quarts of strong and small beer'. The writer continued: 'This customary allowance is excessive; but there are few parts of England where the harvest is got in with such spirit and expedition: but the custom of such excessive drinking ought to be checked, and has been done in the best governed families.'[20] One farmer stated of Shropshire in the same period that 'At present, I give my labourers 14d a day all the year; when the hay-harvest commences, I allow them meat and drink until the end of the corn-harvest. I allow each man two quarts of small beer till harvest and then six quarts each of harvest beer, exclusive of small beer at meals.' This informant added a note that 'The harvest beer is one bushel of malt to eleven gallons, which is always brewed in October.'[21] Henry Hunt recalled that, in his youth in the 1780s, it was customary on his father's farms for the man who constructed the wheat-rick 'a pint of ale as often, during the day, as he chose to ask for it' it being 'much the hardest and most severe work, if done well, belonging to the farming business'. Also, during a record day's work harvesting the last of his father's spring oats, Hunt remembered:

> it being excessively hot, one of the men, the worst mower of course, was principally employed in riding to and from the Inn at Everly, to replenish the bottles. This was indispensible, every man being allowed as much ale as he could drink, with the exception of the two last bottles, containing three quarts each, which I was obliged to prohibit from being tapped till the oats were all down, as some of my partners by this time began to discover evident symptoms of inebriety.[22]

In orchard areas cider was the harvest drink. Significantly, one writer on cider production in 1794 suggested that, in Herefordshire, the principal motivation came from the farm labourers themselves as farmers saw cider-making as a distraction from more important farm operations. He reported that he had overheard 'The following conversation, which passed the other day,'

> "Master, what horse shall I take to drive cider mill?"
> "D-n the cider and the mill too; you waste one-half of your time in making cider, and the other half in drinking it. I wish there was not one apple in the county. You all think of cider, no matter what comes of plough." '[23]

This conversation suggests the centrality of cider-making and cider itself in the relationship between farmer and labourer. Here, the farm labourer is concerned to protect and promote the source of production of his customary perquisite. If no cider was made, then none could be consumed as part of the work contract. The same was true of beer as, in most cases, farmers brewed specially for the needs of harvest when strong ale as well as small beer was required. The defence of the production of the beverage also ensured protection for the custom itself, and with it the promulgation of the customary relationship between master and man.

Worcestershire saw the continuance of the customary allowance of beer into the nineteenth century. William Pomeroy wrote of the expense of the custom in the following terms:

> A true idea of the expense of furnishing drink, will not be formed from the proportion the two prices bear to each other [i.e. the average price of labour with drink is a shilling a day, or fourteen pence without, at the choice of the person employed] or from what is usual in most other parts: two gallons a day is now pretty generally considered as the fixed allowance to each man. In the harvest months there is no restriction. In extenuation of this abuse, it is said that a part is taken home to the families; but this, when it happens, may be set down as an exception to general custom.[24]

The practice of making up low wages with an allowance of beer or cider was also common in the late-eighteenth century in both Gloucestershire and Devon. In the South Hams, Devon, 'Wages are one shilling a day, and a quart of cider. In harvest, the wages much the same, with as much cider as they choose to drink.'[25]

That wages during harvest were not increased, somewhat unusually, in this region, can be seen from the following.

> The wages of the out-door labourer is 7s per week, winter and summer, and from a quart to three pints of drink daily; even in hay-time and harvest, these wages are not increased, although the additional exertions at those seasons are amply compensated by board and very extraordinary drinks and sittings over ale and cider.

This was the case in the second decade of the nineteenth century.[26] It will be seen later that the provision of generous board during harvest remained a source of discontent in early-nineteenth-century Devon. It is probable that these conditions were exceptional and were not repeated to the same degree in other counties. Generous conditions, at least during harvest, were still common in late-eighteenth-century Worcestershire. Sir Frederick Eden reported of Inkborough [Inkberrow] that 'During hay and corn harvests labourers are invariably fed in their masters' houses.'[27] As late as the mid-nineteenth century, it was recorded of the same county that 'Another point of great importance to be here discussed is the system of giving the labourer drink. This varies from two quarts of cider per day in the winter to three quarts in the summer, with four at harvest and hay-making time, and when extra labour is required.'[28]

The Reverend Skinner, in Somerset, not surprisingly, found difficulty in deciding upon the amount of his allowance of beer. He recorded, in July 1828, of his hay harvest that

> After I had left the hayfield the men, I understand, grumbled for not having as much beer as they chose to drink. I therefore made these regulations: That the men who mow are to have a gallon an acre besides money and victuals. The women, three pints and a shilling a piece. I desired the beer to be taken up to the Glebe Farm House, and Heal to see that the people have this allowance. It is most painful to have dealings with the brutified vulgar. Now I have laid down this allowance, those who do not choose to abide by it have orders to leave the ground.[29]

A week later, because of the threat of bad weather, Skinner was obliged, much to his displeasure, to recruit local miners. 'The day has been threatening, but I hope that the hay of the two fields now about will be on the rick, as two waggons and a number of hands from the coal pits are gone to assist. I do not go into the hayfield to witness the saturnalia of the colliers, they have drunken three hogsheads of beer already, and there are seven more acres to mow and make.'[30] He later noted, somewhat resignedly, that 'the haymakers have cost me more than the value of the hay which has been cut since the rain has commenced'.[31] Later in August, during what must have been a long season for Skinner, he found that his allowance no longer satisfied the haymakers. 'The people in the hayfield, who had had a double potation of cider, were not, however, contented; but just as I was stepping into bed, the servant knocked at my door to say they were come for more. I desired her to tell them to go home, that I was sure they had had too much already, and that my parsonage was not a pothouse.'[32] Later the next day, he was obliged to provide an additional 18-gallon cask of small beer as his labourer George had informed him that 'the barrel is out' and that 'he had been working all day without beer, and could do so no longer'. Skinner was disappointed with the progress of his labourers as he had given them an allowance of beer and cider in the expectation that they would complete his hay harvest that day. This they had failed to do.[33]

Increasingly, in the nineteenth century, farmers declined to subscribe to the custom of providing alcoholic beverages in the fields. Sometimes, as Maude Robinson recalled of Sussex in the 1860s, teetotal farmers objected to the giving of beer on moral grounds. She wrote: 'For in the old days shearing was never accomplished without much beer. This my father steadily refused to provide, and although he offered handsome money payments instead the local gang refused to come, but were glad to return when another gang stepped in for one season.'[34] In its place 'stokos' was offered. This was a mixture of oatmeal and water flavoured with lemon. Maude's father maintained this principle with his harvest workers. He refused to give harvest suppers because 'They were too apt to end in drunkenness and the wives and children had no share.' Instead, he sent home joints of mutton to each family.[35]

The provision of drink during harvest continued after 1850, of course, but with increasing reluctance. Drink was still given to Oxfordshire labourers in the 1870s,[36] but, for Richard Jeffries, the quality of the beer provided was poor. The image he depicts of the harvest being gathered in on a regime of weak, unfermented beer, is striking. He wrote of small beer, that

Harvest beer is probably the vilest drink in the world. The men say it is made by pouring muddy water into empty casks returned sour from use, and then brushing them round and round inside with a besom. This liquid leaves a stickiness on the tongue and a harsh feeling at the back of the mouth which soon turns to thirst, so that having once

123

drunk a pint the drinker must go on drinking . . . With it there go down the germs of fermentation, a sour, yeasty, and, as it were, secondary fermentation; not that kind which is necessary to make beer, but the kind that unmakes and spoils beer. It is beer rotting and decomposing in the stomach. Violent diarrhoea often follows . . . Upon this abominable mess the golden harvest of English fields is gathered in.[37]

Whatever the truth of this description, it was the case that the continued expense of brewing harvest beer caused farmers to adulterate or thin out their brew in the fashion described, so that the custom was adhered to at best without enthusiasm, and at worst lethally.

The provision of harvest beer was a welcome indulgence for the harvestmen. It also served a functional purpose in that it provided a source of energy for the arduous labour of the fourteen-hour day in the harvest field. But, more importantly, it cemented, at least symbolically, a customary relationship between farmer and men in which the toil of harvest was given in return for an undertaking from the farmer to provide the expected harvest perquisites. This relationship, strengthened by harvest practice, represented an idea of social harmony in which co-operation, and respect between labourer and farmer, were central. Perhaps the best way to illustrate this normative view is to quote a well-known harvest song, collected at the end of the nineteenth century from many places, although the song itself was probably much older. This version was from North Wiltshire:

When we arise all in the morn,
For to sound our harvest horn,
We will sing to the full jubilee, jubilee;
We will sing to the full jubilee.

The first thing we take in hand
Is the horn all from the can,
And we'll drink to the bottom, you shall find, you shall find,
And we'll drink to the bottom, you shall find.

Our master comes and says,
'We will have this field today,
If the glorious sun it does shine, it does shine;
If the glorious sun it does shine.

'So do not stop to prattle
When you hear the waggons rattle,
For bright Phoebus is drawing to the west, to the west,
For bright Phoebus is drawing to the west.'

Our master's very kind,
So his orders we will mind,
And our mistress is always as good, as good;
And our mistress is always as good.

Sends us plenty of good beer,
And it keeps us in good cheer,
While we pile the heavy sheaves on the load, on the load;
While we pile the heavy sheaves on the load.

Then we'll sing and we will say,
'Heaven bless the happy day
That the harvest was in a flowing bowl, flowing bowl;
That the harvest was in a flowing bowl.'[38]

Despite the overall sense of pastoral, and the obvious signs of literary influences ('bright Phoebus'), this song illustrates well the balance which was the basis of the harvest contract. The day's work is signalled by the harvest horn, but before any work is begun, the harvest beer is sampled. Then the master indicates the work to be completed in the day, with a warning that despatch is required and that the men should not waste time in idle talk. In this instance, the master's words are heeded because he is 'very kind' and his wife is 'as good' because she supplies good beer to the harvestmen in the field, where the work is of a strenuous and strength-sapping kind. Each part of the contract unfolds – good conditions were rewarded with hard work. It is implicit that the converse was also true.

A similar song of the period about sheep-shearing (the first verse of which is quoted at the beginning of this chapter) illustrates the same balance. The shearers contract to work hard 'until our backs do ache', and in return the master 'will bring us beer whenever we do lack'. The two actions are interconnected. It is in this sense that beer at harvest was symbolic of a wider customary significance than the provision of a mere perquisite, or supplement to low wages.

At the conclusion of the harvest, the custom of 'crying the neck' was generally adhered to, particularly in Devon. One commentator described the custom in a letter to the antiquary, John Brand, in 1805:

> When the cutting of the wheat is finished a group or handful of the best ears is selected and being bound together forms what is called the neck. As soon as it is prepared the whole Band of Harvest People, and in general all the household, Master, Mistress, and children, and servants repair to the highest part of the farm; where one of them who possesses the best lungs and clearest voice, advancing before the rest of the Party and holding up the neck with both hands to the fullest extent of his reach commences the following cry or shout, in which he is instantly joined by everyone present.
>
> A . . . . neck
> We . . . . . . ha'en [have it]
> God . . . . . sa'en [save it] [39]

This cry culminated in a series of whoops and loud cheering. The ritual was important to the labourers, not because of any ancient memory or survival of the worship of some pagan earth-mother but because it reflected the co-operation between master and men and reinforced, at least for another year, the sense of community prevailing in the village. By 1826, it was noted that this custom was beginning to decline in Devon. One farmer wrote to William Hone that he would continue to

> patronise it myself, because I take it in the light of a thanksgiving . . . I asked an old fellow about it the other day, and he is the only man who gave me a satisfactory explanation. He says that the object of crying the 'neck' is to give the

surrounding country notice of the end of the harvest, and that they mean by 'we yen' 'we have ended.'[40]

As well as indicating the successful completion of harvest, rituals involving the last sheaf can also be understood by reference to medieval harvest practice. On many manors in medieval England, harvestmen were permitted to carry away part of the harvest for their own use. In fact, Andrew Jones has suggested that even by the thirteenth century this practice was 'both old and widespread'.[41] In some cases, sheaves were given to the harvestmen according to the number of acres harvested. The size of the sheaf was, as with many medieval customary perquisites, dictated not by specific measurement but by reference to customary methods such as grain which could be sheaved within a binding which equalled the circumference of the reeve's head.[42] He has indicated that this customary sheaf, given as part of the harvest contract, was directly replaced by a money payment.[43] Rituals concerning the last sheaf of harvest which are found in the late-eighteenth and nineteenth centuries owe most to this medieval context. It is probable that as the perquisite of actually taking sheaves declined, the last sheaf itself took on a ritual significance, acting as a symbol for the harvestmen of their crucial involvement in the harvest. The grain harvested was not their property and, indeed, they no longer even possessed small amounts of the harvest itself, yet the harvest was still central to the labourer's experience and the rituals involving temporary possession of the last sheaf in the hands of the harvestmen, which signalled the end of the work, were a powerful symbol of group solidarity for them. Gleaning was another illustration of the remaining limited right of property in the harvest which was perceived by the harvest labourers.

Harvest was a corporate activity in which all sections of the community were involved. A sense of this is contained in the following verses from an early-nineteenth-century harvest song:

> The poor old man
> That can hardly stand
> Gets up in the morning and do all he can,

Gets up in the morning and do all he can.
I hope God will reward
Such old Harvest men.

But the man who is lazy
And will not come on,
He slights his good master,
And likewise his men.
We'll pay him his wages
And send him gone,
For why shall we keep
Such a lazy drone.[44]

Despite the suggestion of sentimentality, these verses, sung at the beginning of harvest and drawn from direct experience, illustrate the image of social cohesion which harvest provided for the labouring poor. Also, the self-regulation of the harvest men which formed part of the duties of the harvest lord, is evident in the desire to expel 'the man who is lazy'. The verse recognises that this form of disruption affected the master as well as the men and was behaviour that was not to be tolerated. Recalling the table of fines for non-attendance at harvest which were cited at the beginning of this chapter, the highest fine was reserved for non-attendance at harvest because of incapacity through drunkenness.

Rituals of the last sheaf were increasingly opposed during the nineteenth century along with the customary rights to food and drink in the harvest field by farmers who sought to impose regular work discipline on their harvest force, and were not prepared to endure the expense of the boisterousness of such customary behaviour. The following unsympathetic communication by a Devon farmer to the *Gentleman's Magazine* in 1816 illustrates both the opposition to harvest customs, and the chasm which was developing between the labourer and his master.

The reaping and harvesting of the wheat in the county of Devon is attended with so heavy an expense, and with practices of so very disorderly a nature, as to call for the strongest mark of disapprobation, and their immediate discontinuance, or at least a modification of their pastime after the labours of the day. The wheat being ready to cut down, and amounting to from ten to twenty acres, notice is given in the neighbourhood that a reaping is to be performed on a particular day, when, as the farmer may be more or less liked in the village, on the morning of the day appointed a gang consisting of an indefinite number of men and women assemble in the field and the reaping commences after breakfast, which is seldom over till between eight and nine o'clock. This company is open for additional hands to drop in, at any time before the twelfth hour, to partake of the frolick of the day. By eleven or twelve o'clock the ale and cider has so much warmed and elevated their spirits, that their noisy jokes and ribaldry are heard to a considerable distance, and often serve to draw auxilliary force within the accustomed time. The dinner, consisting of the best meat and vegetables, is carried into the fields between twelve and one o'clock; this is distributed with copious draughts of ale and cider; and by two o'clock the pastime of cutting and binding the wheat is resumed, and continued without other interruption than the squabbles of the party, until about five o'clock, when what is called the drinkings are taken into the field, and under the shade of a hedge-row or a large tree, the panniers are examined, and buns, cakes, and all such articles are found as the confectionary skill of the farmer's wife could produce for gratifying the appetites of her customary guests at this season. After the drinkings are over, which generally consume from half to three quarters of an hour (and even longer if such can be spared from the completion of the field) the amusement of the wheat-harvest is continued with such exertions as draw the reaping and binding of the field together with the close of the evening; this done, a small sheaf is bound up and set upon the top of one of the ridges, when the reapers retiring to a certain distance, each throws his reap-hook at the sheaf until one more fortunate, or less inebriated than the rest, strikes it down. This achievement is accompanied with the utmost stretch and power of the voices of the company, uttering words very indistinctly, but somewhat to this purpose – 'We ha Yn. We ha Yn.' concluding with a horrid yell resembling a war-whoop of the Indian savages,

which noise and tumult continue for about half an hour,
when the company retire to the farmhouse for supper;
which being over, large portions of ale and cider enable
them to carouse and vociferate until two or three o'clock
in the morning. At the same house, or that of a neighbouring farmer, a similar scene is renewed, beginning between
eight and nine o'clock in the morning following, and so
continued through the precious season of the wheat-
harvest in this country. It must be observed, that the
labourers thus employed in reaping, receive no wages; but
in lieu thereof they have an invitation to the farmer's
house, to partake of a harvest frolic, and at Christmas
also, during the whole of which time, and which seldom
continues less than four or five days, the house is kept
open night and day to the guests, whose behaviour during
the time may be assimilated to the frolics of a bear-garden.[45]

The resentment and lack of comprehension of the motives of
last-sheaf rituals is evident, but it is also interesting that the
writer indicates that the harvestmen received no wages
during this period. It is not clear whether this means that
they received no additional harvest wages for harvest work,
or whether no wages were paid at all. The description perhaps
shows that medieval customary labour services still continued
at this period in some parts of Devon. It is also significant
that the customary rights of the labourers included further
feasting at the farmer's expense at Christmas.

In Herefordshire, during the early-nineteenth century the
verse or cry made during the last sheaf ritual was more
elaborate than that of Devon. After the cry of 'I have her',
the rest of the labourers replied ' "what have you?" – "A
mare, a mare, a mare" – 'who is she?" thrice also – "J.B."
[naming the owner three times] – "whither will you send
her?" – "to J. a Nicks" [naming some neighbour who has not
all his corn reaped] then they all shout three times and so the
ceremony ends with good cheer'.[46] In this account the ritual
was used to indicate the labourer's skill in completing the
harvest before the rest of the neighbourhood and thereby to
shame more tardy farmers.

A further part of the harvest contract, customary particularly in East Anglia, was the practice of claiming largess. This

was another way in which harvest wages were supplemented. In Suffolk one commentator recalled of his 'boyish days' probably at the end of the eighteenth century:

> if you were to pass within a field or two of this band of husbandmen, 'my lord' would leave the company, and approaching you with respect, ask of you a largess. Supposing he succeeded, which I know he would, he would hail his companions, and they would thus acknowledge the gift: my lord would place his troop in a circle, suppose fifteen men, and that they were reaping, each one would have a hook in his hand . . . my lord then goes to a distance . . . and repeats a couplet . . . The men still standing in the circle listen with attention to the words of my lord, and at the conclusion each with his reap-hook pointing with his right hand to the centre of the circle . . . they utter together a groan . . . then . . . their eyes are lifted to the heavens above them, their hooks point in the same direction, and at the same time they change the doleful groan to a tremendous shout, which is repeated three distinct times. The money thus got during harvest is saved to make merry with at the neighbouring public house and the evening is spent in shouting of largess, and joyful mirth.[47]

The elaborate ritual of crying largess was not always present, and in some places a simple request for money from passers-by sufficed. Elsewhere, largess was collected by labourers perambulating the houses of the neighbourhood soliciting money from door to door. As with other customary activities, there was an implicit threat for householders who refused to contribute: of which the antiquary, Joseph Haslewood, was fully aware. He observed that, in Hertfordshire:

> a deputation from the men usually traverse the neighbourhood and pray, at the different houses of respectability, largess. On the 30th August, 1819, I was as Broxbourne at a gentleman's house and while sitting after dinner the servant entering said 'There was farmer . . . . . . man to beg largess'. As I knew my friend had little if any arable land, I enquired where the farmer lived and found at

Hoddesdon. The largess was in this instance refused but I found my friend gave to the servants of two or three farmers whose land lay immediately adjacent to his own and it seems possible that the custom has been founded on the propriety, if not necessity, of giving such men what we should call civility money and thereby prevent little infringements or a wanton despoiling of hedges, herbage etc.[48]

The use of the term 'civility money' indicates Haslewood's much deeper comprehension of the nature of popular customs than those who saw them as quaint and picturesque vestiges of bygone days which provided harmonious yet relatively harmless amusement. In this instance deference was a commodity which it was necessary for the farmer to buy, if he was to avoid expressions of popular displeasure.

Largess collection was similar in form and purpose to Christmas boxes which were solicited by tradesmen and appentices in late-eighteenth-century towns. It was an additional levy made on the whole community as a recognition of and reward for the labourer's work during harvest.[49] The custom was also widespread in Norfolk where it was observed in 1826 that

it is a general practice on the first day of harvest, for the men to leave the field about four o'clock, and retire to the alehouse, and have what is here termed a 'whet'; that is a sort of drinking bout to cheer their hearts for labour. They previously solicit any who happen to come within their sight with, 'I hope, sir, you will please to bestow a largess on us?' If the boon is conceded the giver is asked if he would like to have his largess hallooed; if this is assented to, the hallooing is at his service.[50]

This kind of *taxation populaire* was increasingly criticised, as was the disruption caused to harvest work by such practices. Largess collection was satirised in a collection of verses known as the *Norfolk Drollery*:

We have a custom nowhere else is known,
For here we reap where nothing e're was sown,

Our harvestmen shall run ye cap and leg,
And leave their work at any time to beg;
They make a harvest of each passenger;
And therefore have they a lord-treasurer.[51]

The viewpoint that largess collection was the equivalent of begging would not have been accepted by harvest labourers in East Anglia; for them, the collection was part of the harvest contract and was no more than their customary due, forming an essential part of their wages for the work.

Ritual also accompanied the carting of the last load to the farm. John Clare recalled the horkey or hock cart when he wrote: 'When beneath old Lea Close Oak I the bottom branches broke,/To make our harvest cart like so many working folk.'[52]

The last load was decorated with flowers and green boughs. In Norfolk in the 1820s, the cart was thus described: 'The last, or "horkey load" . . . is decorated with flags and streamers, and sometimes a sort of kern baby is placed on top at front of the load. This is commonly called a "ben". This load is attended by all the party, who had been in the field, with hallooing and shouting.'[53] At Whittlesford, in Cambridgeshire, in 1835 the horkey load was described on 1st September: 'The lord walked in front with a large cocked hat on, such as captains in the navy wear with a long staff cap and all decorated with flowers. The lady [a man in woman's clothes] rode on the near fore horse, and four men on the other horses – the whole with flags and the horses with ribbons and flowers – the load was very high and so were the boughs on top.'[54] The central symbolism is of social cohesion. The festivity and floral decorations were visual equivalents of the shout which marked the end of harvest. The effect was to impress upon the employer the efficiency and speed with which his harvest had been completed. The cart was sometimes driven around the village and sometimes directly to the particular farm. At Whittlesford, the cart 'went the whole circuit of the village having come with the load from "Whiteland" round by "Whippity" and Rayners, down to the "Lodge" and then to the farm-yard'.[55] Perambulations of this kind, similar to the journeys of other ritual visitors during the year, were designed to bind the community

133

and to demonstrate group solidarity. As with rituals of the last sheaf, it is likely that the carting of the harvest was also connected to customary perquisites in medieval England.[56]

The image of social cohesion and harmony was also imparted to middle class observers who described the events in glowing if sentimental terms.

> My dear sir, nothing would possibly exceed the heartfelt pleasure I enjoyed when the last load was drawn into the farmyard . . . The farmer's heart gladdened with the reward of his labours. The ale-bottle, when held upward, gurgled its choice liquid into many thirsty throats. Everything and everybody showed satisfaction . . . The increasing pall of dusk . . . drew the labourers into a circle within their master's welcome domicile. Here the farmer and his wife and family were assembled, and without pride's distinction, regaled the sharers of their summer toil with that beverage that warms the feelings of hope into real joy . . . It was a heartfelt celebration. Songs were sung, and they danced down the midnight . . . Sincerity, unity and hospitality was blended: the master was satisfied with his servants – the servants were thankful with their means of support.[57]

This description would perfectly accord with the pastoral poetry of Robert Herrick in the seventeenth century, but it was written on 1 August 1827, three years before the outbreak of the Captain Swing disturbances, when middle-class opinion of the rural labourer was generally of an entirely different kind. Another of Hone's correspondents struck a similar note: 'Here . . . is pomp without pride, liberality without ostentation, cheerfulness without vice, merriment without guilt, and happiness without alloy.'[58]

Despite the symbolism of social unity, the labourer saw himself as claiming nothing more than his customary due, and as reinforcing a view of the community in which the farmers undertook to carry out their customary duties to the labouring poor in return for co-operation in farm work. By the 1870s this relationship had been destroyed and Flora Thompson could write of harvest homes that 'It did not do to look beneath the surface. Laura's father used to say that the farmer paid his men starvation wages all the year and thought to make it up to them by giving them one good meal. The farmer did not think so, because he did not think at all, and the men did not think either on that day; they were too busy enjoying the food and the fun.'[59]

In addition to largess the harvestmen also claimed a harvest home or mell supper as part of their work contract. John Brand, at the end of the eighteenth century, considered that:

> At this entertainment, all are in the modern revolutionary idea of the word, perfectly equal. Here is no distinction of persons but master and servant sit at the same table, converse freely together and spend the remainder of the night in dancing, singing, etc. in the most easy familiarity.[60]

His comment was based upon the earlier writer, Henry Bourne, and the latter part of the statement probably refers to the early decades of the eighteenth century. But the idea that the harvest home was an occasion at which master and men met as equals continued into the early-nineteenth century in as much as the harvest home was claimed as a customary right by the labourers and was not seen as a privilege which could be given at the farmer's discretion. One of the main attacks on harvest homes arose from the sense of 'revolutionary equality' which Brand noted. Thomas Hardy, with characteristic astuteness, observed that a desire to avoid actual familiarity with the labourers was expressed in the arrangements for Bathsheba Everdene's sheep-shearing supper set in the 1840s.

> At the shearing supper, a long table was placed on the grass plot beside the house, the end of the table being thrust over the sill of the wide parlour window and a foot or two into the room. Miss Everdene sat inside the window, facing down the table. She was thus at the head without mingling with the men.[61]

The provision of harvest home, as a general principle, continued well into the nineteenth century. In Herefordshire, in 1819, one commentator wrote, 'In harvest time, the farmer finds it necessary to feed them [the harvest labourers] amply, even with roast beef, geese, good plumb-puddings, and as much liquor as they chuse.'[62] The sense of enforced obligation underlies this report. In the 1830s one account related that 'It has always been the custom at Peak Hall for the master to sit down at this table with the men.' The writer criticised the 'modern refinement which thrusts the peasant at such times to feed in a lower place, without the welcome which the master's presence seems to give'. However, he noted that, in his experience, the farmer should leave before the end of the supper as 'during the latter period of the entertainment . . . beer gets above brains sometimes, and the company think little of an empty chair'. The principal object had been achieved.[63] It was tactful for the farmer now to withdraw before the more boisterous merriment began, in which respect for his status might not always be shown. In some places, such as in parts of Somerset, the harvest home continued in this way until the end of the nineteenth century. S.G. Kendall recalled such an event.

> Amongst a host of other small events there was the Harvest Home, when the younger people of the house decorated the high old kitchen and dining room with emblems of the harvest – the accompaniment of flowers, evergreens and flags, with a variable display of big joints, vegetables, and sweetmeats. The table was laid daintily out and graced with silver prize trophies won on the ploughing fields or at the very far agricultural shows, with the old Sheffield plate candle sticks or old family silver, not always in every day use . . . There will be little need for me to recall how much it was enjoyed by the men, women and boys on such occasions, after which pipes were lit, . . . then songs followed . . . when the oldest Farm hand stood up to give the Toast:

Here's a health unto our master the founder of this feast,
We hope to God his soul may rest where all is love and

peace,

Whilst here it is our duty to consider his demands,
And take it as a pleasure to bow to his command.[64]

The words of the toast were customary, and with some variations, are to be found in the accounts of harvest homes at the beginning of the nineteenth century.[65] As well as social cohesion Kendall's account illustrates the elements of display and public show; of opulence but also of skill – in that ploughing trophies were brought out. The view expressed in the toast was a normative one. The labourers gave deference to the farmer's 'command' implicitly in return for the provision of their customary rights including the harvest home.

The harvest home had its equivalent in the sheep-shearing supper, the hopper's feast, and the marler's feast, when a new marl pit was opened. Indeed in the latter a parallel for the harvest lord can be found as the marlers elected a 'lord of the pit' whose duties included the crying of largess.[66] At the conclusion of the hop-picking, a feast was held and a King and Queen of the hop-pickers were chosen. A procession was then made to the farmhouse from the hopyard. It was noted in 1912 that these festivities could be recalled, in Herefordshire, within living memory, at Hatfield, Blakemere and Ullingswick.[67] One informant of Ella Mary Leather recollected, in 1908, that the 'Man had to be a smock-faced un. We chose a young mon that 'ud make a nice gal like, and a smart woman as ud make a smart boy. It was all a bit o' fun, you'd understand, and the King and Queen opened the ball together.[68] This particular practice of electing young male and female hoppers to the office of King and Queen was recorded in the mid-eighteenth century in Christopher Smart's Georgic, the *Hop-Garden*:

> Then th' exulting band
> of pickers male and female, seize the fair
> Reluctant, and with boist'rous force and brute,
> By cries unmov'd, they bury her i' th' bin.
> Nor does thy youth escape – him too they seize,
> And in such posture place as best may serve
> To hide his charmer's blushes. Then with shouts
> They rend the echoing air, and from them both
> (so custom has ordain'd) a largess claim.[69]

As late as 1931, it was still possible for George Orwell to view this custom. He recorded for 19 September of that year that

137

'on the last morning, when we had picked the last field, there was a queer game of catching the women and putting them in the bins . . . It is evidently an old custom, and all harvests have some custom of this kind attached to them'.[70]

The harvest feast marked the end of harvest work. The labourers, however, claimed one more harvest right. Gleaning or leasing was probably one of the most widespread customary activities during the eighteenth and much of the nineteenth century. Dr Johnson defined gleaning in his *Dictionary* as 'To gather what the gatherers of the harvest leave behind.' This definition centred on the essential source of conflict between farmers and harvesters. The harvest was property, but to permit gleaning meant that the right of property was not absolute. Also, it was the families of the harvestmen who benefitted from gleaning, and it was thus in their best interests to leave a certain amount in the knowledge that their own wives and children would follow at the end of the harvest and collect what remained. At a time when an ideology of private property was becoming dominant, even the intrusion into the field itself was regarded as a threatening invasion. For the labouring poor gleaning in eighteenth century England was a general customary right, and was claimed as an integral part of the harvest contract. In the Middle Ages, gleaning had been of a local character and had been regulated by local custom of the manor. For example, gleaners had to enter the field by certain entrances; gleaning was not permitted until all the sheaves had been carried; was confined to the hours of daylight; was only carried out by those too young or too old to reap.[71] At Welwyn Rectory Manor, Hertfordshire, in 1287, it was ordered that 'men and women who are able to reap be distrained not to glean after the fashion of paupers'. Warren Ault has concluded that no general right for all the poor to glean was claimed during the medieval period, and it is clear from his evidence that local custom and local by-laws regulated the practice specifically.[72]

In the mid-eighteenth century the right to glean by custom was challenged. Arthur Young commented in 1771 that 'The custom of gleaning is universal and very ancient: in this country, however, the poor have no right to glean; but the custom is so old and common, that it is scarcely ever broken through. It behoves the farmer, in some places, where it is carried on to excess, to make rules for the gleaners, and not to suffer them to be broken under any pretence whatever.'[73] To Young and his contemporaries, it appeared that gleaning was being abused and that this abuse was increasing. 'The abuse of gleaning, in many places', he continued, 'is so great as deservedly to be ranked amongst the greatest of evils the farmer undergoes: the poor glean among the sheaves, and too often from them, in so notorious a manner, that complaints of it are innumerable.'[74] Yet whilst Young advised farmers to introduce regulations to restrict gleaners from entering fields until the crop was cleared, he also castigated farmers who, whilst their sheaves remained in the field, turned out hogs and cattle to graze the stubble thereby denying any access to gleaners. To Young, this kind of trick 'is double dealing, and a meanness unpardonable'.[75]

Even the labourers themselves did not necessarily claim gleaning as a right of all. Indeed, it was not to the advantage of local families to permit other families from outside the neighbourhood to glean. The following dispute at Odiham, Hampshire, in 1785 illustrates this point. A case of assault against Sarah Brown and Elizabeth Sparks had been brought for an attack upon one Sarah Cook on 29 August. On that day, Cook had been gleaning in a field when, in the words of the record of one witness, 'the prisoners agreed to take corn from Sarah Cook. Flung her down on the ground and took her petticoats up. Used her she was ashamed to say and Sarah Brown kicked her. Flung many stones but can't say who. Is sure Brown used Sarah Cook very ill. Followed many acres.' Sarah Cook swore that she 'was used very ill by several others who were leasing. Sarah Brown took corn out of hand. Trod on fingers and struck her when she was down – had no quarrel before [with] Brown and Sparks. Followed with many others after them many acres throwing stones. Was in danger of life.' The cause of the assault was that Sarah Cook was 'gleaning in a field not being a parishioner'. It appeared that the quarrelling broke out because several non-parishioners were gleaning. Interestingly, both the accused were found not guilty.[76]

Until 1788 legal opinion differed on the question of

gleaning. Some cited Mosaic law which condemned the restraint of gleaning. 'And when ye reap the harvest of your land, thou shalt not wholly reap the corners of thy field, neither shalt thou gather the gleanings of thy harvest'.[77] Leviticus was even more explicit in the following instruction that 'thou shalt leave them [gleanings] unto the poor and to the stranger'.[78] Even so, scripture allowed for some restriction in a similar way to medieval practice, as is implicit in the latitude with which Boaz allows Ruth to glean 'even among the sheaves' without reproach.[79] Others suggested that Mosaic law was designed for a specific place and time and was not intended to have universal relevance. As Thomas Ruggles pointed out in 1788, the right of gleaning was applied in Mosaic law 'to the vineyard, to the olive grounds; and, by parity of reasoning, in this country, it would go to the orchard, to the hopground; and apples should be left upon the trees, and hops on the bines; and these not for the poor, the fatherless, and the widows only, but for the stranger; not for the poor of a particular village, district, or for our poor countrymen only, but for the whole world.'[80]

William Blackstone noted in his *Commentaries* that 'by the common law and customs of England the poor are allowed to enter and glean on another's ground after harvest without being guilty of trespass'.[81] Whatever the strength of the custom, in the 1780s the practice was under attack. Gleaning was criticised because of the loss of time which resulted. 'How many days, during the harvest', wrote Thomas Ruggles in 1788, 'are lost by the mother of a family and all her children, in wandering about from field to field, to glean what does not repay them the wear of their clothes in seeking; at the same time what a temptation it is to the labourer to gather in his employer's corn in a careless and slovenly manner; and what an early and great inducement to children to pilfer from the swarth or shock, what requires more patience and toil to glean from the harvested field.'[82] The judgement at the Court of Common Pleas of Steel against Houghton and Uxor of 1788 that, 'No person has, at Common Law, a right to glean in the harvest field. Neither have the poor of a parish legally settled any such right', supported Ruggles's view and undermined the customary defence of gleaning. Despite citing an Act of Parliament of only two years earlier for the enclosing of common fields at Basingstoke which implicitly permitted gleaning by including regulations concerning the custom, judgement was given for the plaintiff. One of the justices stated, in giving judgement, that 'No right can exist at common law, unless both the subject of it, and they who claim it, are certain. In this case both are uncertain. The subject is the scattered corn which the farmer chooses to leave on the ground, the quantity depends entirely on his pleasure. The soil is his, the culture is his, the seed his, and in natural justice his also are the profits. Though his conscience may direct him to leave something for the poor, the law does not oblige him to leave anything.'[83]

It remained for Capell Lofft, after the judgement at the Court of Common Pleas, and in conclusion of his published correspondence on gleaning with Thomas Ruggles, to make a last defence. He wrote:

> To a legal custom that it be just in its principle and reasonable in its extent, is indispensibly requisite – A custom founded in benevolence, ascertained by immemorial usage, traceable to a moral precept of divine benevolence, and limited to the indigent, and those who are not of strength or habit to the more profitable labours of the field; nor claimed till the farmer has, in fair construction, carried his crop. – A custom recognised under all these features . . . might, I still think, warrant me, or any man, in the supposition of its legality.[84]

This legal prohibition was similar both in timing and form to the undermining of other customary activities, such as the right to gather dead wood, and was, as in the latter case, difficult to impress upon the popular mind. The judgement merely concluded legal argument, it did not extinguish the custom. In 1794, six years after the judgement, it was recorded of southern England that 'The Wiltshire farmers are very generous in the article of "leasing", the children of the resident labourers being seldom hindered from gleaning, even before the corn is carried off.'[85] In 1797, Eden observed that at Roade, Northamptonshire, the earnings of Richard Walker included £1.10s for gleaning after harvest. 'The poor',

he continued, 'make a great deal by gleaning here, several
families will gather as much wheat as will serve them for
bread the whole year, and as many beans as will keep a
pig.'[86]

In 1869, in some places in Nottinghamshire, gleaning was
heralded by the Church bell.[87] A clergyman wrote to *Notes
and Queries* that:

> In this and several neighbouring villages, it was the custom
> to ring a church bell at 8.00 a.m. to give notice to the
> gleaners that they might begin operations, and another at
> 6.00 p.m. to warn them to give over. Any poor inhabitant
> of the parish was then at liberty to enter into the fields
> which had been cleared. Within the last three or four years,
> however, many of the farmers (my tenants are not of the
> number) refuse to allow any person to glean except the
> wives and children of their own labourers.[88]

Another correspondent, in the same year, confirmed the
clergyman's suspicion that gleaning was being similarly
confined elsewhere. 'In some parts of the neighbourhood of
Alford', wrote 'Alfordiensis', 'it is the custom of some few
of the farmers to allow the wives and families of their regular
labourers to glean the loose ears of corn, even among the
sheaves'. Yet he also noted that 'those restrictions are
generally extended to the inhabitants of the village, as well
as the wives and families of the labourers constantly employed on the farm'.[89]

Gleaning continued to be practiced in Wiltshire in the
1820s[90] and, after harvest, in Kent during the same period.[91]
Indeed, William Cobbett noted that 'Before I got into Folke-
stone I saw no less than eighty-four men, women, and boys
and girls gleaning or leasing in a field of about ten acres.'
Cobbett believed that this great number of gleaners reflected
the difficult economic conditions, and he added: 'The people
all along here complain most bitterly of the change of
times.'[92] This illustrates how gleaning provided, in times of
hardship, a safety net which could partially support the
labouring poor. The produce from gleaning, even towards the
end of the nineteenth century when reaping techniques were
more efficient, continued to make a significant contribution

to the domestic economy. Flora Thompson recalled that the corn, threshed at home from gleaning, was taken to the miller to be ground into flour. 'Great was the excitement', she continued, 'in a good year when the flour came home – one bushel, two bushels, or even more in large, industrious families. The mealy-white sack with its contents was often kept for a time on show on a chair in the living-room and it was a common thing for a passer-by to be invited to "step inside an' see our little bit o' leazings".'[93] Maude Robinson estimated that, in Sussex in the 1860s, an industrious family could glean 'nearly eleven bushels of flour, and what an immense relief it was to the thrifty mother to have no bread bill for which to contrive payment for many weeks.'[94]

Some idea of the economic advantage from gleaning can be seen in the following family account of family earnings from Snettisham, Norfolk in 1799:

	£	s	d
Harvest, 4 weeks	4	14	6
*48 weeks, at 8s per week	18	4	0
Woman's gleanings	0	14	0
48 weeks, at 1s per week	2	8	0
	26	0	6

*Error in original source

This account of income shows that for this particular family the value of gleaning represented 14.8 per cent of the harvest income through wages, 12.9 per cent of the total harvest income, and 2.7 per cent of the total annual earnings.[95] Lord Egremont calculated that a labourer in Sussex at the end of eighteenth century earned a total of £27.2s and that his wife, through gleaning and raking oats and barley, could bring in an additional 20 shillings which represented 3.5 per cent of the family's total income. Capell Lofft suggested in a letter to Lord Egremont that, in Suffolk in 1795, a labourer could earn a total of £27.9s and that a further £4 could be earned in addition by his children spinning, pease and wheat dropping, and gleaning. Assuming that this was about one third of that additional income, gleaning represented 4.1 per cent of the family's total income.[96] Gleaning was significant. Customary perquisites such as gleaning and wood gathering might not represent a large element of the labourer's income but they made up the deficit between structured wages and expenditure.

Farmers and proprietors found it impossible, despite legal sanction, to extinguish the custom. Instead, an attempt was made to limit it. In the 1830s one such limitation was the prohibition of gleaning whilst sheaves remained to be carted. One commentator in 1832 wrote:

> I hear voices, and am apt to think that certain unhired harvest folks have commenced their operations a little too soon. Such, I see, is the case: a party of thirty or forty gleaners, women and children, have made their way in before the sheaves are cleared. This we do not allow; and, I observe, they are aware of their error by decamping at the sight of me . . . There they go, pretty civilly as it happens. We are not, I hope I may say, harsh or inconsiderate with regard to the ancient privileges and important hopes of the poor, at this season. Gleaners, although they have not actual law to authorise their practice, have immemorial usage on their side, in this country, as in most others; and we know that, under the Jewish dispensation, they had a statute right, which the owner of the field dared not infringe. It is evident, however, that as persons are not always to be trusted within arm's length of the rights of others, the farmer is obliged to take care that the labourers, in the first place, do not purposely drop and leave a great deal of corn; and to see, in the next place, that their wives and children do not steal up the sheaves and help themselves at leisure. A family has been known, by mere gleaning, to gather up a quarter of corn, that is, eight threshed and dressed bushels in a season - worth, we may say, three pounds or guineas.[97]

Sanctions which were applied included prosecutions for 'early' gleaning. For example, gleaners near Basingstoke were prosecuted in 1785 for 'gleaning or leasing in a wheatfield last harvest . . . before the corn was carried in'.[98] Some sanctions were not regarded as legitimate and a note of disapprobation was struck in a report of a Lambourn (Berkshire) farmer who set his dog on a woman who was gleaning in

1804.[99] As the Hampshire example cited earlier shows, the gleaners themselves sought to regulate their activities by restricting gleaning to local parishioners. The use of the gleaning bell also reinforced this regulation. The rituals of the last sheaf also had a role as symbolic notification that gleaning could begin, acting as a rite of passage between the harvest itself and customary activities which could only begin upon the conclusion of harvest, such as the harvest home and gleaning.

In late-nineteenth-century Somerset gleaning was restricted by the farmers. One writer recalled that 'when I was a small child permission to glean in the wheat fields was generally granted by Somerset farmers to cottagers who they knew – particularly to the wives and children of their own men.'[100] In this account, coming as it does from a later date, permission was required before gleaning could commence. In 1859 a correspondent to the *Leicester Guardian* noted that in some counties gleaning was denied: 'and the rake closely gathers up the scattered ear; while, what may chance to have been left is abandoned to the pigs'. He went on to describe the revival in his locality of one of the self-regulating gleaning devices, which mirrored in many ways a similar form amongst the harvestmen. This was the election of a 'queen of the gleaners': 'When elected', he continued, 'she is borne in a chair to the first field that is to be gleaned; a crown composed of wild flowers and a few ears of corn is placed upon her head, and she tells her laws to her subjects. They are informed that when there are fields to be gleaned a horn or bell will summon them to the outskirts of the field. The queen then stipulates for a sum to be paid to her attendants who undertake to summon the gleaners.' Models for this kind of office can be found in the lord of the harvest and the marlers' captain, as well as in industrial and trade contexts such as the printing shop. The queen pointed out the particular needs of the elderly and declared 'her will and pleasure' to the effect that her people 'shall not stray from the field' to which she 'leads them' and that anyone who violates this law, 'shall forfeit her gathering, and her corn shall be bestrewed'.[101]

Gleaning continued throughout the nineteenth century partly because, although it was a criminal activity by law, many farmers as well as the labouring poor did not regard it as crime in terms of the prevailing popular morality. The custom of gleaning was associated by members of the 1845 Parliamentary Committee on the Game Laws with other activities which were also not regarded as criminal by the rural labouring poor, such as poaching. This was the implication behind the following exchanges between the committee and one witness. Having elicited that the witness did not believe that smuggling was popularly regarded as a moral offence, the Committee continued:

More especially with respect to gleaning?
– I am not aware that gleaning is an offence at all.
Are you not aware that no one can go and glean without the permission of the proprietor?
– Yes.
Are you aware that the question has been tried?
– I am aware of that.
And decided against the gleaners?
– Yes.
With respect to gleaners, are you prepared to say that gleaners should have a right to glean against the will of the occupier?
– No, unless it were proved out of the divine laws.
Then what is the distinction you draw?
– The distinction I draw is, that I think the existence of a vast quantity of game has such a peculiarly prejudicial effect, that I look upon it in a different light from any other property.
What is the distinction between the man who takes your pheasant, or your hare, or your partridge, and the gleaner who should take a little more corn than would be quite right?
– I should say that the cultivator of the land has been at all the expense which goes to the production of corn; but the land owner upon whose property the game is taken, has, perhaps, been at no expense with regard to the pheasant or the hare.
Of course the labourer can have no more to do with the cost of breeding the pheasant or the hare, than he has with the cost of cultivating the corn?

– The labourer is not entitled to the one or the other . . . but in his own mind he draws a distinction as to the right of property which the owner of the soil has in the one or the other.[102]

It is apparent from this lengthy questioning that the committee wished to establish firmly the illegality of gleaning without permission. Yet in the mind of this particular witness there was a distinction. After some bludgeoning questioning, he conceded that gleaning without authority was an illegal act. Ambivalence towards gleaning contributed to its continuance during the nineteenth century. That it continued can be deduced from the maintenance of the widespread practice of ringing the church bell to indicate the start of gleaning. For example, in Northamptonshire during the 1880s, the gleaning bell 'though by no means so universally rung as was once done' could still be heard or had only recently ceased in some fifty parishes. In twelve of these it was rung at 8 o'clock in the morning only and in a further eleven at 8 o'clock in the morning and at 6 o'clock in the evening. In some cases a small fee was required by the sexton or clerk.[103]

Gleaning became uncommon after the technological innovations towards the end of the nineteenth century which left the harvest field bare. Maude Robinson wrote that the self-binding reaper had contributed to the decline of gleaning. The reaper 'is a blessed invention, clearing the cornfields efficiently. The country folk say that it leaves so little scattered corn that gleaning . . . is not worth doing, but the cheaper price of bread and the higher wage make this work less necessary.'[104] In Hampshire, changes in agricultural practice and more widespread suppression were the causes of the disappearance of gleaning. Charlotte Yonge wrote at the end of the nineteenth century that 'Gleaning is not what it was, mowing and raking leave fewer ears and it is chiefly the holiday of the elder women for old sake's sake, rather than the actual gain; and, indeed, some farmers do not permit it at all. Pigs finish off the remnants, guarded by a boy.'[105]

In the previous century a farmer loosing pigs to eat up the remains of wheat after harvest might be severely dealt with. At Lanshall, in Suffolk in 1772, a man:

who was severe on the poor, by with-holding the corn from them, and not suffering them to glean or gather up the loose-corn dropped by the harvest-men, but would turn in his hogs and cows to eat it, was, on his return from Sudbury market, met in a dark narrow lane by several men in disguise, who pulled him from his horse, and beat him in a most inhuman manner, then dragged him through a little river which ran by the side of a lane, after which they swore they would hang him up to dry, which they did, and then left him, saying they had stopped his oppressing the poor any more.[106]

Such agricultural practice as letting pigs graze the stubble was common by the end of the nineteenth century. Priscilla Savage recalled that, in Blaxhall, Suffolk, gleaning had been discontinued: 'There's no gleaning now, you don't see anybody pick a bit of corn up now, in fact, I don't think the farmers let them . . . but we used to go gleaning . . .'[107]

Harvest and harvest customs provided a context for the labouring poor in the eighteenth and nineteenth centuries within which they set their view of community life and morality. By the twentieth century this context had been destroyed with increased mechanisation of the harvest process. Rituals which had formed rites of passage between harvest work and other harvest perquisites were redundant. John Stewart Collis wrote of a harvest on a farm in southwest England in the 1940s:

We began to get near the last sheaf. Finally we came to it and pitched it up . . . though it nearly fell down again. And as we approached this last sheaf was there any sense of a grand climax? And when it was pitched up, did someone say, – 'Ah, that's the one we've been looking for all this time?' And did 'E say cheerio and give thanks to all and sundry? No, it might have been the first sheaf.[108]

Calendar Rituals and the Shape of the Community

If the old festivals and hearty commemorations in which our land was once so abundant . . . had no other recommendation than their convivial character – the community of enjoyment which they imply – they would, on that account alone, be worthy of all promotion, as an antidote to the cold and selfish spirit which is tainting the life-blood, and freezing the impulses of society.

Thomas K. Hervey[109]

Although Hervey's comments were made in 1836, the promotion of an ideal of community and of social cohesion by the labouring poor remained a significant feature of much customary activity in the eighteenth and nineteenth centuries. The annual mapping of the community which took place in many locations during Rogation week, and elsewhere at other times, was essential to the maintenance of certain calendar rituals which emphasised this view of community solidarity. At various times in the calendar, particularly at Christmas, Easter and Whitsun, these rituals clustered.

The promotion of this image of society was not seen by the labouring poor as mere deferential respect for their superiors but as a concerted attempt to create, albeit temporarily, a corporate society in which the efforts of every individual within that society were directed towards the general well-being of all. Many of these calendar rituals might appear to serve no other purpose than that of providing an opportunity for merriment and festivity, yet their deeper significance can be discovered in the context of an attempt to enforce a view of corporate society.

The physical delineation of the community, in the form either of the parish or the manor, was important. This delineation helped to define those who were inside or part of the individual community. Several common calendar rituals of the eighteenth and nineteenth centuries demonstrate this. A typical account of the Palm Sunday or Easter Sunday custom of sugar-cupping can be cited. The following record of the custom on Easter Sunday is from Ashford-in-the-Water, Derbyshire during the 1840s. One commentator wrote that sugar-cupping

was a custom looked upon as a sort of religious duty, and . . . little parties might be seen going to some neighbouring spring to drink sugar and water . . . I understood the observance of the custom to mean an expression of joy and gladness for the great and important event which the Church considered to be connected with that day. The place most frequented on the occasion [was] . . . a spring of water called 'sinner's well', situated in a curious little dell at the foot of Great Shacklow, a perfect grotto, over-hung with trees.[110]

The religious festival was, at Ashford, marked by a secular observance designed to stress the unity of the community.

Other rituals on Palm Sunday had been popular during the later eighteenth century. Francis Place wrote, in his autobiography, that when he was a youth:

Palm Sunday morning was a grand holiday, a gay jubilee. Thousands of young persons used 'to go a Palming', some in couples, girls and boys, some in parties. I have been Palming many times. We used to set out at daybreak and walk five – six – seven – miles into the country. Dulwich and the valleys among the Surrey Hills, as were indeed all places within the distance named where 'Palm' abounded. All the public houses and small inns round London sold 'Rum and Milk,' and notice thereof was stuck outside their doors and in their windows, thus, – 'The noted Rum and Milk house', . . . Everyone who went out drank 'Rum and milk' on that morning . . .[111]

In Place's account, the custom of 'Palming' was a youth culture activity, and the community defined by adherence to it was therefore a temporarily mobile and urban one.

At Tideswell, Derbyshire, in 1826, sugar-cupping on Easter Sunday had ceased, but could still be recollected by one participant who noted that 'last Sunday, before Easter-day, I walked to the "Dropping tor", the rendezvous of the "sugar-cuppers", but, owing to the extreme inclemency of the weather, no one was there, nor was it, I believe, once visited during the day.'[112] It is clear that these socially cohesive rituals were in decline by the early decades of the nineteenth century; partly because their socially superior patrons were not prepared to tolerate the licence and excess which sometimes occurred on these occasions and partly because the idea of the community as a single unit in which vertical linkage was stressed rather than horizontal division, was no longer in accord with that class's changing value system.

Similar ritual continued in Wiltshire throughout the eighteenth century and until the middle of the nineteenth. It was the custom for the inhabitants of the area around Cley Hill to proceed to its summit on Palm Sunday. Dr Richard Pococke noted the custom in 1754.[113] Further accounts later in the century recorded that 'young people from the adjacent towns and villages 'had a diversion . . . to see one another slip and tumble to the bottom.'[114] The historian of Wiltshire, Sir Richard Colt Hoare, writing in the middle decades of the nineteenth century, wrote: 'It was formerly the custom for the youth of both sexes to assemble on this hill on Palm Sunday, and slide down it; for which purpose horses' skulls were kept in store by the boys, as convenient sledges to sit upon, but of late years this practice has been discontinued.'[115] As with 'Palming' around London, Cley Hill visitations were associated with a youth culture. Elsewhere in Wiltshire, at Silbury Hill, Palm Sunday festivities also occurred. The antiquary, William Stukeley wrote in 1743 that 'the country people have an anniversary meeting on the top of Silbury Hill, on every Palm Sunday, when they make merry with cakes, figs, sugar and water fetched from the swallow head, or spring of the Kennet.'[116] By 1853, the same custom was described: 'The practice of resorting to the top of Silbury Hill is still kept up by the children of the neighbourhood.'[117]

At Pontesford Hill, in Pontesbury, Shropshire, it was customary for crowds of people on Palm Sunday to ascend the hill in search of the 'golden arrow'. This custom occurred until the middle years of the nineteenth century. Furthermore, although it was now confined to 'the wilder spirits of the neighbourhood, and has been little countenanced by the more respectable sort', ascending the hill on Palm Sunday was still undertaken in the 1880s.[118] In 1846 the custom was described as 'a great annual picnic'. 'Every household', the account continued, 'was occupied beforehand in baking cakes and packing up kettles and crockery in preparation for "going Palming" . . . It was said that there was a sort of emulation to be the first to gather "palm" or spray from the ancient "haunted yew-tree" . . . which grows upon the hill.'[119] It was also customary for a race to be held down the hill from the summit to a nearby pool, called Lyde Hole.[120] This custom was very similar to the assemblies held on the Wrekin, in Shropshire, on the first Sunday in May. A full-scale pleasure fair was held on the hill on Wrekin Wakes Sunday, which also included a battle between local inhabitants for possession of the hill. This fighting was so violent that when the Cludde family took over the manorial rights for a part of the hill, the wakes were suppressed, although the practice of assembling on the hill continued. Charlotte Burne, who collected this information, was unable to identify the precise date of this suppression.[121] A correspondent to William Hone's *Everyday Book* referred to the decline of the custom in the 1820s. 'It has been usual', he wrote 'for the people in this neighbourhood to assemble on the Wrekin-hill on the Sunday after May-day, and the three successive Sundays, to drink a health "to all friends round the Wrekin", but as on this annual festival, various scenes of drunkness and licentiousness were frequently exhibited, its celebration has, of late, been very properly discouraged by the magistracy, and is going deservedly to decay.'[122]

The use of high features in the local landscape, or of sites of archaeological remains, for convivial meetings at various times in the year was common in the organisation of some fairs and rural sports. An annual sports was held on Halgaver Moor, near Bodmin towards the end of July. A description of 1789 observed that

> Besides the common exhibitions at fairs, wrestling, cudgelling etc, one of the diversions is to draw the unwary into a quagmire and assist in keeping him there till he pulls another into the same situation. – In addition to maurice [*sic*] dancing, grinning through a horse's collar, and other grotesque performances . . . there is also a mock court held here at this time, whose president is then called the Mayor of Halgaver, and where persons found guilty of an infringement upon the rules of the place, etc, are punished by being rendered ridiculous in appearance, as being obliged to ride woman-wise through the place, have their clothes turned inside out, etc.[123]

Great Wishford. Oak Apple Day 1906. Figures on the left are dressed in costume which was
eady anachronistic to commemorate an early defender of the custom, Grace Reed.

Great Wishford. Early twentieth century. The villagers collecting green boughs in Grovely
rest on Oak Apple Day. The banner is again present with the words 'Unity is strength'.

3. *Gleaners*. W.H. Pyne. *Microcosm* 1808. Women and children, in gleaning after harvest, supplemented the meagre incomes of labouring families.

4. *The Gleaning Field*. Samuel Palmer. 1833. By permission of the Trustees of the Tate Gallery, London. In Palmer's painting, the gleaners have entered the field before all the sheaves have been carted away.

(*top*) *Hereford . . . Harvest Scene, Afternoon*. George Robert Lewis. 1815. By permission of the
stees of the Tate Gallery, London. An impression of the large numbers of harvestmen
uired can be gained from this painting.

(*below*) The sheep shearing supper from *Far From the Madding Crowd*. Thomas Hardy.
hsheba Everdene sits in her parlour window, avoiding any compromise of her social and
ssibly sexual position.

7. *Country Around Dixton Manor.* By permission of Cheltenham Art Gallery and Museum. This detail shows the festivities associated with the eighteenth-century harvest including musicians and morris dancers.

By permission of Cheltenham Art Gallery and Museum. Here the detail is of the procession which followed the last harvest load. A large number of people is shown in the picture which should probably read like a cartoon strip.

9. Gathering firewood. Photograph by Greystone Bird. By permission of the Mary Evans Picture Library. Collectors of dead wood for fuel would not be met by an open gate by the late nineteenth century.

10. Overton mummers. G. Long. Annual Christmas visitants like the mummers were less welcome by the middle of the nineteenth century when such customary folk doles were increasingly opposed.

11. *(above)* The Chulkhurst Charity, Biddenden, Kent. On Easter Monday, bread and cheese and Biddenden cakes are still given out, from the benefaction of the Chulkhursts who were Siamese twins.

12. *(right)* Notice prohibiting the collection of Christmas boxes in Trowbridge, Wiltshire. 1825. By courtesy of the Wiltshire Library and Museum Service.

13. *The May Day Procession of Queen Eva.* Anna Richards. 1902. By courtesy of Whitelands College, London. This depicts a May festival, instituted in 1881, at the suggestion of John Ruskin, which is still annually performed. Ruskin was attempting to create an

The rural sports and the mock court can be seen as mechanisms of social cohesion for the surrounding district. The location was a prominent part of the physical appearance of the area and provided the venue for the custom itself. This prominence was also significant within the mental map for the neighbouring communities.

Perhaps the best-known example of this type of custom was the Scouring of the White Horse at Uffington and the sports and festivities which accompanied it. The 'Scouring' was first described in 1738, although earlier writers alluded to it.[124] Thomas Hughes's novel *The Scouring of the White Horse*, which was published in 1857, contains much information about the custom and cites some ten occasions when the figure was cleaned from 1755 to 1843.[125] Drawing from an account published in the *Reading Mercury*, Hughes reports that, in 1780, on Whit Monday some 30,000 people were present at the festival which accompanied the scouring, including most of the county notability.[126]

In 1776, the scouring was held on 27 May, and among the sports which took place was the usual canon of rustic play including 'A good hat to be run for by men in sacks, every man to bring his own sack . . . A waistcoat, 10s 6d value, to be given to the person who shall take a bullet out of the tub of flour with his mouth in the shortest time. – A cheese to be run for down the White Horse manger.'[127] It is easy to dismiss these festive sports as mere horseplay but it is significant that cheese-rolling figured in other customary activities, such as the similar event at Cooper's Hill, Gloucestershire and at Randwick Mop in the same county.[128] Both of these festivals occurred through the nineteenth century. In the case of Randwick a cheese was rolled round the churchyard at the election of a mock mayor, and at Cooper's Hill it was believed that the cheese rolling down the Hill preserved certain grazing rights. Activities like cheese-rolling within the public context of a socially important festival were methods of preserving customary economic rights to land. The festivals both defended the use of the ground by the local community or by several neighbouring communities for pleasure activities, and emphasised older economic uses to which the land was put by the community. Cheese-rolling acted as a mechanism of record. It is in this way that the

historian should view the cheese-rolling at Uffington in
particular, and the total festival of the scouring itself. These
events demonstrated the group identity of the community
or the neighbourhood and provided physical proof of its
cohesion. Denial of the legitimacy of the festival was also
a denial of the community's right of access to the venue
itself for any purpose and also, in some cases, destroyed the
original economic function which the festival safeguarded
and reaffirmed.

A further example of this kind of defence of customary
right can be found in certain Whit Sunday festivals, during
the eighteenth century, held by the inhabitants of the town
of Burford. In 1779 the Whit festival was described in the
following terms:

> The parish consists chiefly of arable lands and woodlands.
> A house called Cap's Lodge, though lying within the boun-
> daries of the forest of Whichwood, belongs to Widford,
> where, by ancient custom, the inhabitants of the town of
> Burford assemble, on Whit Sunday yearly, and choose a
> Lord and Lady. They likewise claim the privilege of
> cutting wood, and of hunting with dogs, and killing deer
> in the forest; but the latter is compounded for, by deliver-
> ing to them two bucks annually, on a certain day, with
> which the principal inhabitants of the town made an
> entertainment.[129]

Another account makes it clear that not only Burford, but
many local communities, were involved in similar festivals
at Whitsuntide connected with the forest of Wychwood, and
that these continued well into the 1840s.[130] The custom of
the 'Whithunt' in Wychwood, as well as providing an occasion
for merriment, defended a real economic right. The deer hunt
itself not only brought the carcass for the distribution of
meat, but also protected other rights of access to the forest
for such uses as collecting dead wood for fuel. The 'Whithunt' acted as a symbol of the solidarity of particular local
communities in preserving their rights.

The map of the community which 'processioning' provided
was used by the participants throughout the year as a frame
of reference for the customary activities which occurred on

other key calendar dates. Whilst this map might be only of the parish, wider cognizance of the surrounding locality can be seen in the socially-cohesive festivals which occurred at Palm Sunday, Easter, Whitsun and Christmas. Over the Christmas period, it was customary for the parish to be traversed by many parties of ritual visitors including mummers, church singers, ringers and wassailers. Some of these visits had a similar function to the largess-collection and work rituals of harvest. One of the most widespread during the eighteenth and early nineteenth centuries was the practice of apple-tree wassailing.

In most of the counties of southern England, parties of labourers visited the orchards of their farming masters during winter, and particularly upon Twelfth Night, to wassail the trees and to demand, in return, the hospitality of the farmer. The ceremony performed was elaborate and was redolent of pagan beginnings. Howitt wrote of the custom in the 1840s that

> In some places, they walk in procession to the principal orchards in the parish. In each orchard one tree is selected as the representative of the rest; and is saluted with a certain form of words. They then sprinkle the tree with cider, or dash a bowl of cider against it. In other places, only the farmer and his servants assemble on the occasion and after immersing cakes in cider, hang them on the apple-trees. They then sprinkle the trees with cider; pronounce their incantation, dance about the tree, and then go home to feast.[131]

The rituals of sprinkling the tree and chanting incantations have been cited by some folklorists as proof of the continued belief in tree-magic and vegetative divinities.[132] It would be more relevant to consider the activity in terms of the promotion of social cohesion within the community. As with many similar customs, and particularly harvest, the elements of commensality and group solidarity were combined. The parish or, in the smaller cases, the farmer and his men, were linked together by vertical and horizontal threads, and the prevailing social hierarchy and its conventions were set aside.

In Sussex, during the 1820s the emphasis on largess and

commensality was clear. One writer noted that, having performed the requisite actions in the orchard, the labourers
'proceed to the home of the owner, and sing at the door a
song common on the occasion. They are admitted, and
placing themselves around the kitchen fire, enjoy the spark-
ling ale, and festivities of the season.'[133] In Sussex, the
custom was referred to as 'apple howling', which was a
corruption in the popular tongue of 'apple yuling'. A correspondent of the antiquary, John Brand, described 'the custom
of singing and drinking to the apple trees' in 1805:

> In most places where there are orchards of any conse-
> quence it is usual for large parties annually to assemble on
> the evening of Twelfth Day for the purpose of making a
> copious libation to the Goddess Pomona . . . when the
> requisite arrangements are made and the hour arrives, the
> Person who leads the ceremony, advancing to the finest
> and largest tree of the orchard, takes hold of a limb with
> one hand and holding up a jug of cider in the other sings to
> the following purpose:

> > Huzza, Huzza in our good town
> > The Bread shall be white, and the liquor be brown
> > So here my old fellow I drink to thee
> > And the very good health of each other tree.
> > Well may ye blow well may ye bear
> > Blossom and fruit both apple and pear.
> > So that every Bough and every twig
> > May bend with a Burthen both fair and big
> > May ye bear us and yield us fruit such a store
> > That the Bags and the chambers and house run o'er.

> . . . At the conclusion all the persons present join in shout-
> ing and halloing with every possible vehemence, so that at
> times the county for many miles around resounds with
> their noisy festivity.[134]

This form of wassailing allowed for much convivial enjoyment, as the correspondent made clear.

Dancing contributes to enliven the scene, and a loose is

given to every species of rural fun and frolic. the
you may imagine is not dealt out with a p?
hand: it more frequently flows with such ?
profusion that many of the Devotees are soon u.
stand and it is not uncommon for some of the most ie.
vent of them when in this state to continue stretched on
the ground (either snoring aloud or vociferating with all
imaginable custom and no doubt with much sincerity their
wishes for a plentiful crop) throughout the whole of the
night.[135]

Apple-tree wassailing emphasised the bonds of rural
society and stressed commensality on the part of the farmers.
Food and plentiful supplies of cider were used to strengthen
these bonds. Elsewhere in England, a similar form of customary behaviour was adopted in the ritual of wassailing the
farm beasts. In Hereford, in 1832, this practice pertained.
One account reported:

On the eve of old Christmas day, there are thirteen fires
lighted in the cornfields of many of the farmers, twelve of
them in a circle, and one round a pole, much larger and
higher than the rest, and in the centre. These fires are
dignified with the names of the Virgin Mary and the
twelve apostles, the lady being in the middle; and, while
they are burning, the labourers retire into some shed or
outhouse . . . In this shed they lead a cow, on whose horns
a plum-cake has been stuck and having assembled round
the animal, the oldest labourer takes a pail of cider and
addresses the following lines to the cow with great solemnity:

Here's to thy pretty face, and thy white horn,
God send thy master a good crop of corn,
Both wheat, rye and barley, of grains of all sort,
And next year, if we lives, we'll drink to thee again.

After which the verse is chanted in chorus by all present.
They then dash the cider in the cow's face, when, by a
violent toss of her head, she throws the plum-cake on the
ground; and if it falls forward, it is an omen that the next

157

harvest will be good; and if backward, that it will be unfavourable. This is the commencement of the rural feast which is generally prolonged till the following morning.[136]

The similarity between the verses sung and the customary forms used illustrates the common function which underlined apple-tree wassailing and beast wassailing. These were regarded as mid-winter versions of the harvest home, and provided the labouring poor with an opportunity to regale themselves at the expense of the farmers.

By the beginning of the nineteenth century some critics noted that the country gentry were already withdrawing support for these and similar customs. Dr Falconer wrote that

> However ridiculous and absurd these customs may appear to the enlightened mind of the present generation, they had undoubtedly their advantages. The nobility and gentry before they adopted the pernicioues custom of deserting their native mansions and misspending their time and sub-stance in the levities predominant in foreign countries, thought it sufficient entertainment and recreation for themselves and their children to attend them. Uncouth as some of these amusements may be deemed by our modern refined taste, they had their charms and their utility; the novelty and dexterity of them excited admiration; they did not tend to promote vice and immorality, and they afforded an opportunity for all ranks of people to assemble and spend their time in innocent mirth and hilarity.[137]

'All ranks of people' as a description of the participants in customs which emphasised social cohesion became increasingly inappropriate as the nineteenth century progressed. Harvest and its customary perquisites, and similar calendar events, became less festivals of the whole community than of the labouring poor. The visits of wassailers or mummers at Christmas, or mayers during the spring became less common. William Hone was conscious of this trend when he wrote in the 1820s of sheep-shearing suppers that they were 'fast sinking into disuse, as a scene of mirth and revelry, for the want of being duly encouraged and partaken in by the "great ones of the earth"; without whose countenance and example it is questionable whether eating, drinking, and sleeping, would not soon become vulgar practices, and be discontinued accordingly.'[138]

In Wiltshire, the visits of the Christmas waits continued until the last third of the nineteenth century. A gradation of visits occurred, with children beginning the season a month before Christmas. These children's visits finished with a general request for largess in the following terms:

> God bless the master of the house,
> Likewise the mistress too,
> And all the little children
> That go by two and two
> Please to gee us a penny apiece
> It's all we do desire.
> We wish you a merry Kersmass
> And a joyful Near Year.

After this, on Christmas Eve night itself, the waits appeared.

> The last really primitive carol-singing I heard was eighteen years ago [i.e. 1870s], in a small Wiltshire town [wrote one observer]. Sometime about one o'clock in the morning we were aroused by hearing distant strains of music, which presently approached nearer, and finally broke still and clear in front of the house . . . On drawing aside the window curtains we saw about twelve men and women, old men and maidens, young men (not children: they had been earlier in the evening) with lanterns, fiddles, bass viols, and voices . . . when they had sung their carols, they all shouted at the top of their voices, 'Good marnin', Mr and Mrs Jones, and all the Miss and Master Joneses, we wish you a merry Kersmass and an Happy New Year.' In the morning as we sat at breakfast two of their number apppeared with a collecting box.[139]

Support was less frequently forthcoming by the date of that particular recollection. The shape of the local community had been transformed. The map which was traced by carol singers and others was no longer relevant. Neither was the

159

By Rite

earlier social structure of the village in which, at least in the
view of those who were structually inferior, the structurally
superior fulfilled their responsibilities towards the poor.
Customs of social cohesion no longer draw upon the support
of the whole community.

Notes

1   N.P. Blaker, *Sussex in Bygone Days: Reminiscences of Nathaniel
    Paine Blaker* (Hove, 1919), p. 13. For other variants of the song
    see Bob Copper, *A Song for Every Season: A Hundred Years of
    a Sussex Farming Family* (London, 1971), pp. 256–7; Barclay
    Wills, *Shepherds of Sussex* (London, n.d.), pp. 157–8; C.F. Cook
    (ed.), *The Book of Sussex Verse* (Hove, 1920), pp. 192–3; R.W.
    Blencowe, 'South-Down Shepheards, and their songs at the sheep-
    shearings', *Sussex Archaeological Collections*, vol. II, 1849, p. 251.
2   'Wiltshire and General: Folklore and Tales. Notes on Beacons,
    Gibbets, Holy Wells', collected by Cecil V. Goddard, F. 97. Wilt-
    shire Archaeological and Natural History Society Headquarters,
    Devizes, Wiltshire.
3   R. Chambers (ed.), *The Book of Days: A Miscellany of Popular
    Antiquities* (London, 1888), vol. II, p. 376.
4   Lilias Rider Haggard (ed.), *I walked by night: The Life of the
    King of the Poachers* (London, 1935), pp. 91–2.
5   See Andrew Jones, 'Harvest Customs and Labourers' Perquisites
    in Southern England, 1150–1350: the Corn Harvest', *Agricultural
    History Review*, vol. 25, 1977, Part I, p. 21. Andrew Jones's work
    is extremely important for an understanding of the medieval con-
    text of much eighteenth-century and nineteenth-century harvest
    custom.
6   *Sussex Notes and Queries: A Quarterly Journal of the Sussex
    Archaelogical Society*, vol. II, 1928–9, pp. 24–5.
7   Wills, *Shepherds of Sussex*, p. 155.
8   Ibid., pp. 157, 162–4.
9   'With no idea that they were at the end of a long tradition, they
    still kept up the old country custom of choosing as their leader
    the tallest and most highly skilled man amongst them, who was
    then called "King of the Mowers". For several harvests in the
    'eighties they were led by the man known as Boamer. He had
    served in the Army and was still a fine, well-set-up young fellow
    with flashing white teeth and a skin darkened by fiercer than
    English suns' – Flora Thompson, *Lark Rise to Candleford* (Lon-
    don, 1973), p. 257.
10 Clare, *Selected Poems*, ed. J.W. Tibble and Anne Tibble (London,
    1976), p. 40.
11 A.E. Baker, *Glossary of Northamptonshire Words and Phrases*

160

(London, 1854), entry under 'Booting'.

12 Joseph Stevens, *A Parochial History of St Mary Bourne* (London, 1888), p. 338.

13 See W. Carew Hazlitt, *Faiths and Folklore of the British Isles* (London, 1905; reprinted New York, 1965), p. 585.

14 See William Hone, *Everyday Book* (London, 1864), vol. I, p. 573.

15 For the Army see J. Keegan, *The Face of Battle* (London, 1978), pp. 181-2. For the Navy see Eric Partridge, *A Dictionary of Historical Slang* (London, 1972). Entry for 'Cob' – the term used in the Navy.

16 Variants of this cry can be found in G.F. Northall, *English Folk Rhymes* (London, 1982), pp. 261-3.

17 *Bristol and Gloucestershire Archaeological Society Transactions*, vol. II, 1877-8, p. 19.

18 F.H. Hinton, 'Notes on the Court Books of the Manors of Lacock, Charlton, Liddington with Cote, and Nethermore (chiefly 1583 to 1603)', *Wiltshire Archaeological and Natural History Magazine*, vol. I, 1944, pp. 475-6.

19 William Marshall, *Review and Abstract of the County Reports to the Board of Agriculture* (York, 1818), vol. V, p. 268, which quotes William Stevenson, *General view of the Agriculture of the County of Dorset* (London, 1812), p. 428.

20 Ibid., vol. II, pp. 181-2, which quotes J. Bishton, *General view of the Agriculture of the County of Salop* (Brentford, 1794), p. 36.

21 Ibid., vol. II, pp. 241-2, which quotes Joseph Plymley, *General views of the Agriculture of Shropshire* (London, 1805), p. 139. Information from Mr Flavel.

22 Henry Hunt, *Memoirs* (London, 1820), pp. 182, 280. The harvest-bottles were usually small barrels.

23 Marshall, *Review and Abstract*, vol. II, p. 294, which quotes John Clark, *General view of the Agriculture of the County of Herefordshire* (London, 1794), p. 40.

24 Ibid., vol. II, p. 374, which quotes William Thomas Pomeroy, *General view of the Agriculture of the County of Worcester* (London, 1794), p. 17.

25 Ibid., vol. II. For Gloucestershire see p. 407, which quotes George Turner, *General view of the County of Gloucestershire* (London, 1794), pp. 20, 39, 44. For Devon see Ibid., vol. V, p. 554, which quotes Robert Fraser, *General view of the County of Devon* (London, 1794), p. 43.

26 Ibid., vol. V, p. 574, which quotes Charles Vancouver, *General View of the Agriculture of the County of Devon* (London, 1813), p. 361.

27 Sir Frederick Eden, *The State of the Poor* (3 vols., 1797), vol. III, p. 805.

28 Clement Cadle, 'The Agriculture of Worcestershire', *Journal of the Royal Agricultural Society of England*, Second Series, vol. III, 1867, p. 463.

161

29   Reverend Skinner, *Journal of a Somersetshire Rector*, ed. Howard Coombs and Reverend A.N. Bax (London, 1930), Entry for Thursday, 3 July 1828.

30   Ibid., pp. 175-6. Entry for Saturday, 12 July 1828.

31   Ibid., p. 193. Entry for Monday, 11 August 1828.

32   Ibid., p. 201. Entry from Thursday, 21 August 1828.

33   Ibid.

34   Maude Robinson, *A South Down Farm in the Sixties* (London, 1947), p. 10.

35   Ibid., p. 16.

36   Thompson, *Lark Rise to Candleford*, pp. 257, 259. The harvestmen at Lark Rise continued to use a song which, in their eyes, encapsulated the bargain with the farmer – see Chapter 2, pp. 42-3.

37   'One of the New Voters' in *The Pageant of Summer: Essays by Richard Jefferies*, ed. Andrew Rossati (London, 1979), pp. 137-8. This essay first appeared in Richard Jefferies, *The Open Air* (London, 1885).

38   Alfred Williams, *Folk Songs of the Upper Thames* (London, 1923), p. 55. Williams notes: 'This fine song was prevalent about the Wiltshire Downs and was sung at the Harvest-homes held in times past.'

39   British Library. Additional MSS 41313, F. 86. This is a letter from Robert Studley Vidal to the antiquary, John Brand, dated Cornborough (Devon), 28 September 1805.

40   Hone, *Everyday Book*, vol. II, p. 586. Letter dated July 1826.

41   Jones, 'Harvest Customs', p. 14.

42   Ibid., p. 15.

43   See also the companion article by Andrew Jones, 'Harvest customs and Labourers' Requisites in Southern England, 1150-1350: the Hay Harvest', *Agricultural History Review*, vol. 25, Part II, 1977, pp. 98-107. I find his comments on the customary provision of food and drink to hay makers particular significant.

44   Hone, *Everyday Book*, vol. II, p. 585.

45   George L. Gomme, *Extracts from the 'Gentleman's Magazine' on Manners and Customs* (London, 1885), pp. 45-6.

46   Hone, *Everyday Book*, vol. II, p. 582. This account is taken from John Brand, *Observations on Popular Antiquities*, ed. Sir Henry Ellis (London, 1813), vol. I, pp. 443-4.

47   Hone, *Everyday Book*, vol. II, p. 583.

48   Joseph Haslewood's copy of John Brand, *Observations on Popular Antiquities*, ed. Henry Ellis (London, 1813) (BL, 142.4.1,2) contains his own interleaved manuscript notes. For largess, see the note in vol. I between pp. 447 and 448.

49   On Christmas boxes and opposition to the custom see a newspaper cutting affixed before the title page in Thomas Park's copy of John Brand, *Observations on Popular Antiquities* (Newcastle upon Tyne, 1777) in the British Library (801.e.4).

50   Hone, *Everyday Book*, vol. II, p. 583. Letter to William Hone

dated 14 August 1826 from Norfolk.
51 Quoted in R.M. Garnier, *Annals of the British Peasantry* (1895), pp. 154-5.
52 Clare, *Selected Poems*, p. 221. The lines are taken from Clare's poem *Remembrances*.
53 Hone, *Everyday Book*, vol. II, p. 583.
54 Judith Allen, 'It is the Custom in this Village', *Folklore*, vol. 92 (i), 1981, pp. 71-2.
55 Ibid. Whitelands was a field name and Whippity was a road.
56 See Jones, 'Corn Harvest', particularly pp. 18-19.
57 William Hone, *The Talk Book* (London, 1864), p. 524.
58 Hone, *Everyday Book*, vol. II, p. 582.
59 Thompson, *Lark Rise to Candleford*, p. 261.
60 Brand, *Observations* (1813), vol. I, p. 439.
61 Thomas Hardy, *Far from the Madding Crowd* (London, 1974), p. 185.
62 See Gomme, *Extracts from the 'Gentleman's Magazine'*, p. 17. The account is taken from the *Gentleman's Magazine*, 1819, Part I, p. 109.
63 Jefferys Taylor, *The Farm: A New Account of Rural Toils and Produce* (London, 1832), p. 142. This work describes 'Peak Hall' - a fictional estate in Essex.
64 S.G. Kendall, *Farming Memoirs of a West Country Yeoman* (London, 1944), p. 36.
65 See, for example, Hone, *Everyday Book*, vol. Iı, pp. 584, 586.
66 See F. Llewellyn Jewitt, 'On Ancient Customs of Cheshire', *Journal of the British Archeological Association*, vol. V, October 1849, pp. 254-5 and, for an earlier account, see Robert W. Malcolmson, *Popular Recreations in English Society, 1700-1850* (Cambridge, 1973), pp. 62-4.
67 Ella Mary Leather, *The Folklore of Herefordshire* (London, 1912; reprinted 1973), p. 106.
68 Ibid.
69 Christopher Smart, *The Hop-Garden: A Georgic* (1752) in *The Works of the English Poets from Chaucer to Cowper*, ed. Alexander Chalmers (London, 1810), Vol. 16, p. 39.
70 George Orwell, *The Collected Essays, Journalism and Letters of George Orwell*, Vol. 1 (London, 1971), p. 92. Entry for 19 September 1931. See also *Old Days in the Kent Hop Gardens*, ed. West Kent Federation of Women's Institutes (Maidstone, 1962; reprinted, 1981), particularly p. 34 where an informant recalls the custom in the late-nineteenth century and recalls that the fattest woman was put in the bin and effigies were burned.
71 W.O. Ault, *Open-field Farming in Medieval England* (London, 1972), pp. 31-2, 180.
72 Ibid., p. 82.
73 Arthur Young, *The Farmer's Kalendar* (London, 1773; reprinted 1973), pp. 246-7.

74 Ibid., p. 247.
75 Ibid.
76 This case is to be found in the Hampshire Record Office. Quarter Sessions Rough Minute Books QMP/III Epiphany Sessions 1785. FF. 185-6.
77 Leviticus, xix, 9.
78 Leviticus, xxiii, 22.
79 Ruth, ii, 15.
80 Thomas Ruggles, 'On Gleaning', *Annals of Agriculture* (London, 1788), ed. Arthur Young, vol. IX, p. 639.
81 Ibid., p. 640, which quotes Sir William Blackstone, *Commentaries on the laws of England* (London, 1765-9), vol. III, p. 212.
82 Thomas Ruggles, 'Picturesque Farming', *Annals of Agriculture* (London, 1788), ed. Arthur Young, vol. IX, p. 14.
83 See Steel against Houghton and Uxor 1788 in *The English Reports*, vol. CXXXV: Common Pleas 125 IV, pp. 32-7. Quotation p. 38.
84 Capell Lofft, 'On the Gleaning Question', *Annals of Agriculture* (London, 1788), ed. Arthur Young, vol. X, p. 227. Capell Lofft (1751-1824), described by Boswell as 'This little David of popular spirit' (*Life of Johnson*, chapter LXXIII; see James Boswell, *Life of Johnson*, ed. R.W. Chapman, London, 1970, p. 1281) was struck off the roll of magistrates in 1800 because of his 'improper interference' in attempting to save the life of a poor girl who had been capitally convicted of theft by Sir Nash Grose at the Suffolk Assizes. See *Dictionary of National Biography*, vol. XII, pp. 69-70.
85 Marshall, *Review and Abstract*, vol. V, p. 218 which quotes Thomas Davis, *General view of the Agriculture of the County of Wiltshire* (London, 1794), p. 89.
86 Sir Frederick Eden, *The State of the Poor* (3 vols., 1798), vol. II, pp. 546-7.
87 See Chapter 2, pp. 50-1.
88 *Notes and Queries*, 4th series, vol. IV (London, 1869 July–December), p. 216.
89 Ibid., p. 286.
90 William Cobbett, *Rural Rides* (London, Everyman Edition, 1973), vol. II, p. 68.
91 Ibid., vol. I, p. 245.
92 Ibid., vol. I, p. 237.
93 Thompson, *Lark Rise to Candleford*, p. 15.
94 Robinson, *A South Down Farm*, p. 15.
95 Arthur Young, *General view of the Agriculture of the County of Norfolk* (London, 1804), pp. 493-4, cited in G.E. Mingay, *Arthur Young and his Times* (London, 1975), p. 123.
96 See Arthur Young, *General view of the Agriculture of the County of Sussex* (London, 1813), pp. 407-9.
97 Taylor, *The Farm*, pp. 139-41.
98 *Hampshire Chronicle*, 23 May 1785.

99   *Reading Mercury*, 1 October 1804.
100 W.G. Willis Watson (ed.), *Calendar of Customs* (1920), p. 336.
101 A clipping from the *Leicester Guardian* dated Rempstone, Lough-
     borough 17 October 1859 interleaved in William Kelly's copy of
     John Brand, *Observations on Popular Antiquities* (London,
     1841), located in the Library of the Folklore Society, University
     College, vol. II, p. 12. addition A. For another set of gleaning
     rules see *The Evesham Journal*, 30 September 1899. For another
     account of the Queen's duties see Enid Porter, *Cambridgeshire
     Customs and Folklore* (London, 1969), p. 124.
102 Parliamentary papers. Report from the select Committee on the
     Game Laws, 1846, pt. I, pp. 71-2, Questions 1453-1465. Evi-
     dence of Sir Henry Verney.
103 *Northamptonshire Notes and Queries*, vol. I, 1886, p. 248, which
     quotes Thomas North, *The Church Bells of Northamptonshire*.
104 Robinson, *A South Down Farm*, p. 15.
105 Charlotte M. Yonge, *An Old Woman's Outlook in a Hampshire
     Village* (London, 1896), p. 197.
106 E.A. Goodwyn, *Selections from Norwich Newspapers 1760-1790*
     (Ipswich, n.d.), p. 20, quoting the *Norwich Mercury* for 1772.
107 Ginette Dunn, *The Fellowship of Song: Popular Singing Tradi-
     tions in East Suffolk* (London, 1980), pp. 35-6.
108 John Stewart Collis, *The Worm Forgives the Plough* (London,
     1975), p. 197.
109 Thomas K. Hervey, *The Book of Christmas* (London, 1836),
     pp. 14-5.
110 T. Brushfield, 'Notices of some customs and observances at
     Ashford-in-the-Water', *The Reliquary*, vol. IV, 1863-4, p. 207.
111 Mary Thrale, *Autobiography of Francis Place* (Cambridge, 1972),
     p. 77.
112 Hone, *Everyday Book*, vol. II, p. 226.
113 Dr Richard Pococke, *The Travels Through England* (Camden
     Society, 1888-9), two vols., cited in Jean Morrison, 'Folklore
     of Cley Hill', *Wiltshire Folklore*, vol. 1, Autumn 1977, pp.
     35-6.
114 Ibid., quoting *A Geographical Description of Wiltshire*, 1762.
115 Ibid., quoting Sir Richard Colt Hoare, *The History of Modern
     Wiltshire* (6 vols., 1822-1852).
116 William Stukeley, *Abury Described* (London, 1743), p. 43, cited
     in Michael Dames, *The Silbury Treasure* (London, 1976), pp.
     96-7.
117 William Long, *Wiltshire Archaeological Magazine*, vol. 4, 1858,
     p. 340, cited in Michael Dames, *The Silbury Treasure*, p. 97.
118 Charlotte S. Burne, *Shropshire Folklore: A Sheaf of Gleanings*
     (London, 1883; reprinted 1973), p. 331.
119 Ibid.
120 Ibid.
121 Ibid., p. 363.
122 Hone, *Everyday Book*, vol. II, p. 300.

123   *The Western County Magazine*, 1789 (Salisbury, n.d.), vol. III, p. 245.
124   See Morris Marples, *White Horses and other Hill Figures* (London, 1949; reprinted 1980), p. 55, which quotes Reverend Francis Wise's pamphlet, *Letter to Dr Mead concerning some Antiquities in Berkshire* (1738).
125   Marples, *White Horses*, p. 57.
126   Ibid.
127   Handbill quoted by Marples, *White Horses*, p. 58.
128   For Cooper's Hill see Homer Sykes, *Once a Year* (London, 1977), p. 85, which cites an account of 1836. For Randwick see *County Folklore*, ed. Edwin S. Hartland (London, 1885), vol. I, p. 18 for an account of the Randwick custom in the mid-nineteenth century, and p. 34 for an account of 1784 which illustrates how Randwick's custom was connected with the election of a mock-mayor. See also Hone, *Talk Book*, p. 277.
129   Rudder, *A New History of Gloucestershire* (Cirencester, 1779), p. 822.
130   See Percy Manning, 'Some Oxfordshire Seasonal Festivals: with notes on Morris-Dancing in Oxfordshire', *Folklore*, vol. VIII, 1897, pp. 310-12.
131   Howitt, *The Rural Life of England* (London, 1841), pp. 396-7.
132   The classic view is to be found in the descriptions of the customs throughout Europe in Sir James Frazer, *The Golden Bough* (abridged edition, London, 1922; reprinted 1971), pp. 800-1. See also Hole, *A Dictionary of British Folk Customs*, p. 317.
133   Reverend T.W. Horsfield, *The History and Antiquities of Lewes* (Lewes, 1824-7), vol. II, p. 267.
134   British Library Additional MSS 41313, pp. 85-6, letter from Robert Studley Vidal to John Brand, dated 28 September 1805 from Cornborough.
135   Ibid.
136   British Library Additional MSS. 24545: Joseph Hunter's copy of John Brand, *Observations on Popular Antiquities*, newspaper clipping interleaved at F.62 from *The Courier*, 29 December 1832.
137   British Library: Joseph Haslewood's interleaved copy of John Brand, *Observations on Popular Antiquities*, advertisement interleaved at beginning of vol. I which announced the publication of No. III of 'Popular Pastimes, Being Picturesque Representations of the Customs and Amusements of Great Britain, in Ancient and Modern Times'.
138   Hone, *Everday Book*, vol. II, p. 394.
139   *Wiltshire Notes and Queries*, vol. I, 1893-4, pp. 150-1.

5 The Rituals of Privation and Protest

Custom, Conflict and Commensality

> Upon approaching the village towards 3 o'clock, I heard
> a good deal of uproar and tumult, intermingled at times
> with the heavy monotonous sound produced by blowing
> a cow's horn . . . I did not actually see the people by
> whom the noise was occasioned but took it for granted
> that it was one of those ebullitions of popular feeling
> which are sometimes occasioned in country villages, by
> a man's beating his wife, or other flagrant violation of
> the marriage vow.[1]

This account is taken from an anonymous pamphlet published at Oxford in 1830 entitled 'Machine-breaking and the
changes occasioned by it in the village of Turvey Down: a
tale of the times', a fictionalised description of the Captain
Swing riots of the winter of 1830–1, written by someone
who appeared to be well-acquainted both with the background to the disturbances and the form which they took.
The author aimed to trace the causes of the riots and to show
the futility of breaking agricultural machinery. However,
the quotation well illustrates the theme of this chapter. A
machine-breaking riot is mistaken for a gathering of 'rough
music' – the common punishment for wife-beaters in the
village community.[2] It will be argued that organised forms of
protest such as the Captain Swing disturbances of 1830 and
some popular customs both sprang from the same cultural
experience and are consciously (in the sense of providing
models for behaviour) or unconsciously inter-related.

Some popular customs and ceremonies during the eighteenth and nineteenth centuries in themselves embodied a
strong element of confrontation. Social anthropologists have
emphasised that certain rituals in which conflict between

167

groups is a central feature, and in which disruptive or anti-social behaviour is tolerated, can be interpreted as a demonstration of strength and importance by those normally regarded as the powerless group in the usual social hierarchy. These rituals occur most frequently when such groups feel threatened or are under some external pressure. Victor Turner has identified rites of liminality as a significant factor in certain rituals. 'Liminality', he writes, 'implies that the high could not be high unless the low existed, and he who is high must experience what it is like to be low.'[3] Turner characterises one type of liminality as 'frequently found in cyclical and calendrical ritual, usually of a collective kind, in which, at certain culturally defined points in the seasonal cycle, groups or categories of persons who habitually occupy low status positions in the social structure are positively enjoined to exercise ritual authority over their superiors'.[4] These calendrical rituals 'are performed at well-delineated points in the annual productive cycle, and attest to the passage from scarcity to plenty (as at first fruits or harvest festivals) or from plenty to scarcity (as when the hardships of winter are anticipated and magically guarded against.)'[5] Turner argues that these rituals can reorder the prevailing social structure as a 'communitas', which he defines as 'society as an undifferentiated, homogeneous whole, in which individuals confront one another integrally, and not as "segmentalised" into status and roles.'[6]

The English ritual calendar during the eighteenth and nineteenth centuries gives evidence of ritual demonstrations of strength at certain times of the year when deprivation threatened, was at its worst, or was soon to disappear. The labouring poor sought to demonstrate their strength or assert their importance or reconstruct the social hierarchy as a 'communitas'. Such calendrical rites of passage were observed during the months before Christmas, at Epiphany and around May Day.

William Howitt, writing in the 1840s about the steady decline of folk custom, described Plough Monday ceremonies and their disruptive elements: 'The insolence of these Plough-bullocks as they are called, which might accord with ancient licence, but does not at all suit modern habits, has contributed more than anything else to put them down.'[7] The plough-bullocks to which he referred were teams of labourers who went in procession from house to house on Plough Monday, the first Monday after Epiphany, in some areas of the Midlands. Llewellyn Jewitt recorded these gatherings much later in the century in Derbyshire when they were no longer common:

> On Plough Monday, the 'Plough-bullocks' are still occasionally seen; they consist of a number of young men from various farmhouses, who are dressed up in ribbands, their shirts (for they wear no coats or undercoats) literally covered with rosettes of various colours, and their hats bound round with ribbands, and decorated with every kind of ornament that comes in their way; these young men yoke themselves to a plough, which they draw about, preceded by a band of music, from house to house collecting money; they are accompanied by the fool and Bessy; the fool being dressed in the skin of a calf, with the tail hanging down behind, and Bessy, generally a young man in female attire, covered with a profusion of ribbands and other meretricious finery. The fool carries an inflated bladder tied to the end of a long stick, by way of a whip, and which he does not fail to apply pretty soundly to the heads and shoulders of his team; to these personages are usually two or three more drivers, armed with similar bladders, and a ploughman and attendants. When anything is given, a cry of largess is raised, and a dance performed around the plough; but if a refusal to their application for money is made, they not infrequently plough up the pathway, door stone, or any other portion of the premises that happen to be near.[8]

The sanction of ploughing up the property of ungenerous neighbours was present in the ceremony a century earlier, as the following account confirms: 'On this day [Plough Monday] the young men yoke themselves and draw a plough about with musick, and one or two persons in antic dresses like Jack-Puddings, go from house to house to gather money to drink. If you refuse them, they plough up your dunghill.'[9] The original purpose of these visits was to solicit money for the upkeep of the 'plough light' in the parish church, but after the Reformation the money collected by the men was spent on drink and festivity. The more respectable inhabitants were increasingly reluctant to permit such behaviour. Howitt noted:

> In some places I have known them enter houses, whence they could only be ejected by the main power of the collected neighbours; for they extended their excursions often to a distance of ten miles or more, and where they were the most unknown, there practised the most insolence. Nobody regrets the discontinuance of this usage.[10]

It is interesting to note the concentration upon largess and the threat of abuse of property or person for those who did not comply with their requests, and Howitt makes it clear that their behaviour was far from deferential: 'They visited every house of any account and solicited a contribution in no very humble terms.'[11] Another account of Plough Monday stresses that faction fights between rival groups were common.[12]

In the counties of southern England, Plough Monday was apparently not observed with the same degree of aggression. Yet other ceremonies can be found which embody the central elements of the soliciting of charitable doles, and the sanction of damage to property for non-compliance. The custom of lent-crocking was common in the eighteenth and nineteenth centuries, particularly in Dorset, Wiltshire, Somerset and Devon. On Shrove Tuesday, parties of youths went from house to house soliciting pancakes or other food, drink or money contributions. At any house where such bounty was not forthcoming, they exacted a violent penalty. Retiring to some distance, the boys subjected the front door of the house to a shower of broken crockery, to the annoyance of the inhabitants. It would seem that the original customary format depended to some extent on the skill of the boys who, if they were able, tried to reach the kitchen undetected and place a piece of china on the table, thereby entitling themselves to demand a reward. If they were detected the pancakes were not given. Access was given by leaving the front door upon the latch. By the early-nineteenth century the intricacy of the custom had disappeared, perhaps because of the declining support of householders. The sanction of showering the door with sherds became the custom's dominant feature. In one account of the custom as it prevailed in some parts of Devon, other motives are made apparent. Lent-crocking, it was observed:

> appears to be now persisted in from no other motive than that of insulting and annoying many of the most peaceable and deserving inhabitants of the neighbourhood. In fact, it at present takes no other character than that of a sorry despicable method which the most worthless and disorderly of the rabble use to express their dislike and hatred of those who least resemble themselves; and consists of throwing a quantity of potsherds and filth into the principal Passage of the House; or if the door be secured, in dashing materials of this description against it with such vehemence as not infrequently to break it or otherwise injure it so as to render a new one necessary.[13]

This is how the custom was observed in some Devon towns in 1805 by Robert Studley Vidal, where the idea of soliciting pancakes was done away with, the crowd merely being content to damage the doors of respectable inhabitants. In the neighbouring villages the custom retained its original purpose, although the sanction of crocking was still an integral part of the observance. Vidal continued: 'The heaving . . . at the door of the House from where nothing could be obtained, was probably designed to show that the owner was a person so inhospitable, so destitute of common charity, as to refuse even a Pancake to the Poor on Shrove Tuesday.' He also commented that the ungenerous inhabitant had to endure for the rest of the year 'the notion of scandal and disgrace which the Common people annex to anyone's having Potsherds thrown at his Door at this particular Season.'[14]

In Dorset, where lent-crocking prevailed until the end of the nineteenth century, it was reported that the throwing of potsherds at people's doors was acceptable but that youths were not allowed to throw stones. Various rhymes have been noted which were chanted by the assembly, the following verse coming from Milton Abbey during the latter half of the century.

> Please I've come a-shroving
> For a piece of pancake
> Or a little ruckle cheese
> Of your own making
> If you don't give me some,
> If you don't give me none,
> I'll knock down your door
> With a great marrow bone
> And away I'll run.

This was no idle threat, as the account continued that 'in this way real damage was done'.[15] However, the custom was gradually .brought under control by the increased exercise of the law. A report in the *Bridport News* in the 1880s described a visit made by a party of lent-crockers to the house of a widow. Receiving no pancakes, they pelted the door with sherds and damaged it in the process. The case was brought to court and: 'The bench thought that sufficient evidence had been given to prove guilt, and fined the defendants six shillings and costs, as well as ordering them to pay eight shillings damages. After some protest the money was paid.'[16]

By the late-nineteenth century in Somerset the sherding was more often merely a threat: 'A stone or a shard is kept ready to carry out the threat, but is rarely used, for usually a pancake is given to the singers. Sometimes, in the case of a known niggard, the dole is not waited for, the stone is thrown, and a scatter of scampering feet denotes the hurried decamping of the serenaders.'[17] The law was also used at Crewkerne in 1858 to prosecute lent-crockers who had 'done malicious injury to the door of the National School-rooms by throwing dirt against it on the evening of Shrove Tuesday.'[18]

The custom of 'lifting' or 'hocking' on the Monday and Tuesday following Easter, or, in some places, the second Sunday after Easter, also contained the motif of payment to avoid rough treatment if no largess was given. A clergyman related his experience of a Lancashire 'lifting' Tuesday in the mid-nineteenth century. He was 'astonished by three or four lusty women rushing into his room, exclaiming that they had come to lift him . . . "Lift me because it is Easter Tuesday?

I don't understand. Is there any such custom here?" "Yes, to be sure, why don't you know? All us women were lifted yesterday; and us lifts the men today in turn." '[19] The clergyman avoided the customary action by paying a small money contribution to the women. In the case of 'lifting', not only were barriers of status surmounted but gender-role reversal occurred. In this example, respect for prevailing sexual propriety and the clergyman's social position was overridden by the needs of customary folk action. In the early part of the nineteenth century, the custom prevailed at Ludlow in Shropshire. On the Monday following Easter, parties of men went from house to house with a chair decorated with greenery and flowers. Women were hoisted in the chair and their feet were sprinkled with water from a bunch of flowers dipped in a basin. Money was given by the victims when the men were lifted on Tuesday. If no money was forthcoming, a forfeit was seized. 'Your cap or your money' was the threat.[20] Elsewhere in Shropshire, in the 1830s, it was the practice for servants to lift their masters. One participant recalled that the old squire had said, when confronting the prospect of 'heaving', ' "John, don't let the wenches come to me today, I canna bear it; give 'em this instead:" for of course we looked for a present.'[21] The feature of gender-role reversal was strong, as the following account illustrates:

> I recollect a few years ago accompanying my excellent friend Joseph Palmer Esq. to Acton Reynald Hall on the privileged day and being there very much amused. My friend had a particular aversion to the custom of lifting; he had escaped from a posse of his own tenants' wives and daughters in Coleham, Shrewsbury, and fought through a host of resolute females assembled in the Castle Foregate; but at Acton Reynald he could neither fight not run away.

Mr Palmer was eventually lifted on Easter Tuesday 1838 only after his host 'the distinguished owner of the mansion' had previously been lifted.[22] The custom was particularly strong in the coal-mining areas of Shropshire, and was eventually extinguished only by the end of the nineteenth century.

It would be easy to underestimate the impact of this ceremony on a strictly hierarchical community, and one in which the behaviour and image of women was delineated by reference to a male-dominated society. Most of the descriptions which are recorded give the impression of a rather picturesque custom. Yet the undertones of sexual threat are evident and strong in the ceremony as it occurred on Easter Tuesday. A later folklorist remarked that lifting 'could only be popular in ruder times when manners were coarser, and the standard of national education ignored the refinements of social intercourse'.[23] A description of Easter heaving in Wolverhampton in 1838 brings out the sense of sexual aggression which was inherent in the custom. 'Not bearing in mind the season of the year, he ventured on a short cut into Darlington Street through Townell-Fold. Until halfway through there was no sign of danger, but when fairly in the net, out bounced a bevy of beautiful nymphs who barred further passage, and one of the most stalwart seized and fairly heaved him off the ground, claiming and receiving the silver guerdon demanded as the forfeit.'[24] The notion of the possession of certain areas of the town is implicit in the above account. One writer further recorded that 'it was a problem every Easter Tuesday morning for masters, managers and clerks to get to their respective offices without having to submit to the unwelcome kisses of these amorous Amazons. No respect was ever paid to personal dignity or social position.'[25]

This form of behaviour was particularly threatening to middle class genteel male society. One critic wrote of the custom in 1784 that it was 'a rude, indecent and dangerous diversion, practised chiefly by the lower class people. Our magistrates constantly prohibit it by the bellman, but it subsists at the end of town; and the women have of late years converted it into a money job.'[26] The rough treatment of gentility and other sexually aggressive behaviour by women, at other ritual occasions such as fairs was commented upon by eighteenth-century writers. Daniel Defore wrote of the Horn Fair at Charlton:

> The mob indeed at that time take all kinds of liberties, and the women are especially impudent for that day; as if it was a day that justified the giving themselves a lease to all manner of indecency and immodesty, without any

reproach, or without suffering the censure which such behaviour would deserve at another time . . . I rather recommend it to public justice to be suppressed as a nuisance and offence to all sober people, than to spend any time to enquire into its origin.[27]

He was equally critical of moral behaviour at Bloxham mop in Oxfordshire. 'This I christened by the name of a Jade-Fair, at which some of the poor girls began to be angry, but we appeased them with better words.'[28] Later in the eighteenth century, an observer recorded the following description of Greenwich Easter Monday Fair:

it is conjectured that there were not less than 15,000. We do not hear that any mischief has been done in the Park, or elsewhere, or that there were any excesses of any kind committed; but they were extremely facetious on their return journey . . . Meeting a single gentleman on horse-back, (who seemed to me to be a clergyman) holding hands with each other, they formed a line, the extremities of which reached the opposite ditches. When they had thus effectively retarded his progress, they insisted upon his getting down and saluting one of their nymphs, that they averred, by repeated assurances, had the most beauty and the softest lips of any girl in the Park. The young gentleman, sensible of his embarrassment, and probably fearing the consequences of non-compliance, shewed his sense in dismounting without hesitation, which, as soon as they perceived his alacrity in doing, he was dismissed with a general plaudit.

But it faired far otherwise with a fat surly curmudgeon just behind him in a one horse chair, of whom the same tribute was in like manner exacted. Whether it was the consciousness of his own weight, and the mighty inconvenience of ingress and egress, from and into the narrow compass he was confined, or for fear of his wife's resentment, should the story come to her ears, or for both, or neither of these reasons, instead of complying, he began to expostulate with them. After a prelude of smart altercation, and abusing him for a woman-hater, they handled him so roughly, that he would have been glad to have kissed a more ignoble part of the lady than her face, to have avoided such familiarities.[29]

As this record is of Easter Monday, it is not unlikely that the correspondent was observing a form of Easter lifting custom. In any event, the elements of status reversal and sexual threat are again evident; particularly as the first victim was a clergyman.

Other fairs, such as Pack Monday Fair at Sherborne in Dorset, were heralded by the aggressive activities of local youths.

> To the present time [September 1826] Pack Monday Fair, is annually announced three or four weeks previous by all the little urchins who can procure and blow a cow's horn, parading the streets in the evenings and sending forth different tones of their horny bugles, sometimes beating an old saucepan for a drum . . . and not infrequently a whistle-pipe or a fife is added to the band. The clock's striking twelve on the Sunday night previous, is the summons for ushering in the fair, when the boys assemble with their horns, and parade the town with a noisy shout and prepare to forage for fuel to light a bonfire, generally of straw, obtained from some of the neighbouring farmyards, which are sure to be plundered, without respect to the owners . . . In this way the youths enjoy themselves in boisterous triumph, to the annoyance of the sleeping part of the inhabitants, many of whom deplore, whilst others, who entertain respect for old customs, delight in the deafening mirth.[30]

Pack Monday Fair was formerly held in the churchyard itself but was removed from that venue sometime around the beginning of the nineteenth century. The clamour made to herald the fair is also recorded as an immemorial custom during the eighteenth century.[31] This rough music continued as a central feature of the fair until 1964.[32] At Horn Fair, disguise was employed by fair-goers. In 1703 William Fuller attended, 'dressed in my land-lady's best gown and other women's attire, and to Horn Fair we went, and as we were coming back by water, all the clothes were spoiled by dirty water that was flung on us in an inundation'.[33] This remained the practice into the nineteenth century.[34]

Other calendar festivities witnessed the overruling of normal respect for property or person. On Furry day at Helston in Cornwall in 1826, a procession of dancers was formed to dance through the borough. Furry day was and is 8 May and anyone found working was 'instantly seized and set astride a pole, and jolted away on men's shoulders, amidst thousands of huzzas'.[35] To avoid the penalty of jumping across a nearby river, the exaction of a small fine was made. When the procession reached Helston 'they go through every house and garden they please without distinction; all doors are opened, and, in fact, it is thought much of by the house-holders to be thus favoured.'[36]

Rituals of status reversal and the ceremonial abuse of property and person invested the date and the event with great social significance for the labouring poor. The fair was a centre of social activity in which, at least for a time, the normal structure of society could be set aside or even over-turned. Rituals of initiation to fairs were also common whereby newcomers were brought into temporary 'com-munitas'. These occurred at Weyhill where the custom of 'horning the colt' was recorded and also at Stourbridge near Cambridge (known colloquially as Stirbitch fair) where strangers were christened.[37] Fairs, during the Middle Ages, had been established upon legal foundations such as royal charters, and had often been regulated by borough courts similar to manorial courts, such as courts of Pie Powder, or were governed by Quarter Sessions. It is not surprising, therefore, that the poor annexed these defences of fair rights by elaborating rituals for the recognition and initiation of strangers.

At Weyhill, the ceremony of horning colts or newcomers was also referred to in terms of the initiate being 'made free'. The ceremony at Stourbridge was perhaps consciously modelled on early apprenticeship initiations which were common among groups like printers and coopers. There the stranger was known as an infidel and was presented to the 'court' for 'instruction'.[38] The fair, then could be a place and an event where a temporary reordering of the normal hierarchy, in ritual terms, took place. Strangers had to be initiated into its ways and, in some cases, the fair needed to be defended against outsiders who sought to disrupt the temporary communitas or to intimidate its members. At Leatherhead in 1803 such a defence occurred. The fair at Leatherhead took place on 11 October and, according to one account, 'was attended by almost all the respectability of the neighbourhood'. However, the fair was disturbed by the arrival of a party of the 10th Light Dragoons who

> began to display their address in performing the sword exercise, which created some confusion, and drew on them the displeasure of the crowd, who attacked them; and, driving them into a field, assailed them with stones. The soldiers charged the people with drawn swords, but the crowd stood firm, and proved victorious. One soldier was severely wounded in the face and eyes. A poor woman received a cut across her arm and breast, but supposed not dangerously; and a man had his hand or fingers nearly cut off. Two officers arriving interfered, and put an end to the affray . . . and ordered full amends to be made to the wounded parties; and the soldiers soon after left the place for Guildford.[39]

The behaviour of the soldiers was seen as a direct provocation by the fair goers, who perhaps took their presence as a threat, and their sword play as intimidatory. The fair was defended by the crowd against the dragoons who had invaded the temporary 'communitas'. Interestingly, there is no mention of legal redress being sought against the crowd although the account makes it clear that the affray was begun by them. The arrival of the officers occurred only after the crowd had, in the words of the report, been 'victorious'.

Anti-social behaviour was the central feature of 'Lawless Day' at Exeter on Oak Apple Day. This custom was reported in 1831 as consisting of 'squads of the mischief-loving parts of the mobility with large bludgeons' taking over different areas of the town for the purpose of damming up the kennels to form pools of water. These were known as 'bays' and passers-by, in order to avoid being drenched from them, were obliged to pay a contribution to the attendants of the bays:

At a short distance from the 'Bay', its boundaries are marked out, and at each bay one of the party belonging to it is stationed to solicit donations from passengers. If a gift be refused he makes a signal by whistling to his companions, and they directly commence splashing and bedabbling most lustily and render it impossible for any one to pass by without a thorough drenching; but if a trifle, however small, is bestowed, the donor is allowed safe conduct, and three cheers for liberality.

This kind of ritual 'pass of arms' often led to more explicit violence: 'The effects of the liquor is soon perceived in the conduct of the various parties. The more they drink the more outrageous they become, and it mostly happens that the interference of the beadles and constables is absolutely necessary to put an end to the violence, by locking up some of the ringleaders, who are thus taught that, if there is no law upon "lawless day" there is law the next day.'[40]

Interestingly, an older account makes it apparent that the actions of Lawless Day had previously taken place during Rogation week. A report of 1750 states:

At Exeter, in Devon, the boys have an annual custom of damming-up the channel in the streets, and going the bounds of the several parishes of the City, and of splashing water upon people passing by . . . Neighbours as well as strangers are forced to compound hostilities, by giving the boys of each parish money to pass without ducking: each parish asserting its prerogative, in this respect.[41]

At Leicester, until the middle of the nineteenth century, a similar form of customary behaviour took place during the Shrove Tuesday Fair when the precincts of Leicester Castle, known as the Newark, were possessed by parties of 'Whipping Toms'. It is probable that these were originally city officials whose purpose, after the bellman had rung the end of the Shrovetide Fair, was to drive away late revellers from the fairground. At some point this activity was converted into a form of sport. At one o'clock, the Whipping Toms appeared in the Newark. As one commentator who observed the custom in his youth, wrote: 'After that hour any persons passing through the Newark was liable to be whipped, unless they paid a fee to any or all of the Whipping Toms by whom they might be met or pursued, who, however, were not by custom allowed to whip above the knee, and any one kneeling down was safe from attack so long as he retained that posture.'[42] The Whipping Toms were permitted to whip passers-by only when the bellman was ringing the bell. Another report early in the nineteenth century stated that 'The amusement consists in surrounding the bell-man, and silencing his bell; for during the cessation of ringing the whipper is powerless'.[43]

The activities of the Whipping Toms on Shrove Tuesday, and of those who made dams at Exeter on Lawless Day (Oak Apple Day), are similar in the way each group took possession of areas in the town and set up ritualised 'pass of arms' where forfeits were levied on, or punishments meted out to, passers-by. Status reversals and assaults on private persons were also common to both forms, as was the inherent boisterousness and general rough treatment of Shrove Tuesday and Oak Apple Day. As has clearly been seen, these were important festival dates in the English customary calendar, occurring at strategic points in the cycle of production. Also, links with old practice can be seen, at least in the case of the Whipping Toms, where a more utilitarian function probably underlay the ceremony. The elements of conflict between groups within the social hierarchy are strong and emphasise the ritual demonstration of strength by the labouring poor at these times of the year.

In rural areas similar patterns can be observed. The months of November and December were very hard for the labouring poor. Harvest earnings were exhausted and work was scarce at what was traditionally a slack period in the farming cycle. The clustering of several 'doleing' customs in the weeks preceding Christmas was a reflection of this pressure. One custom which took place on St Andrew's day (30 November) embodied a strong protest element and again took the form of a collective demonstration of strength. The diversion of 'squirrel hunting' was common in several places in southern England on this day. At Eastling in Kent:

the labourers and the lower kind of people, assembling

together, form a lawless rabble, and being accoutred with guns, poles, clubs, and other such weapons, spend the greatest part of the day in parading through the woods and grounds with loud shoutings; and, under the pretence of demolishing the squirrels, some few of which they kill, they destroy numbers of hares, pheasants, partridges, and in short whatever comes their way, breaking down hedges, and doing much mischief, and in the evening betaking themselves to the ale-houses, finish their career there as is usual with such sort of gentry.[44]

The custom of 'St Andr'ng' was also kept up, in similar fashion, in parts of Sussex until the early-nineteenth century, when stricter protection of game and further enclosure of coppices led to its discontinuance.[45] There, as in Kent, the primary aim was to do damage to the fences and hedges and to take game. The assembled crowd directed their actions against the preserves of propertied men, mapped out in the Acts of Enclosure and protected by the increasingly severe game laws. Research has not yet uncovered earlier references to the custom in the particular form recorded for the period under analysis, although squirrel hunting was widespread as an amusement throughout much of southern England, especially in the New Forest.[46] Ceremony and social conflict were intermixed in the .practice of 'St Andr'ng' in a way which throws different light on the view that there was little popular protest against enclosure.

At Duffield in Derbyshire, the squirrel hunt took place on Wakes Monday, and the right of gathering wood was preserved by collective action which was more implicit. A more overt defence of wood rights was made at Great Wishford, as will be seen in the next chapter. Llewellyn Jewitt recounted that:

The young men of the village assemble together on the Wakes Monday, each provided with a horn, a pan, or something capable of making a noise, and proceed to Kedleston Park, where with shouting and the discordant noise of the instruments, they frighten the poor little squirrels until they drop from the trees. Several having been thus captured, the hunters return to Duffield, and having released the squirrels amongst some trees re-commence the hunt. At the same place, the right of collecting wood in the forest is singularly observed, – for the young men in considerable number collect together, and having taken possession of any cart they can find, yoke themselves to it, and preceded by horns, remove any trees or other wood from the various lanes and hedge-rows; this is done almost nightly between September and the Wakes, in the first week in November, when a huge bonfire is made of the wood collected, on the Wakes Monday.[47]

The central elements of the invasion of private property, and the disorderly behaviour of the crowd, were present at Duffield. As these elements were implicit, it is perhaps the reason for the survival of the custom until a late date in Derbyshire. The activites of the crowd were less destructive and less obviously directed against rural privilege.

The folk, therefore, were not only tenacious in promoting customs and ceremonies where the elements of conflict and rough treatment were central, but found in some of them a vehicle for protest against the destruction of customary society and, indeed, a legitimating agent in their defence of some collective rights which were in danger of being revoked. Custom permitted excesses and affronts at times when economic pressure was great. A pattern of folk activity emerges which, for the eighteenth century and part of the nineteenth century, was robust, aggressive, demanding and far from deferential. Customary society with its emphasis upon reciprocal dues and responsibilities was being challenged by the emergence of social thinking more attuned to the needs and requirements of the market economy.

The feasts of All Souls, St Clement, St Catherine, St Andrew and St Thomas were very important for the labouring poor. These occurred on 2 November, 23 November, 25 November, 30 November and 21 December respectively. After the Reformation and their decreased significance in the ecclesiastical calendar, these Saints days continued to provide opportunities for the poor to perambulate the parish, soliciting doles of food, drink and money. At All Souls or on All Souls' Eve, small cakes were given in response to the chanting of a rhyme. This varied from place to place, but

one version which was recorded towards the end of the nineteenth century ran as follows:

> Soul day, Soul day,
> We be come a-souling.
> Pray good people remember the poor,
> And give us a soul cake.
> One for Peter, two for Paul,
> Three for him who made us all.
> An apple, a pear, a plum or a cherry,
> Or any good thing to make us merry.
>
> Soul day, Soul day,
> We have been praying for the soul departed.
> So pray good people give us a cake,
> For we are all poor people,
> Well known to you before.
> So give us a cake for charity's sake,
> And our blessing we'll leave at your door.
>
> Soul! Soul! For an apple or two,
> If you have no apples, pears will do
> If pears are scarce, then cakes from your pan,
> Give us our souling and we'll be gone.[48]

Going a-souling was an important part of the economy of
the labouring poor. The rhyme indicates that the poor concerned were 'well known to you before', that is, formed part
of the local community and were not beggars.

In parts of Cheshire, the soulers consisted of men who
performed a mummer's play with a hobby horse which was
permitted great license to deal with recalcitrant householders.
This play is still performed at Antrobus where, it has been
recently argued, it continues to reinforce the sense of solidarity within the community and has little to do with the
folklorist's obsession with life-cycle fertility rites.[49]

The table (overleaf) based upon Charlotte Burne's distribution map, indicates the incidence of the three rituals of
souling, clementing and cattern in the West Midlands, as
summarised in 1914, and represents information gathered
throughout the last decades of the nineteenth century.

Table of Distribution

	Cheshire	Shropshire	Stafford-shire	Worcester-shire
Souling	14	15	15	0
Clementing	14	16	22	0
Catterning	0	0	2	9

Source: Charlotte S. Burne, 'Souling, Clementing and Catterning: Three November customs of the Western Midlands', *Folklore*, vol. 25, 1914, pp. 285-99.

Clementing and catterning partially overlap and it is evident that catterning existed in the southern part of the district where souling and clementing did not take place. Equally clear is the indication that catterning did not exist in the northern part of the region where souling and clementing held sway. Yet the rituals were very similar in form. In Shropshire in 1881 the following rhyme was recorded in which the adjacent feasts of St Clement and St Catherine were cojoined. Also the verse includes a specific reference to Rogation week parish perambulations and illustrates how the annual reaffirmation of the boundary provided a mental map for the inhabitants which was employed during more informal visitations such as catterning and clementing.

> Cattern and Clemen's come year by year,
> Some of your apples and some of your beer,
> Trowl' Trowl'
> Gentleman butler fill your bowl:
> If you fill it of the best,
> You shall have a good night's rest;
> If you fill it of the small,
> You shall have no rest at all.
> Apple, pear, plum and cherry,
> Anything to make us merry,
> One for Peter, Two for Paul,
> Three for the merry men under the wall,
> Master and Misses sit by the fire,
> While we poor children trudge through the mire.
> We go from Bickbury and Badger to Stoke on the Clee,
> To Monkhopton, Round Acton, and so return we.[50]

As with souling, the visitants solicited doles of food and drink in return for bringing good luck.

The custom existed elsewhere in England and a Sussex version of the mid-nineteenth century ran:

> Cattern' and Clemen' be here, here, here
> Give us your apples and give us your beer,
> One for Peter, Two for Paul,
> Three for Him who made us all;
> Clemen' was a good man,
> Cattern' was his mother;
> Give us your best,
> And not your worst,
> And God will give your soul good rest.[51]

It is significant that most of these dole chants included reference to fruit, particularly apples and pears, as the occurrence of the rituals coincided with the completion of the apple harvest and the making of cider.

In some places these rural rituals were matched by more industrial versions. St Catherine was the patron Saint of rope-makers, and in Kent, at Chatham, Rochester and Brompton, her embodiment was placed in a chair and paraded round the town wearing a gilt crown.[52] The Saint was also chosen as their patron by Buckinghamshire lace-makers who held an annual feast on 25 November at which 'wigs' or small cakes were consumed.[53] St Clement was the patron saint of blacksmiths and of anchor-makers. The custom of 'firing the anvil' which was common on St Clement's day, when a small quantity of gunpowder was ignited on the anvil, was suppressed in Brighton in the 1840s.[54] The suppression was probably occasioned not so much by the disruption of the ritual, but because of the leaving-off of work to celebrate the festival. A supper was held in the evening similar to the feast provided for printers. Because of the association of anchors with St Clement (he was supposed to have been martyred by being drowned in the sea with an anchor round his neck) the festival was generally celebrated in Naval dockyards. The following account is of Woolwich in the 1820s:

185

One of the senior apprentices being chosen to serve as 'Old Clem' . . . is attired in a great coat, having his head covered with an Oakham wig, face masked, and a long white beard flowing therefrom; thus attired he seats himself in a large wooden chair . . . with a crown and anchor, made of wood, on the top. . . . He has before him a wooden anvil, and in his hands a pair of tongs and wooden hammer which, in general, he makes good use of whilst reciting his speech . . . This procession, headed by a drum and fife, and six men with old Clem mounted on their shoulders, proceed round the town, stopping and refreshing at nearly every public house (which, by and by, are pretty numerous) not forgetting to call on the blacksmiths and officers of the dockyard: there the money-box is pretty freely handed . . . [55]

A statement of 'Old Clem's' credentials was made to prove his authenticity and the greatness of his deeds. This statement was very similar to some of the declarations contained in mummer's plays in which lists of great travels were made.

I am the real St. Clement, the first founder of brass, iron, and steel from the ore. I have been to Mount Etna, where the god Vulcan first built his forge, and forged the armour and thunderbolts for the god Jupiter. I have been through the deserts of Arabia; through Asia, Africa and America; through the City of Pongrove; through the land of Tipmingo; and all the Northern parts of Scotland. I arrived in London on the twenty-third of November, and came down to his majesty's dockyard at Woolwich, to see how all the gentlemen Vulcans came on there. I found them all hard at work, and wish to leave them well on the twenty-fourth.

The money collected was then spent on a supper in the evening.[56]

The crucial element in both rural and industrial charity customs was the collection of dole either in kind or in money. A Clem Feast was held at the Bugle Inn in Twyford, Hampshire, by blacksmiths for, at least, a continuous period of fifty years before 1912 when the feast, together with the legends and tales always repeated on the occasion, was recorded.[57]

St Andrew's Day, as well as having significance for squirrel hunters in Kent and Sussex, was celebrated in Northampton-shire and Bedfordshire by lace-makers. 'Tanders' cakes were eaten with tea or metheglin. At Olney, in the early-nine-teenth century, the owners of the Honey House in the High Street took out a three day licence to supply metheglin to the surrounding neighbourhood.[58]

The most widespread of all the 'doleing days' was the Feast of St Thomas on 21 December. It was known colloquially by different names in different places; going a-mumping in Herefordshire, going a-corning in Warwickshire, going a-Thomasin in Cheshire. Parties of poor people visited houses in the neighbourhood and solicited doles of food, drink or money. This sometimes took the form of small quantities of corn with which the poor used to make furmety. One account stated that St Thomasin was 'generally done by poor widows, but also often by people who would never think of begging at any other time of the year. Formerly, every farmer set aside a sack of corn for the mumpers, some of them needy widows, some of them married women with their families, wives of the holders of cottages on the farm. These all went to receive each a dole of corn.'[59] The day was also referred to as 'gooding day' because of the good things poor people hoped to solicit. In Staffordshire in the 1850s, good-ing was not confined to poor widows 'but representatives from every poor family in the parish, make their rounds in quest of alms. The Clergyman is expected to give a shilling to each person, and at all houses a subsidy is looked for either in money or kind'. The account continued: 'a sum of money is collected from the wealthier inhabitants of the parish, and placed in the hands of the clergyman and church-wardens, who on the Sunday nearest to St. Thomas's day, distribute it in the evening, under the name of "St. Thomas's Dole".'[60] In this account, institutionalised charity is also involved. Many bequests or local charities for the poor were distributed on St Thomas's Day so that the poor could benefit from the bequest prior to Christmas.

In 1825, at Loose in Kent, doleing day saw the distribution of quantities of wheat to the poor 'who, at the same time, go to the other respectable inhabitants of the place to solicit the normal donation, and it is not an uncommon thing for a family to get in this way six or seven shillings'.[61] In Cheshire, in 1849, the St Thomas's Day doleing was described as 'Universal'.[62] The custom, as it existed in Hampshire in the 1820s, was recalled in the following terms:

> I remember when a boy, some seventy years since, being with my grandfather in the house of a respectable farmer on the morning of the 21st of December, and seeing in the kitchen a large tub standing, filled with wheat, and the recipients consisting of women and children, the latter predominating, coming trooping in, each carrying a bag to receive the customary 'gooding', which was afterwards taken to the nearest mill to be exchanged for an equal value of flour.[63]

In Sussex and Hampshire, widows were entitled to a double dole.[64]

These doleing customs or folk charities which occurred in the months before Christmas can be seen on the merely functional level as providing opportunities for the labouring poor to collect not inconsiderable contributions. Yet, on another level, they had the function of reinforcing the labourer's normative view of the social structure, in which there was a reciprocal relationship between the responsibilities of the wealthy for their poorer neighbours and the dues owed by the labouring community to the governors of rural society. Doleing rituals also represented an attempt to establish a temporary form of 'communitas' within the local society. This explains why most of the salutations recorded of the seasonal visitants include statements which identify the singers as members of that particular parish rather than general and unspecified poor. The verses also served the purpose of giving notice of the labouring poor's actions. Each verse specified the particular festival date which was being celebrated. Thus, the contributor could be assured that the request for charity was legitimate and authentic. In this way, the poor went 'a-gooding', 'a-catterning', 'a-clementing', 'a-souling', 'a-corning', 'a-mumping', 'a-st'andring', but never 'a-begging'. It was the specificity of the custom which prevented the stigma of begging from being attached to the action. In many cases, the verses indicated that these particular folk charities were to be regarded as 'once-a-year' visitations, and not as irregular or more frequent cadging or begging.

Although the operation of doleing customs appears to emphasise the normal paternalism-deference continuum in which charity was used by the wealthy as an instrument of control in the community, it is important to stress the essential differences between these folk charities and the distribution of institutionalised charities and bequests. When contributing to the folk dole, the householder was not permitted to discriminate between deserving and undeserving cases. Clearly, in some areas, the dole was restricted to certain categories of poor, but beyond this, the contributor was not able to discriminate. In short, the initiative lay with the poor themselves who were not, as in the case of institutionalised charity, the passive recipients of benefit but were active and vociferous claimants of the particular folk dole. The householder could, of course, decide to make no contribution, but then ran the risk of being ritually punished as in the case of lent-crocking and Plough Monday visitations. In other cases, the claim for largess took the form of a kind of forfeit or tax on passers-by which, if they chose not to contribute, was followed by some form of sanction. This was particularly strong in certain environments such as fairs where the poor perhaps established a temporary new relationship between themselves and the wealthy.

There was also a strong element of communal hospitality in the doleing customs. Contributions were often in the form of food and drink, and when money was provided this was usually spent in conviviality. The wealthier inhabitants of the community were helping their poorer neighbours to enjoy, at least temporarily, some of the benefits of wealth. It is for this reason that it is significant that many of these customary doles were claimed in the lean winter months, leading to Christmas. Ritual demonstrations of strength, including status reversals, were a major part of this pattern. It is also for this reason that the dolers did not regard themselves as beggars. Beggars subsisted on charity for the whole year, whereas the labouring poor who went doleing on these specific occasions were merely claiming customary largess to which they were entitled and which the more affluent members of the community were duty-bound to give. Adherence to these folk charities confirmed, for the labouring poor, the notion that there was a wider consensus for their corporate view of society. Support for the poor lay at the root of folk charity. As shrovers chanted on Shrove Tuesday at Shrewton in Wiltshire in the late nineteenth century:

> Is the pan hot?
> Is the pan cold?
> Is the best barrel tap't?
> Is the bread and cheese cut?
> Please ma'am I'm come shroving here.
> Eggs and lard and butter is dear,
> That's what makes me come shroving here.[65]

Protest and the Enemies of the Community

It should not be surprising to find that a similar pattern of customary behaviour can be deduced in more orthodox movements of social protest. Historians are well aware of ritual and ceremonial forms in such movements. The study of food riots in the eighteenth century has demonstrated the widespread use of symbols of protest, ritual rough handling of the enemies of customary society and the parading of effigies.[66] The activities of Rebecca and her followers in Wales, also embodied much ritual behaviour, inspired by the Welsh folk experience.[67] Ceremonial activity, accompanying popular disturbance, had more significance for the participants than merely the preservation of their anonymity or the addition of a sense of drama to the proceedings. By examining some events which occurred during the Captain Swing disturbances in the winter of 1830–1, it is hoped to demonstrate that a pattern of folk activity, not dissimilar to much of the ceremonial experience of the rural labouring poor, asserted itself, both as a model for behaviour and as the basis for the defence of customary morality. We are, in a

sense not looking at two distinctive types of collective behaviour but at a single phenomenon. Customary behaviour and
social conflict were inter-related in the activities of Captain
Swing and his adherents not in a picturesque way but in direct
opposition to the official views of the relationship between
groups in the community.

The riots in 1830, or 'mobbings' as they were known
colloquially, were an attempt by the farm labourers to
reverse the course of agricultural change and to return to the
security of an older popular morality when farmers recognised their responsibility to provide employment for their
men. Therefore agricultural machinery, especially threshing
machines which reduced the amount of winter employment,
was a principal target for the riots. Also, poor law overseers
found themselves in some areas the object of the crowd's
attentions because of the harsh and degrading treatment of
the unemployed in receipt of parish relief.

Contemporarily with the Captain Swing disturbances
arose a mythology that rural society faced a violent up-
rising of disaffected labourers which took the form of bloody
insurrection. This view concentrated on reports of labourers
supposedly attempting to seize weapons or of threats made
by men armed with firearms. In fact, it was not the case.
'The mob have in no cases been armed except with
bludgeons, iron bars, and scythes', wrote one correspondent
to the Home Office.[68] Violence, in the sense of attacks on
individuals, was also rare. One Berkshire correspondent
informed the Home Office that he saw 'no reason for any
extraordinary alarm as to the state of this county . . . Hither-
to no violence, no outrage, but on the contrary a singular
degree of peaceable respectful demeanour, even in the
assemblages of labourers that have occurred, which have
never been numerous, but chiefly confined to their respective villages. Today when something like a general rising
seemed to be apprehended, nothing has appeared but a very
few straggling parties, asking, with moderation, for an increase of wages, and where refused, retiring without ill
treating or insulting anybody.'[69]

In the entire episode only one life was lost (other than
prisoners who were hanged)[70] and few of the affrays were
anything more than scuffles. In fact, rather than rise in

191

torrents of blood the labouring poor turned to older, customary forms of behaviour to seek redress. What did the followers of Captain Swing do?[71] Notoriously they burned ricks. Rick-burning was a customary way of making protest or settling grievances in rural England. However, this was a covert act and was probably seen as an individual kind of behaviour not supported by the labourers themselves. 'They appear totally distinct', John Pearse wrote to the Home Office, 'from the Incendiaries for whom they express great horror.'[72]

The most common form of activity involved large groups of labourers visiting farms and villages, asking for higher wages, or for food and drink, or breaking threshing machines. For example, at Henfield in Sussex in late November 1830,

> A large meeting of the farming labourers took place . . . for the purpose of obtaining an increase in wages. They were met by the gentlemen of the parish. After the terms had been stated, upon which they were in future to be employed, and which were highly satisfactory to the assembled poor, Mr Nelson Morgan addressed them, in a manly, kind, and energetic speech, as did other gentlemen in a conciliating manner, and the labourers repeatedly cheered. Refreshments were given them in a field opposite the George Inn, and they afterwards paraded the town, headed by a band of music, and dispersed without the occurrence of the least unpleasant circumstance.[73]

The style of this report is very reminiscent of accounts of village club days or other parish festivals. It is important to note the general consensus which existed for the proceedings, and, in particular, the presence of commensality in the form of the provision of refreshments. Also, a note of festivity is struck with the parade through the town accompanied by the local band. In this account, negotiations between farm labourers and their masters for higher wages were conducted within a customary framework. The new form of proto-political activity was channelled through the medium of older ceremonial forms.

Elsewhere, negotiations were conducted at the local vestry meeting. Here, local unity could be expressed and if a consensus could not be found then sentiments of peaceful harmony could be balanced by threat. At one parish in Sussex, such a meeting took place at which the farm labourers were reported to have said: 'comply . . . with our demand, and we will stand by you; refuse, and there are 100 men ready to join us at a moment's notice'.[74]

At Canterbury, a mixed body of the labouring poor paraded the city. 'About 7 o'clock this morning a large body of labourers, attended by a concourse of men, women, and children, paraded the streets . . . and proceeded to the city workhouse, where they made a demand for either work, or a sufficient maintenance for themselves and their families.' Although there are no mentions of violence of person or property in this account, it was further reported that 'The guardians of the poor were much alarmed at this demand.'[75]

In Hampshire, Sussex, Berkshire, Wiltshire and Dorset, the prevalent form of disturbance was the assembly of bodies of men who marched from village to village destroying machinery and demanding money, food or drink, sometimes as a 'reward' for their work. Collective begging was an integral part of the proceedings and this form of charity was common to many ceremonies, such as Christmas wassailing and mummers' visits. A 'treasurer' was appointed to collect the money and to act as overseer for its distribution. This was again, common practice in ceremonial visitations. Joseph Carter was treasurer for the crowd at Barton Stacey. He told Alexander Somerville some fifteen years later that: 'they said I wor honest, and they gave it to me to carry. I had £40 at one time – £40 every shilling'.[76]

Collective begging was no new development. A food riot at Norwich in 1740 followed much the same pattern:

Early on Thursday Morning, by sound of Horns, they met again; and after a short confabulation, divided into Parties, and march'd out of Town at different Gates, with a long streamer carried before them, purposing to visit the Gentlemen and Farmers in the neighbouring villages, in order to extort Money, Strong Ale, etc from them. At many places, where the Generosity of People answer'd not their Expectations, 'tis said they shew'd their Resentment by treading down the Corn in the fields.[77]

193

This pattern was common during the Captain Swing disturbances. Henry Leeke, a magistrate at West Leigh in Hampshire reported that the district had 'experienced no other absolute act of Riot excepting the destruction of seven or eight threshing machines – no fires, no molesting of other property, or person, and in a few instances only, asking for, or may I say demanding Beer and provisions'.[78] From Andover, this activity was described as 'a system of pillage' which implied a degree of organisation which probably did not exist.[79] Even the act of breaking threshing machines was regarded as a job of work which demanded monetary reward. Around Hungerford the labourers were determined, according to one account, 'to break up all the farmers' thrashing machines in the Parish and neighbourhood which they accomplished and made demand on the proprietor of every machine that they broke of twenty shillings for so doing and would not depart from the premises without food and beer being given them.'[80]

The demand for food, and particularly, drink was common. In Chichester, parties of labourers visited houses and demanded beer. At one house they were met by a woman who did not possess any threshing machines yet 'The party . . . called out for Drink. The woman said if they would injure nothing she would give them some Beer and she then went away and got some jugs full and then some Bottles and brought out to us . . . We then went to Mrs Blunden's but did no mischief – she gave us some beer and bread and cheese.'[81] These contributions of beer and food were made much in the same way as to visitations of wassailers at Christmas, or of parties of St Thomas day dolers. It is also evident that, in many cases, the labourers stayed within their own parish and visited houses and farms that were known to them.

The summoning of the crowd by the blowing of cows' horns was general practice in the 1830 disturbances. However, the 'doleing riots', as this form of action might be termed, not only utilised random elements of folk behaviour as a model. November and December were the principal months in which the upheavals occurred, and it was not surprising that Captain Swing's operations took place at this point of 'life crisis' in the year. Charity was customarily expected at times of most economic pressure by the labouring poor. The doleing customs provided a model for action and it is possible that members of the crowd felt that their behaviour was legitimated by references to customary practice and to the concept of popular moral behaviour which acted as a force for both forms of activity. They had stepped beyond the bounds of custom but had adapted its mechanism for use in more direct forms of behaviour. The riots were, with some exceptions, well-disciplined and restrained. In Dorset it was reported that: 'The mob, urged on from behind hedges, by a number of women and children, advanced rather respectfully, and with their hats in their hands, to demand increases in wages.' Some of the country gentry who had been despatched to quell the riots 'described the mob they had encountered as being in general very fine-looking young men, and particularly well dressed, as if they had put on their best clothes for the occasion'.[82] The wearing of Sunday clothes was a feature of much customary behaviour.

The demand for contributions was a general feature of the disturbances and the legal position regarding such levies was clarified in the address to the Grand Jury at Winchester Assizes when the Hampshire rioters were tried.

> The cases of robbery from the person, likely to become the subject of our present inquiry, may be found to differ in the circumstances, but not in principle, from the ordinary attacks of robbers, familiar to all who are in the habit of frequenting our Courts of Criminal Justice. They will as far as I am able to judge from the depositions, be found to have been perpetrated by tumultous mobs, armed with offensive weapons, traversing the country, and requiring money, victuals, drink, and other articles, sometimes under the pretence of alms or contributions to relieve some real or supposed grievance.[83]

At the Winchester Assizes, legal precedents were cited by way of illustration. Mr Justice Alderson related of riots in London that 'a boy knocked at the door and said "God bless your honour, give something to the mob", he told him to get away, which he did, and said he would fetch his captain. The mob afterwards met the person, and said, "This gentleman is always generous, give us something." The party said "How much?" They said half a crown and he gave it them. This cause was similar to those.'[84]

Perhaps the most interesting example of the 'doleing' behaviour during the Captain Swing disturbances occurred during the 'attack' on Eyre Coote's house at West Park. Mr Eyre Coote had received information that his residence was a likely target, and he had gathered together his keepers and house guests to defend the house. 'About eleven', he reported, 'a party came demanding if I possessed any machines. I told them I had none, and expostulated with them on the impropriety of their conduct. They were exceedingly civil and on promising to pass peaceably through the village I gave them a very little beer.' The first visitors to West Park responded to this show of hospitality and departed. However, he continued: 'About an hour afterwards a much stronger body of about one hundred persons came headed by a person on horseback whom they called Hunt, they all departed in the same peaceable manner.' This second much larger group also departed without any disturbance. Yet, at about two o'clock a further party was heard breaking windows in the village. They were also, in Eyre Coote's words, 'extorting money and victuals from the inhabitants.' This party came up to the house and Eyre Coote's party 'drew under the portico of my house, to wait their arrival'. These men were not to be dissuaded by the provision of food and drink and an affray developed.[85]

The significance of this account for the understanding of the action of the crowd is the length of time necessary for the normal forms of behaviour in the relationship between local gentry and the labouring poor to disintegrate. The first party to visit West Park received a customary form of response from Mr Eyre Coote, in the provision of drink. This would have been the pattern for any number of more ceremonial visits from wassailers to harvestmen claiming largess. The second party were equally slow to react in any different way, and it was only with the third, perhaps more determined party, that the code of behaviour broke down and violence erupted. At the Assizes in Winchester, the Grand Jury was directed to pay great attention to the affray at West Park. This was perhaps partially due to the obvious failure of customary ways of dealing with visits from the labouring poor and the direct threat to the established social order. Elsewhere, the crowd refused the offers of bread and beer. At Bircham in Norfolk 'the party that broke the machines and fired the stacks . . . were offered money and beer. Neither of which they would accept! – they said they neither wanted money or beer. They went after they had done the mischief to a neighbouring public house and ordered beer and bread and cheese and threw down bank notes, and never asked for change.'[86] It is clear that the refusal to take food and drink and the bravado with which they purchased their own was a conscious demonstration of the poor's independence from the customary relationships which operated within rural society. The bank notes were, however, doubtless obtained from local farms and houses.

In several cases, either implicitly or explicitly, the poor adopted or made reference to customary practice, particularly with regard to the treatment given to one of the major 'enemies' – the Overseer to the poor or his assistant. At Lewes, in November 1830, parties of labourers assembled and moved on to Ringmer Green where they were met by Lord Gage. He promised to reduce his rents so that his tenant farmers would be able to pay higher wages. At this the crowd gave three cheers. 'A grindstone in front of the poor house', it was reported, 'used for employing paupers at 9d per day, was next pulled down. The mob then adjourned to the public house, where they received some beer, which was paid for by subscription, and afterwards quietly dispersed.'[87] After demanding increased wages at Tunbridge Wells, the crowd 'regaled themselves with bread and cheese and ale promising the Overseer a good ducking if they could catch him, which, however, they had not the opportunity of putting into execution'.[88] Having assembled at Mayfield, to be confronted by military brought from Battle, the labourers dispersed and gathered at Rotherfield. There they proceeded to several houses in the neighbourhood, demanding food and ale and destroying machines. One account stated that 'The cry then was, "To Eridge Castle"; but many of them said, "No, tomorrow is Mayfield fair, and let us go tomorrow to the Castle".'[89] In this case, the labourers restrained their initial fervour until the more significant local event – the fair –

perhaps in order to make a more dramatic and public statement of their grievances.

Elsewhere in Sussex, forms of ritual were noticeably present. The expulsion of poor law officials and holders of tithes either occurred or was threatened in some ten Sussex communities: Battle, Brede, Brightling, Burwash, Fairlight, Heatherfield, Mayfield, Ninfield, Ticehurst and Warbleton.[90] It is perhaps not surprising that poor law officials should have found themselves targets. They stood between the labouring poor and the farmers and wealthier rural residents. They were, to some extent, professional men, whose main function was to reduce the parish poor rate and to administer the poor as efficiently as possible. The Assistant Overseer's duties were summarised in 1832 as follows:

> It is his duty to make himself intimately acquainted with the situation of every family or person who usually claims relief, with the amount of his wages, the person by whom employed, the number in each family, the ages of the children, their health and various wants; and to be prepared at all times to give every information concerning these objects to the Vestry or any of its members, without whose consent and directions (except in case of necessity) no relief can be given. By these means frauds and impositions are detected, and such is the difficulty of practising them, that they are not often attempted. Since this plan has been adopted, the amount of the poor-rates has been gradually abating.[91]

This intrusiveness made the Assistant Overseer particularly hated by the labouring poor. Where the office of Overseer was not held by a professional, it usually rotated among reluctant leading inhabitants. One commentator noted that 'In a large parish, an overseer cannot become acquainted with the real situation of all the poor persons belonging to it . . . hence the concerns of the poor are liable to be less kindly or partially investigated.'[92]

The well-documented events which took place at Brede in Sussex where Mr Thomas Abel was Assistant Overseer and Governor of the Poor House, illustrate the extent of the ritual activity of the crowd. Some one hundred and fifty persons, including many women and children, assembled before Mr Abel's house and tried to force an entry. They brought with them the handcart used by the unemployed on parish relief to haul stones when working on the road. Their intention was to secure Abel and transport him, in the cart, to the parish limits. After some initial resistance, Abel surrendered himself to the crowd, on the promise that he would not be harmed, and took his place in the cart. In fact, he was given the opportunity to choose where he wanted to be taken and, at his request, the crowd conveyed him to Vinehall, some six miles from the parish. The cart was pulled by women and children and a group of labourers marched alongside in mock imitation of a military bodyguard, carrying their staves over their shoulders like rifles. The whole occasion appeared to be accompanied with great festivity and Abel recounted in his deposition: 'that many of the persons wore ribbands in their hats'.[93]

A report of the incident illustrates the close similarity of the crowd's actions to the rituals associated with 'rough music':

> The villagers brought the cart to Abel's door, seized him and placed him in it with a rope round his neck, to which a large stone was tied. Without scarcely an exception, the whole of the inhabitants accompanied the labourers, who thus drew him out the parish attended by 'rough music'. They at first fixed on the parish of Westfield to deposit their load; but his fame having extended to that hamlet, he was rejected by the people, and the procession bent their steps to Vinehall, near Robertsbridge, where it appears, rubbish-like, he was 'shot out' of the cart into the road and there left with this blessing, – that if ever he made his appearance again at Brede he would get his head broke.[94]

Joseph Bryant, one of the leaders of the crowd, described the events, emphasising the use of the parish cart as the mode of transport:

> We sent back to the workhouse and the cart that Mr Abel had made for the men to draw on the Road was there and

then the farmers went in and persuaded Mr Abel to come out and then he came out with them and got into the Cart himself . . . and we carried him there [Vinehall] or drew him there in the cart the women and the men altogether.[95]

It is significant that women and children played an active role in the ritual drawing of the cart to Vinehall. Women and children were not normally regarded as powerful elements in the structure of the community and their central role was, therefore, a symbolic demonstration of strength and an added humiliation in what was a form of role reversal. Mr Abel was ritually demoted and the normally powerless members of the community performed the main task, thereby confirming his total degradation and emphasising their triumph. It is perhaps also significant that the events at Brede took place on 5 November 1830. This ritual degradation was so potent that it was only 'after an absence of some time he was reinstated in his situation at the workhouse'.[96]

The element of community was also central to the proceedings at Brede. In this case ritual emphasised unity between groups in the community in opposition to an outside agent. The labourers were not acting alone but were supported by many of the leading farmers, as Bryant's statement made evident:

When we came back . . . Mr Coleman was there of Chitcomb and he gave every one of us half a pint of Beer women and men and Mr Reed of Brede High gave us a Barrel because we had done such a great thing in the Parish as to carry that man away and Mr Coleman said he never was better pleased in his life than with the day's work which had been done.[97]

Abel's expulsion was central to the unity between farmers and labourers and the commensality accompanying the proceedings was indicative of their cooperation and confirmation of the customary pattern of relationships. It cannot be overlooked that such commensality was a common feature of many folk customs and ceremonies and that the concept of reward for due labour lay at the heart of much folk activity. It is also important that, rightly or wrongly, many of the labourers involved in machine-breaking often demanded their contribution in the form of money or victuals as a reward for their destructive work and, when such donations were forthcoming, they gave hearty thanks before the crowd moved on to the next farm. By referring to elements common to certain folk usages such as solidarity between groups in the community, expressed in commensality and exchange of service, the labourers, in the collective action of machine-breaking, wished to eliminate the stigma of illegality. At Brede, the crowd were supported in their actions by the farmers and the hospitality extended to them after Abel's removal must have acted as a strong legitimating influence. Bryant continued: 'We told the farmers when we come back that we would always assist them as far as laid in our power all of us'.[98] In fact their support was required some days later at the tithe audit, when some of the farmers asked the labourers to put their case so that tithes might be reduced. This they did and it seems that some agreement was reached after which the tithe-holder was given three cheers and they 'set the bells ringing as [we] were all as well pleased as could be at what we had done'.[99]

Similar ritual humiliation of poor law officials occurred in 1837 during the anti-poor-law agitations. For example, at Illogen in Cornwall the parish Overseer, whilst attempting to remove paupers to the workhouse, was seized by 'not very gentle sample of the female sex; held forcibly in his own cart, and carried off in triumph to another part of the parish'.[100] This kind of 'rough music' was employed elsewhere in Sussex in 1830. Similar occurrences took place at Warbleton where a crowd gathered, 'for the purpose of compelling the assistant overseer to leave the parish against his will'. While at Ninfield the labourers were later accused of: 'forcibly removing Samuel Skinner the assistant overseer from whence they took him to Battle in a cart drawn by women and children'.[101] Here the ritual role of usually powerless groups in the community was again stressed.

In 1893, the Reverend T. Roach took down an account as well as a song about the Swing disturbances at Owslebury in Hampshire from an informant whom he referred to only as 'M.H.' in order to protect his identity. He recalled that the labourers had marched to the house of the bailiff to the Earl of Northesk to demand some of 'my Lord's money'. This money, and other contributions was divided among the party to the amount of two shillings per head. 'M.H.' remembered that the 'next day it was put about that those who gave back their two shillings to the vicar of Owslebury would not be proceeded against, and a number of them accordingly did so.' Although 'M.H.' also gave back his share, to use his own words 'they put him away'.[102] The rumour that contributions were refundable perhaps indicated that, at least in Owslebury, they had been voluntarily given, and that there was genuine surprise at the reaction of the authorities. The customary form adopted, in levying largess, possibly legitimated the poor's activities in their view despite their departure from calendar practice. In any event, the activities were similar and provided a framework within which the labourers conducted relations with the local farmers. This relationship, then, was a customary one based on ritual forms, and was understood by both parties in the negotiations as can be illustrated from the common response of the local farmers and householders in the resort to commensality. The concept of riot in rural society could encompass most forms of collective behaviour from the local Plough Monday visits to sustained periods of agitation and disorder, involving less ceremonial activities such as collective wage bargaining. A continuum existed which linked the ritual activity of the labouring poor in the rural community and which informed much of their behaviour. Both orthodox protest and ceremonies of privation sprang from the same cultural background, and it is not surprising that the forms adopted by the poor should be similar. The followers of Captain Swing, the heroes of local mummers plays, and the participants in parish calendar rituals were the same people. In many cases, their motives and their actions were also the same.

Notes

1   Anonymous, *Machine-breaking and the changes occasioned by it in the village of Turvey Down: a tale of the times* (about 1830); reprinted in *The Rising of the Agricultural Labourers: Nine Pamphlets and Six Broadsides, 1830-31* (British Labour Struggles series, New York: Arno Press, 1972), p. 20.

2   For a full account of 'rough music' see: Edward P. Thompson ' "Rough music" – le charivari Anglais', *Annales*, 27 (1972), pp. 285–312.

3   Victor W. Turner, *The Ritual Process: Structure and Anti-Structure* (London, 1969), p. 97.

4   Ibid., p. 167.

5   Ibid., p. 169.

6   Ibid., p. 177.

7   William Howitt, *The Rural life of England* (London, 1841), p. 397.

8   Frederick W. Llewellyn Jewitt, 'On ancient customs and sports of the country of Derby', *Journal of the British Archaeological Society*, VII (1851), pp. 201–2.

9   *The Gentleman's Magazine*, December 1762. Cited in William Carew Hazlitt, *Faiths and Folklore of the British Isles* (2 vols, London, 1905; reprinted New York, 1965), p. 496.

10   Howitt, *Rural life*, p. 397.

11   Ibid.

12   *County Folklore*, vol. V, ed. Mrs E. Gutch and Mabel Peacock London, 1905; reprinted New York, 1965), p. 496.

13   BL. Add.Mss 41313. f. 80. A letter from Robert Studley Vidal to John Brand, dated 10 July 1805.

14   BL. Add.Mss 41313, f. 81.

15   Udal, *Dorsetshire Folklore* (Hertford, 1922), pp. 24–5.

16   Ibid., p. 26.

17   W.G. Willis Watson (ed.), *Calendar of Customs* (1920), p. 53.

18   Ibid., pp. 64–5.

19   R. Chambers (ed.), *The Book of Days: A Miscellany of Popular Antiquities* (London, 1888), vol. I, p. 425.

20   Charlotte S. Burne, *Shropshire Folklore* (London, 1883; reprinted 1973), pp. 336–7.

21   Ibid., p. 339.

22   Ibid.

23   Frederick W. Hackwood, *Staffordshire Customs* (Lichfield, 1924; reprinted 1974), p. 13.

24   Ibid.

25   Ibid.

26   *The Gentleman's Magazine*, February 1784, vol. 54, p. 9.

27   Daniel Defoe, *A Tour Through England and Wales* (London, 1927), vol. I, p. 97.

28   Ibid., vol. II, p. 31.

29   *Lloyd's Evening Post*, 24 March 1761. A clipping attached opposite p. 150 of Haslewood's edition of John Brand's *Observations on Popular Antiquities* in British Library.

30   Hone, *Everyday Book* (London, 1864), vol. II, p. 654.

31   Ibid.

32   Hole, *A Dictionary*, pp. 291–2: 'The parade was held as usual in 1963, but because of hooliganism and malicious damage on that occasion, it was banned by the police in 1964, and this ban has

since been annually repeated.'

33 John Brand, *Observations on Popular Antiquities*, ed. Sir Henry Ellis (London, 1813), vol. II, p. 112.
34 Hone, *Everyday Book*, vol. I, p. 697.
35 Ibid., vol. II, p. 325.
36 Ibid.
37 For Weyhill see Reverend R. Clutterbuck, 'Notes on the Fair at Weyhill', *Hampshire field club and Archaeological Society Papers*, vol. III, 1907–9, pp. 127–42. For Stourbridge see William Hone, *Year Book* (London 1864), pp. 772–3.
38 Ibid., p. 772.
39 *The Gentleman's Magazine*, vol. 73 (1), 1803, p. 971.
40 Hone, *Year Book*, p. 319.
41 Brand, *Observations on Popular Antiquities*, vol. I, p. 176.
42 *Notices Illustrative of Drama and other Popular Amusements* . . . *Extracted from the Chamberlain's Accounts and other MS of the Borough of Leicester*. William Kelly (London, 1865), p. 174. Quoted in *County Folklore*, vol. I, p. 113.
43 Hone, *Year Book*, p. 270.
44 Brand, *Observations on Popular Antiquities*, vol. I, p. 323.
45 Frederick E. Sawyer, 'Sussex folk-lore and customs connected with the seasons', *Sussex Archaeological Collections*, XXXIII (1883), p. 253.
46 See D.H. Moutray Read, 'Hampshire folklore', *Folklore*, XXII (1911), pp. 323–4; John R. Wise, *The New Forest: its history and scenery* (London, 1863), p. 182.
47 Jewitt, 'On ancient customs', pp. 208–9.
48 G.F. Northall, *English Folk Rhymes* (London, 1892), pp. 225–6, which quotes R.H. Poole, *The Customs, Superstitions and legends of the County of Stafford* (n.d. – c. 1875), which in turn quotes from the *British Mercury*.
49 See Susan Pattison, 'The Antrobus Soulcaking Play: An Alternative Approach to the Mummer's Play', *Folklife*, vol. 15, 1977, pp. 5–11.
50 Northall, *English Folk Rhymes*, p. 226.
51 F.E. Sawyer, 'Sussex Folklore and customs connected with the seasons', *Sussex Archaeological Collections*, vol. 33, p. 252.
52 Northall, *English Folk Rhymes*, p. 228, which quotes *Notes and Queries*, 2nd Series, vol. 5, p. 47.
53 Ibid.
54 Gordon P.G. Hills, 'Notes on Some Blacksmiths' legends and the observance of St. Clement's Day', *Hampshire Field Club Papers*, vol. 8, 1917–18, p. 65.
55 Hone, *Everyday Book*, vol. I, p. 755.
56 Ibid.
57 Gordon Hills, 'Notes on Some Blacksmiths' Legends', pp. 73–4.
58 Thomas Wright, *The Romance of the Lace Pillow* (1919), pp. 197–8. I wish to thank Maggie Black for pointing me towards this source.

59   Elizabeth Mary Wright, *Rustic Speech and Folklore* Oxford, 1913), p. 302.
60   Chambers, *The Book of Days*, vol. II, p. 724.
61   Hone, *Everyday Book*, vol. II, p. 814.
62   F. Llewellyn Jewitt, 'On Ancient Customs of Cheshire', *Journal of the British Archaeological Association*, vol. V, 1849, p. 253.
63   Hampshire Newspaper Cuttings. Vol. I. (Ref. Sh. 08) in Hampshire County Reference Library. F. 96. Cutting dated 20 July 1890.
64   For Sussex see Sawyer, *Sussex Folklore*, p. 253. For Hampshire see Charlotte M. Yonge, *An Old Woman's Outlook in a Hampshire Village* (London, 1896), p. 280.
65   'Wiltshire and General: folklore and Tales. Notes on Beacons, Gibbets, Holy Wells,' collected by Cecil V. Goddard. F. 87. Wiltshire Natural History Society Headquarters, Devizes, Wiltshire. Mr Goddard died 12 September 1933, aged 75. The rhyme was collected by him at Shrewton. A further version is also recorded on F. 142 from C.G. Blake (who died in 1932). He recalled singing the rhyme at the houses of South Newton gentry.
66   See Edward P. Thompson, 'The moral economy of the English crowd in the eighteenth century', particularly pp. 135-6.
67   See David Williams, *The Rebecca Riots: a study in agrarian discontent* (Cardiff: University of Wales Press, 1953). See also 'Rebecca', *Quarterly Review*, LXXIV (1844), pp. 225-7.
68   Public Record Office. (PRO) Home Office correspondence HO 52 (7) Hampshire. Letter from Winchester dated 26 November 1830.
69   PRO HO 40/27 (iii) F. 184. Letter from Boxford dated 13 December 1830.
70   See W.H. Hudson, *A Shepherd's Life* (London, 1910; reprinted 1981), pp. 174-5.
71   A full analysis of the types of activity can be found in: E.J. Hobsbawm and G. Rude, *Captain Swing* (London, 1973), pp. 269-316.
72   PRO HO 52 (6) letter from John Pearse, Chilton Lodge dated 22 November 1830.
73   *The Sussex Advertiser*, 29 November 1830.
74   *The Hampshire Advertiser and Salisbury Guardian*, 13 November 1830.
75   Ibid., 20 November 1830.
76   Alexander Somerville, *The Whistler at the Plough* (Manchester, 1852), p. 263.
77   Thompson, 'Moral economy', p. 111.
78   PRO HO 52 (7) letter from Henry Leeke, West Leigh, near Havant, dated 21 November 1830.
79   Ibid., letter from Andover, dated 26 November 1830.
80   PRO HO 53 (6) letter from J. Westall, Hungerford, dated 22 November 1830.
81   West Sussex Record Office. *Goodwood* MS 1477A Depositions of

Rioters. The examination of Richard Caplin, the Younger.

82 W.H. Parry Okeden, 'The agricultural riots in Dorset in 1830', *Dorset Natural History and Archaeological Society*, LII (1930), pp. 90–1.

83 *A report of the proceedings at the Special Commission holden at Winchester, December 20th 1830, and eight following days* (London, 1831), pp. 11–12.

84 *Hampshire Advertiser and Salisbury Guardian*, 25 December 1830.

85 PRO HO 52 (7), letter from Eyre Coote, West Park, Hampshire, dated 26 November 1830.

86 PRO HO 40/25 (ii) F. 308, letter dated 27 November 1830.

87 *Hampshire Advertiser and Salisbury Guardian*, 20 November 1830.

88 Ibid.

89 Ibid.

90 Hobsbawm and Rude, *Captain Swing*, p. 79.

91 Henry Gawler, *Farm Reports, or Accounts of the management of Select Farms, No. 1. North Hampshire* (*c*. 1832), Cope pamphlets, vol. 44, no. 1, p. 23. Located in the Cope Library, University of Southampton.

92 William Marshall, *Review and Abstract of the County Reports*, vol. II, *Western Division*, p. 213.

93 Thomas Abel's deposition, dated 6 November 1830 (PRO, HO 52/10, ff. 402–3).

94 Bernard Reaney, *The class struggle in 19th century Oxfordshire*, Oxford History Workshop Pamphlet, no. 3 (1971), p. 111.

95 Deposition of Joseph Bryant concerning Mr Abel, dated 19 November 1830 (PRO, HO 52/10, f. 488).

96 Parliamentary Papers Report of the Royal Commission on the Poor Laws, 1834, XXVIII, p. 200.A. I should like to thank Mr F.C. Mather for this reference.

97 Deposition of Joseph Bryant.

98 Ibid.

99 Ibid.

100 *Cornwall Royal Gazette*, 23 August 1837. I thank Dr J.G. Rule for drawing my attention to this reference.

101 PRO HO 52/10 f. 501.

102 *Hampshire Notes and Queries*, vol. VII, 1893, pp. 97–8.

6 Crime, Custom, and Popular Legitimacy

John Evelyn's great work 'Sylvia, or a Discourse on Forest Trees and the Propagation and Improvement of Timber in his Majesties Dominions' contains a chapter entitled 'Of the laws and Statutes for the preservation and Improvement of Woods' from which the following sanguinary statement is taken:

> Severer punishments have lately been ordained against our wood-stealers, destroyers of young trees and etc. By an ancient law of some Nations I read he forfeited a hand, who beheaded a tree without permission of the owner; and I cannot say they are sharp ones, when I compare the severity of our laws against mare stealers; nor am I by inclination the least cruel but I do affirm, we might as well live without Mares, as without Masts and ships, which are our wooden, but no less profitable horses.[1]

Legal sanctions against wood-stealers never quite invoked the harsh, retribution penalties advocated by Evelyn. However, the eighteenth century saw the progressive strengthening of those sanctions in a way which would have, in part, satisfied the celebrated diarist. English landowners did not abandon the source of supply for England's 'wooden horses' to 'wood-stealers and destroyers of young trees'.

Wood-stealing has never attracted the student of eighteenth-century social history in the same way as the more dramatic infringements of the law which have received ready attention.[2] The armed affrays between poachers and game-keepers which frequently occurred in the copses and coverts of the English countryside are reasonably well chronicled, although much more remains to be done in terms of motivation, and the relationship of the crime to the community.[3] We now also know of the bitter conflict which took place between small farmers and royal officials in the Royal

By Rite

Forests of Hampshire and Surrey and which took the form of bands of disguised men poaching deer.[4] Also, smuggling was tolerated in some areas and promoted by the local inhabitants to such a degree that the authority of government excisemen was openly and defiantly challenged to the extent that for some of the time these areas were beyond the force of the king's law.[5] For example, in March 1775 a 'posse comitatus' was raised in Hampshire to protect and escort some witnesses to the Winchester Assize, who were to give evidence against a smuggler. The first attempt to escort the witnesses to Winchester ended in failure as the party was forced back to Southampton by 'a large, regular body of smugglers, all armed and mounted'.[6]

The dramatic nature of the tensions and conflicts aroused by these forms of crime marks them as particularly attractive to the social historian, concerned to dispel the myth of the tranquillity of eighteenth-century English society. As well as being dramatic, such crime was aggressive, confident and often explicitly or implicitly violent. The punishments for such violations of the Palladian peace of mind were severe. Transportation, hanging or periods of imprisonment awaited the poacher, deer-stealer or smuggler.

Possibly the most common way in which the law and rights of property were infringed, was by the taking of wood from the parks, woodlands, copses and hedgerows of private landowners. A study of summary conviction records for the county of Wiltshire indicates that wood theft or damage was a consistent and frequent occurrence. Furthermore, the difficulties involved in detection and prosecution of wood-theft – that is, unless caught red-handed or convicted on the evidence of witnesses, it was difficult to prove guilt – make it seem probable that the number of crimes reported and from which conviction resulted represents only a very small proportion of the number of crimes committed, and that illegal wood-gathering was widespread.

Poaching, smuggling and deer-stealing were always acknowledged as infringements of the law, despite popular sympathy and encouragement for the poacher, smuggler or deer-stealer. Indeed in the case of deer-stealing, the criminal became folk hero and entered the mythology of British history.[7] However, Robin Hood retained his potency because he stole from the rich and gave to the poor, rather than because he opposed oppressive forest laws. It is the nature of Robin Hood himself which makes the crime acceptable. The taking of dead wood was anciently a popular right protected by customary law and sometimes recorded in manorial charters. Wood-gathering occupied a central position in the popular view of relationships within the community, similar in importance to such practices as gleaning, the claim to harvest perquisites, including harvest homes and largess, and to certain other annual ceremonial claims and doles. Possibly, also, the protection of public rights of way across private land (usually enclosed) can be placed in this category, as this could involve disputes about access to commons. The transition from custom to crime occurred in the late-seventeenth and eighteenth centuries as the wood-gatherer faced increased legal sanctions, and was more regularly stigmatised as wood-stealer.

'Through all the woodland parts of this country', wrote Charles Vancouver in his account of agriculture in Hampshire, 'the peasantry are tolerably well supplied with fuel, and which is obtained by a claim they exercise pretty freely, of taking what is called "snapwood"; that is all the fallen branches, and such as they can snap off by hand, or break down with a hook fixed in the end of a long pole; for this purpose they have been observed to visit most of the demesnes and private as well as other woodlands through the country.'[8]

The custom of taking snapwood existed also in Wiltshire where the specific rights of tenants to wood can be seen in an early-seventeenth-century charter relating to the inhabitants of Great Wishford. This charter, known as 'The sum of the Ancient Customs belonging to Wishford and Barford out of the Forest of Grovely', sets out the precise nature of the customary rights belonging to the inhabitants of Great Wishford with respect to wood gathering in nearby Grovely Forest. In fact the charter specifies a whole series of common rights such as pannage and grazing for cattle. The rights are extensive:

> Item the lordes and freeholders of Wishford and Barford for themselves and all their tenants and all inhabitants in the said mannor of Wishford and Barford St. Martyn have

209

an auntient custome and ever tyme out of minde have used
to fetch and of right may fetch and bring away Bowes at
theire pleasure from the woodes of Grovely from maye
daie in the morninge untill Whit-Monday at night every
Saterdaye and half Hollydaie once vizt in the eveninge and
every hollydaie and sabbath daie twice vizt in the morninge and in the Eveninge.[9]

Item the lordes and freeholders of Wishford for themselves
and theire Tennants have ever by auntient custome and
tyme out of mind used to fell in Grovely and in right may
lawfullie fell and bring away aboute Holie Thursday everie
yeare one loade of trees uppon a Cart to be drawen by
strength of people and the lord and freeholders of Barford
for themselves and their tennants have used and in right
may fetch one other loade of Trees uppon Whitson Mundy
uppon a Carte to be drawen also by strength of peopell.[10]

Item the olde custome is and time out of mind hath byn
that the people and Inhabitance of Wishford and Barford
aforesaide may lawfully geather and bring away all kinde
of deade snappinge woode Boughes and Stickes that be
in the woodes at Grovely at their pleasure without controlment and none other besides them may lawfully fetch any
there at any tyme.[11]

In order to reaffirm these rights each year it was laid down
that

the lords freeholders Tennants and Inhabitance of the
Mannor of greate Wishford or soe many of them as would in
auntient tyme have used to goe in a daunce to the Cathe-
drall Church of our blessed Ladie in the Cittie of new
sarum on Whit Tuesdaie in the said Countie of Wiltes,
and theire made theire clayme to theire custome in the
Forrest of Grovely in these words: Groveley Groveley and
all Groveley.[12]

Other ceremonies associated with wood gathering can be
identified. In Huntingdonshire the following custom was
observed: 'It is the custom at Warboys for certain of the poor
of the parish to be allowed to go into Warboys Wood on
May-day morning for the purpose of gathering and taking

away bundles of sticks. It may possibly be a relic of the old custom of going to a wood in the early morning of may-day for the purpose of gathering may dew.'[13] On the fifth November at Charlton on Otmoor, children sang:

> The fifth of November, since I can remember,
> Was Guy Faux, Guy, poke him in the eye,
> Shove him up the chimney-pot, and there let him die.
> A stick and a stake, for King George's sake,
> If you don't give me one, I'll take two,
> The better for me, and the worse for you,
> Ricket-a-racket your hedges shall go.[14]

Yet another custom connected with wood gathering prevailed, as mentioned previously, at St Briavels in Gloucestershire.[15] An assessment of 2d was made on every householder to buy the bread and cheese which was distributed. This assessment per household is probably a survival of 'wood coin' – a payment formerly made by tenants of some manors to the lord for their right of gathering dead wood.

The Great Wishford charter shows the familiar manorial customs of Plowbote, Hedgebote, Housebote and Firebote. These customs were reserved for the tenants and inhabitants of Great Wishford and Barford St Martin. Indeed the charter further contains a number of presentments for infringement of these rights by outsiders:

> we present that the Inhabitants of Barwicke St. James, Stapleford, Stoford, Newton, Chilhampton, Dichampton and Wilton do often use as namelie goodwife White of Stapleford and others there, John Hoop of Stoford and divers others there, John Baker of Everall the Clark of Newton and divers others there, Robert Blake of Chilhampton and divers there, and out of Ditchampton some and out of Wilton very many doe often resort into Groveley woodes and fetche fearne and wood there without any auethoritie for the doeinge thereof.[16]

Of the forms of wood custom, firebote seems to have been the one which survived longest and was most jealously guarded. At Great Wishford as specified in the charter, the right to 'snappinge woode' was open to all people and inhabitants of the village. The right to 'snapping wood' assumed a significance in the popular mind for two reasons. Firstly fuel was a most important commodity and one which was expensive. Secondly, the right to gather dead wood in areas where this was plentiful helped shape a view of the relationships within the community between the poor inhabitants and their richer neighbours in which notions of unity and corporate identity were central.

The taking of green wood, on certain days and for certain periods in the year, by tenants for building purposes was also a right which was common in customary relationships. Mayday figured importantly as one of the days when the taking of green wood was legitimate. It is for this reason that Mayday is associated, even today, with so great a variety of ceremonial practices which are connected with wood and wood use. The Maypole itself was no more than a tree taken from the woods and set up on the village green. John Evelyn pointed to this when he wrote:

> And here we cannot but persistringe those Riotous Assemblies of idle people, who under pretence of going a maying (as they term it) do oftentimes cut down, and carry away fine straight trees, to set up before some Ale-house, or revelling-place, where they keep their drunken Bacchanalias . . . I think it were better to be quite abolished amongst us, for many reasons, besides that of occasioning so much waste and spoil as we find is done to trees at that season, under this wanton pretence by breaking, mangling, and tearing down of branches, and entire arms of trees, to adorne their wooden idols . . .[17]

For example, the notion that the tree was usually stolen can be seen in the following: 'What adoe make our young men at the time of May? Do they not use "night watchings" to rob and steale young trees out of other mens grounde and bringe them home into their parishe with minstrels playing before.'[18] It is clear that this practice persisted into the seventeenth and eighteenth centuries:

The most of these May-poles are stolen, yet they give out

212

that the poles are given them – There are two may-poles set up in my parish [King's Norton]; the one was stolen and the other was given by a profest papist. That which was stollen was said to bee given, when 'twas proved to their faces that 'twas stollen, and they were made to acknowledge their offence. This pole that was stollen was rated at five shillings: if all the poles one with another were so rated, which were stollen this may, what a considerable sume would it amount to.[19]

Indeed, the custom of taking a growing tree for May-day survived in the late-nineteenth century in Herefordshire at Letton[20] and at Upper Chilstone, Madley.[21]

Oak Apple day, 29 May, was another occasion for the ritual taking of wood (and was the day that the inhabitants of Great Wishford ritually defended their right to gather dead wood).[22] Karl Marx pointed to the essential ambivalence towards property rights in wood: 'It will be found that the customs which are customs of the entire poor class are based with a sure instinct on the indeterminate aspect of property; it will be found not only that this class feels an urge to satisfy a natural need, but equally that it feels that need to satisfy a rightful wage. Fallen wood provides an example of this.'[23] It is against the background of custom that we should view what can only be described as a battle which took place in the eighteenth and early-nineteenth centuries between landowners and wood gatherers.

The belief that there existed a customary right to collect dead wood for fuel, which included the taking of wood from growing trees 'by hook or by crook' or by 'snapping', as well as from the ground, prevailed in the popular mind. In order to gain a proper impression of what was implied by the act of gathering wood, the historian must lay aside the image of the poor man gathering sticks in the King Wenceslas carol. Wood gathering involved the taking of all forms of wood where such wood could be gathered either from the ground or from the branches with only the effort of snapping it off, or by using a crooked pole. The use of any other tools such as saws or billhooks was not legitimate with regard to growing timber. This was a systematic and regular method of obtaining fuel and should not be viewed as sporadic or casual.

However, the distinction between green and dead wood had grown up in manorial custom with regard to firebote, and was clearly open to much dispute. Overzealous gleaning of the branches of a growing tree obviously brought down much live wood as well as dead and in practice the distinction was hard to define. The whole pattern of legal sanction in the eighteenth century was to prohibit even the smallest infringement of the rights of property in wood in order to prevent widespread ravages and despoiling. It is probable that abuse resulted from generous interpretations of the term 'snapping wood' in the seventeenth century.

Sir Frederick Eden noted of a family budget he recorded for Seend in Wiltshire:

> Nothing is stated for fuel. If the labourer is employed in hedging he is allowed to take home a faggot every evening, while the work lasts: but this is by no means sufficient for his consumption: his children therefore, are sent into the fields, to collect wood where they can; and neither hedges nor trees are spared by the young marauders who are thus, in some degree, calculated in the art of thieving, till, from being accustomed to small thefts, they hesitate not to commit greater deprivations on the public: this, perhaps, might be prevented, if every parish would lay in a stock of fuel, and sell it at somewhat below the market price, instead of giving their poor an allowance in money to purchase it.[24]

Eden clearly saw wood gathering in Wiltshire as a criminal activity, not defended by reference to custom. This view was increasingly held after the passage of legislation.

There were two crucial periods of legislation relating to offences concerning wood. The first of these periods occurred in the early years of the Restoration. During the seventeenth century, enclosure, particularly in wooded areas, provoked several sustained, determined and organised disturbances. In the 1630s, in the South and West, particularly in Dorset and Wiltshire, opposition to enclosure of forests was strong. Disturbances occurred at Braydon in Wiltshire and Feckenham in Worcestershire in 1632, and in 1634 in Gillingham in Dorset. A figure, dressed in woman's clothes, and referred to as 'Lady Skimmington' led a determined band in the destruction of enclosures in the Forest of Braydon, near Purton in Wiltshire.[25] Three of the ringleaders were eventually arrested, each fined £500 and were ordered: 'to be set in the Pillory in women's clothes as they were disguised in the Riots, with papers on their heads declaring their offences and be there well whipped'.[26] This serves as a remarkable reminder of the potency of the symbolic dressing in women's clothes during popular disturbances and in this case illustrates how the authorities attempted to defuse the symbolism by turning it back on the rioters in the form of ridicule.

Rioters in women's clothes and wood-gatherers might not, at first, appear to be associated, but it should not be overlooked that, as well as being concerned with their immediate target in the enclosure fences themselves, the rioters were mainly concerned to establish the general right of access to the woodlands and to secure for the local community benefits of pannage, grazing for cattle and the gathering of wood for fuel.

In the Civil War it is probable that forest and woods were further exposed to visitations of wood-gatherers, 'without controlment', to use the phrase employed in the Great Wishford charter, so that by the Restoration it was necessary to extend statute law in that area. A statute in 1663, the legal change to which John Evelyn referred, gave 'full power and authority to apprehend . . . all and every person or persons they shall suspect, having or carrying, or any ways conveying, any burthen or bundles of wood, underwood, poles or young trees, or bark or bast of trees, or any gates, stiles, posts, pales, rails, or hedgewood, broom or furze.'[27] The statute covered a wide variety of wood forms, and points at the strong anti-enclosure elements involved in the committing of wood offences. Hedges and fences in themselves were ready sources of wood for fuel, and constant despoiling could lead to the barrier being rendered ineffective. On the other hand, more malicious offenders deliberately threw down fences or gates to gain access to woodlands and then, having destroyed the obstacles, removed them as general wood for fuel.

This motive can be found in the following extract from the Game Laws Parliamentary enquiry of 1845:

I had some sheep in the neighbourhood of Luton, just by the town, and I frequently missed stakes, pulled up of a night and hurdles pulled up, and the sheep were let out over the fresh turnips; the consequence was, that one evening my shepherd went and took a person that had taken a hurdle and broken it up. I went down and found the hurdle underneath a heap of stubble. The man was found guilty? Yes; the punishment was about 6s or 7s, and he had a fortnight to pay it in; . . . Was the charge against the man before the magistrates a charge of stealing? – It was for stealing; it was not for letting out the sheep, but for taking a hurdle out of the field, and breaking it up for firewood. Was it malicious damage that you complained of, or felony? I did not consider it felony; it was taking the hurdle, and breaking it up for firewood.[28]

A certain amount of ambivalence existed regarding the taking of wood from fences and hedges. It appears that the law generally acknowledged that the crime was one of theft rather than anything more serious. This supports the view that the wood was stolen for fuel rather than as an act of malicious damage. This can be seen in the following account of wood theft tried at the Easter Sessions in Winchester 1784, when William and Thomas Smith were charged that on 6 February 1784, they 'feloniously stole ten pales of wood value 10d property of the Earl of Portsmouth'. William and Thomas Smith had been detected in making up two bundles of pales from the fencing round Portsmouth Park where 'great many pales [had been] carried away this winter'. Both men were found guilty and received sentences of one week's imprisonment and a public whipping at Whitchurch. No attempt was made to magnify their offence so that a charge could be brought under the notorious Black Act.[29]

Also, powers of search were given to constables and officers. They could search, on suspicion only, any property thought to conceal stolen wood. If the accused, before a magistrate, could not give good account of how he came by the wood or produce evidence of purchase, then he was 'deemed and adjudged as convicted of the . . . offence of cutting and spoiling of the woods, underwood, poles or young trees' concerned.[30] The penalty for the first offence was fixed at a maximum fine of 10 shillings with the offender being made liable for any damages. Failure to pay the fine resulted in the offender being sent to the House of Correction for up to one month or to be whipped. The second offence carried the penalty of one month's imprisonment with hard labour. Buying stolen wood was also made an offence. The statute has its significance in the comprehensive and thorough treatment of takers of all types of wood. This can only be viewed as a departure from the form of rights to wood specified in manorial custom. A further statute in the reign of Charles II separated malicious damage to timber trees from the lesser offence of wood-stealing.

The second significant strengthening of the law occurred in 1766.[31] The reaction of local communities in Wiltshire has indicated to M.J. Ingram in a recent study on 'Law and Disorder in early seventeenth century Wiltshire' that wood-gathering was regarded as 'an equivocal area of behaviour'.[32] The strengthening of the law in 1766 aimed to remove all possible equivocation and to establish firmly the criminality of wood-gathering. It was made an offence to 'wilfully cut or break down, bark, burn, pluck up, lop, top, crop, or otherwise deface, damage, despoil or destroy or carry away any Timber tree'.[33] The punishment for the first offence upon conviction on the evidence of one witness before a magistrate, was a fine of £20 or six to twelve months imprisonment. The second offence was punishable by an increased fine and longer period of imprisonment. However, a third offence could be punished by transportation for seven years.[34] Timber trees were oak, beech, chestnut, walnut, ash, elm, cedar, fir, aspen, lime, sycamore and birch trees, within the meaning of the Act. To this list were later added poplar, alder, larch, maple and horn beam.[35] The offence of taking wood from other than timber trees, that is, underwood, hedgewood, hollies and thorns was punishable by a fine of forty shillings or one month's hard labour, and a whipping.[36] As with other crimes in the eighteenth century, detection was to be encouraged by the offer of rewards to informers. Anyone attempting to aid an offender to resist arrest was also liable to a heavy fine. A further statute added that, if the offence was committed by night, an offender could be transported for seven years as the crime was then treated as a felony.[37]

Before considering what can best be described as certain key battle grounds in Hampshire where the issue of taking wood was disputed hotly in the eighteenth century, a brief note on the nature of the evidence is necessary. Under the terms of the statute, an offender was brought before a magistrate and if he was convicted upon the evidence of one witness the details of his crime and the degree of his penalty were recorded in the form of a paper slip which followed a standard form of words: 'Be it remembered that on the — day of — in the year —, A.B. was upon the complaint of C.D. convicted before — for — in pursuance with an act . . .' This was duly signed, sealed and dated and then was certified and filed amongst the records of the next sessions. Such summary conviction records rarely survive. Wiltshire, however, has a full series of such evidence.

Except in cases where the crime was committed by night or where it was a third offence, summary conviction records are the only source. In the case of night or third offences, Quarter Session records prove more useful, although the full details of the cases are not often recorded. A major source for detailed case studies is the local press, which for Hampshire and Wiltshire (and also Berkshire) is rich and rewarding. By definition, it is the more dramatic cases which were reported in the local newspapers, but this serves to highlight the key areas involved. Advertisements offering rewards for information leading to the conviction of wood-stealers or notices warning possible illegal gatherers of wood are also frequently to be found in their columns. So the historian can, at best, expect only to glimpse the tensions and conflicts which often ran deep in eighteenth-century woodland society in Hampshire and Wiltshire. Yet these glimpses, tantalisingly brief though they may be, give witness to powerful and determined resistance in some areas to legal sanctions against the right to gather wood for fuel, which was so deeply fixed in the popular mind.

In October 1787 an anxious and doubtless law-abiding correspondent to the *Hampshire County Magazine* gave the following warning to his fellow readers:

You cannot render your Magazine more useful at this

season than by giving a place for the following extract from the act of the 6th of his present Majesty, of the law relative to woods, as many people under the pretence of going a nutting may subject themselves to great punishment, without being fully apprised of the risque they run. The Act recites that many idle and disorderly persons have made a practice of going into woods, underwoods and wood-grounds, and cutting and carrying away great quantities of young wood of various kinds for making poles, walking-sticks and for other uses; and under pretence of getting fire-wood, have cut down, boughed, split off or otherwise damaged or destroyed the growth of said woods and underwoods to the great injury of the lawful owners.[38]

The correspondent, warning against unwitting contravention of the strengthened law, indicates a genuine conviction which was held widely enough for him to think it important to warn the inhabitants of Hampshire that they were not aware of the risk they ran when exercising long-established customary rights to go nutting or to collect firewood.

Further warning of a different kind was given to Hampshire wood-gatherers on 13 August 1792:

Whereas the Timber growing on the estates in the Parish of Eling, which belong to Winchester College, have been cut, lopped and stolen by certain iniquitous and daring plunderers of property who are supposed to live in the neighbourhood of Bartley: A Reward of Twenty Guineas is hereby promised to anyone who will give such information as may convict any person or persons so injuring the estates aforesaid.[39]

The advertisement continued further and indicates another and obviously connected crime:

And whereas many encroachments have from time to time been made on the wast of the college Manor, to the great prejudice of the College tenants, notice is hereby given that in future, neither the College nor homage of the manor, will consent that coppices should be granted for such encroachments; but all buildings hereafter erected on

219

the waste by trespass shall be pulled down, and all land taken in from the waste by trespass shall be laid open.[40]

Winchester College had several estates in Hampshire, in particular the manor of Eling on the edge of the New Forest and on the west bank of Southampton Water. This manor was well-wooded and from the College's Wood Account Books it can be seen that the sale of timber was a valuable and regular source of income. It would also seem that at this time the College decided to improve the development and maintenance of its wooded estates. It was apparent that a major problem had developed in Eling with respect to wood stealing and encroachment.[41] In many ways these are twin issues. Some inhabitants of Eling lived a marginal existence on the edge of the woods, putting up buildings, taking waste land into rough cultivation or for grazing, and gathering wood for fuel. The tenants of the College benfited from the proximity of supplies of wood for fuel and timber for building purposes.

In December 1794 the Wood Minute Book recorded that: 'Whereas great injury has been done to the woods at Eling, particularly at Birchwood and Polsom Bushes. It is resolved that a stipend usually paid the warden and Wood-Burser be discontinued in order that a proper salary may be allowed out of the same, for the better management of these woods.'[42] It was recorded elsewhere that the number of 'trees carried away and injured' amounted to some 1,200.[43] Another estimate put it much higher: 'upon a moderate calculation there have been near 3000 trees belonging to the College cut down, lopt, and otherwise injured within the last six or seven years'.[44] Such despoiling clearly required action and the College was not slow in this respect. In 1792, two men gave information on behalf and at the expense of the College against some wood-stealers at Eling.[45]

In 1793 a thorough enquiry into the condition of the woods in the manor of Eling was mounted by the College.[46] The result was that the College concluded that whereas the land was much suited to the growth of good timber it was ravaged by wood-stealers: 'Fletchwood is peculiarly adapted to the growth of oak timber. It has however been much injured by wood stealers. The cottagers in the neighbourhood of Fletchwood do great injury to the wood, and it is their common practice to cut down trees from the Frittern to trees of 20 or 30 feet timber.'[47] The report added that, 'This wood is however less liable to Depredation than others.'[48] Warden's Thorn's, the report continued, 'has likewise been much injured, tho' a small wood. Trees have there been cut and carried away, that have contained 30 feet and upwards of timber.' 'Halfpenny Hern has suffered in like manner. Paulsham Bushes, a wood more adapted to the growth of Beech than other timber, (tho' favourable to the growth of oak) has been extremely abused. It is a fact, that great part of the timber now standing in this wood has either been lopped, or otherwise injured. In many parts, trees have been cut or sawed off in the middle, and frequently near the stool; or where the trunk remains the most considerable lengths have been cut away.'[49]

This remarkable report detailed other abuses: 'The Ash timber on the Manor has been much injured by the keepers in the New Forest, who lop them for browsing their deer.'[50] It also indicates the reason why the Minute Book recorded that the stipend which had usually been paid to the warden was to be set aside to pay a woodward. His responsibility was to protect the interests of Winchester College in the Manor of Eling:

> The extent of the college woods in Eling, and their situation in the New Forest, making them liable to great Depredations; it becomes necessary to employ some active man in that department only. The care of the woods and the labour necessary in keeping up the fences, will fully employ one man; and should be his only concern. A salary adequate to 9s a week would be sufficient wages, and the Society would be amply compensated by the preservation of its timber. It does not appear that a plan of this kind has yet been adopted by the College. Sir Charles Mill employs a man constantly at the above salary.[51]

The report concludes, rather fatalistically, that, 'Notwithstanding all possible care, the Society must expect that these woods will be liable to considerable depredations.'[52] In fact, 'all possible care' was taken to protect their woodlands. In

January 1793 one John Whicker was 'convicted of cutting
and lopping beech timber, the property of the warden and
fellows of Winchester College' and was imprisoned for a
year.[53]

The depredations in the woods of Eling do not appear to
have been carried out by poor and landless men. On the
contrary it would seem that Winchester College faced such
damage from some of the tenants. The problem of encroachment of wastes indicates that squatters were no doubt
attracted to forest areas to live marginal existences on their
limits. However, an earlier document for 1760 in the College
records shows that encroachment was in fact undertaken
by a good many of the College's tenants.[54]

A far more sustained effort was mounted later in the
decade when the College achieved something of a break-
through in its battle with the 'iniquitous and daring plunderers' of its property. There were two major trials of Eling
wood-stealers in the period. The first occurred in 1798
at the Easter Sessions – 'The King on the prosecution of the
warden and scholars of Winchester College, against William
Gould, Edward Gould, Thomas Wolfe and Stephen Hatch.'
These men were charged with 'cutting down and taking away
in the night of the 28th February last, a beech timber tree,
at a place called Balsome Bushes, in the parish of Eling,
belonging to the warden and scholars of Winchester College,
lords of the manor of Eling.'[55] During the trial no specific
mention of the use of tools was made and it is probable that
the accused used none, as the prosecution would have
referred to tools to ensure conviction. It is more likely that
the men were merely gleaning the trees for fuel. 'Balsome
Bushes' is the 'Paulsham Bushes' of the College's report. The
woodward, Richard Light, gave evidence of the amount of
damage in the last six to seven years, stating that in that
time, 'near 3000 trees' had been injured.[56] The principal
evidence came from William Hatch, who was one of the
accomplices and was related to Stephen Hatch, one of
the accused. He had 'voluntarily come forward as a witness'
and 'swore to the prisoners cutting down the timber and
putting the same into a cart which he had procured in order
to carry it away.'[57] As the offence was committed by night,
the full force of the law was invoked and the prisoners were

all sentenced to be transported for seven years.[58] A study of the lease records of the College indicates that these men, in so far as the names can be positively identified, were not squatters or poor labourers, but were probably tenants of the College.

At the Midsummer Sessions in 1798 a further case was tried, against one Peter Gray.[59] Gray was indicted for 'lopping two beech trees standing on Balsome Beeches, the property of the warden and scholars of Winchester College, without their consent' on the night of 3 May. (An interesting date bearing in mind the variety of May ceremonies and customs associated with wood, and the citing of May in some instances as one of the permitted periods for legal wood taking in the Great Wishford Charter.) It seems that Gray was an habitual offender, having been convicted in 1795 for the lopping of a beech tree belonging to the College and, on the nonpayment of ten pounds which it was adjudged he had forfeited for the offence, was committed to gaol for six months. Furthermore, he had been a witness at the last Sessions called to give characters for the prisoners who had been convicted and transported. John Steed, who had given evidence against the prisoners at the last Session 'swore to his having seen [Gray] cut a large limb from a beech tree, belonging to the College . . . (it being moonlight) which the prisoner carried home with him'. Steed further stated that previous to that in the night 'he saw and heard the prisoner bark and cut down a great many young trees of different kinds'.[60] Again, it is noteworthy that no specific mention is made of the use of tools; it is probable that Gray used none.

An alibi was attempted on Gray's part. Two or three witnesses were called to prove that he was elsewhere at the time when he was charged with having committed the offence. However, 'after a very minute examination of them, two of whom were his sister and her husband, and who very grossly prevaricated from what they had said before Mr. Poulter, the Magistrate who committed the prisoner, of which prevarication he gave evidence as being directly contrary to what they swore before him . . . the court overruled the plea'. 'The whole of the evidence being summed up to the jury in a very satisfactory manner by the chairman of the Court, the jury gave a verdict of guilty.' Gray was sentenced to transportation for seven years.[61] There is some suspicion in all this that Gray was deliberately 'set up' because he gave evidence at the first trial. If we accept that this was not the case, then it was probably of considerable relief to the College to rid themselves of one more desperate wood-stealer from Eling. It would seem again probable, although no positive identification in the leases can be made, that Gray was a tenant of the College. The name certainly occurs and reoccurs in the eighteenth-century records for that manor.

This somewhat lengthy reconstruction of the details of the conflict which occurred in the late-eighteenth century between Winchester College and some of the inhabitants of its manor at Eling, represents one of those glimpses we are afforded of the tensions which wood rights aroused. It is perhaps likely that after a lax period in the management of its affairs the College sought to stiffen its attitude over the taking of wood, and to develop its estates as regards the very valuable commodity of timber – not an unusual entre-preneurial decision at that time. William Cobbett recom-mended the growing of timber as a reliable and speedy means of making profit when he wrote in 1825: 'The inducements to create property by tree-planting are so many and so powerful, that, to the greater part of those who possess the means, little, I hope, need be said, to urge them to the employing of those means. Occasions enough will offer for showing how quickly the profits come.'[62] It also appears that in so doing the College faced resistance not merely from a few individuals, but from a woodland community who depended upon the benefits of access to wood for their marginal economies. Some of the features of this communal solidarity can be seen in details of the trial. First there is Gray's evidence as to the characters of the accused in the first trial, then the attempt to establish an alibi at his own trial. More-over, it is only with the aid of an informer related to the group that evidence was found for the trial of the two Goulds, Hatch and Wolfe. These men were not idle and disreputable criminals but were from families living in a community with close proximity to woods and forest, who believed that taking wood on a regular basis from the College estate was not a crime but a custom, at least defended by common practice. No more than three months after the first trial, Gray had been detected taking wood, by night, in the same area. In the early-nineteenth century Eling manor was enclosed and certain specific fuel rights to turf were set aside for tenants of the College.[63] The sharp lessons of 1798 were not enough for the inhabitants of Eling and further trouble seems to have occurred during the early part of the nineteenth century. Indeed, one writer saw wood-stealing as the first step on the road to other forms of rural crime:

> The poor of Eling derive considerable advantage from the vicinity of the New Forest. A cottage and garden are obtainable at a moderate rent (from £2.10s to £5.). Pigs are easily kept. Fuel, whether of turf or wood, is cheap, and the climate is such that a day's work is rarely lost through inclemency of weather. On the other hand, the Forest tempts the poor to become poachers and timber-stealers, and these nightly depredations lead to the robbing of out-houses of poultry and calves, and sometimes to house-breaking, and to dissolute habits of every description.[64]

Earlier in the eighteenth century a similar pattern of events, although of a less dramatic nature, can be seen in another part of the country. In this case, the cause of the access to the woodland was championed by legal test. At the Assizes at Winchester in March 1776, a case was heard against one Jevoise Clark of Belmount.[65] Clark was accused by Peter Taylor Esq. of Pembroke Park (and M.P. for Portsmouth) of breaking down his park pales. Clark justified his action by claiming a right of way across Taylor's parkland to Purbrook Heath, and also a right of common in 'a certain close which, though formerly inclosed, has lain open for several years back'. The land in dispute was of little value 'never worth a shilling an acre, being morassy and barren, part a rabbit warren, and the remainder a peat moor'.[66] Several ancient witnesses were summoned to testify to these claims ('upwards of four score years of age'), and they testified that no road had formerly laid across the land 'until the fences being entirely neglected and broken down, people and carriages went over it at their pleasure'.[67] The report in the *Hampshire Chronicle* continued: 'All the evidences brought on the

Defendent's side were of modern date, and mostly persons in some degree interested in the decision, as wanting a road from Havant to Purbrook Heath.' The *Chronicle* added that 'to the surprise of most of the spectators a verdict was found, in part, for the Defendent, Mr Clark'.[68]

At the same time as the effects of this decision were reported, 'We are informed from Havant, Bedhampton and the villages adjacent, that the inhabitants of those places met [after the case between Peter Taylor and Jevoise Clark, Esqs. was decided], and spent an evening shewing the most evident proofs of joy, by ringing of bells, firing of guns, and every demonstrative gladness that could be shewn, at having regained a right which was attempted to be wrested from them.'[69] This popular expression of joy did not sweeten Mr Taylor. In September 1776, the following warning appeared:

Wood stealers
Whereas several idle and disorderly persons have, under a pretence of gathering dead wood, made a practice of going into and damaging the woods and coppices of Peter Taylor, Esq. of Purbrook Park, in this county; now this is to give notice, that any person who shall hereafter be found in the woods and coppices of Peter Taylor Esq. or within his Manors of Farlington and Drayton, trespassing against the Statute . . . in such case made and provided, shall be prosecuted as the law directs. And any person giving information to Mr. James Newland, in Havant, shall receive a reward of two guineas, on conviction of the offender, over and above the moiety of the forfeiture allowed by the statute.[70]

This advertisement was again carried by the *Hampshire Chronicle* on 7 October 1776.[71]

An interruption in the campaign occurred the following year with the death of Mr Taylor. His heirs, however, took up the cause, for in April 1778 one 'William Langley, of Plant Farm, in the Parish of Southwick, was convicted, at Fareham before Richard Bangus Esq. . . . for having in his possession a quantity of thorn bushes cut on Red-hill Plain, in the forest of Bere the property of the heirs of the late Peter Taylor Esq.'[72]

Some similarities with the conflict between Winchester College and the inhabitants of Eling can be identified. Firstly, in both cases it would appear that control of the woodland was lax or had been allowed to slacken over a period of years. After the Act of 1766 and in response to the increasing attractions of efficient cultivation of timber, the landowner sought to reassert his control over the woodland areas in dispute. Secondly, the conflicts occurred on manors close to Royal Forests – Eling near the New Forest and, in the second case, in the villages and hamlets around the Forest of Bere. A third case, which will be referred to in more detail later, that of the Forest of Alice Holt on the Hampshire/Surrey border, can also be added to this list. Thirdly, the pattern of advertisements warning potential offenders and offering rewards leading to the successful prosecution of wood-stealers, and of cases brought to trial as reminders of the potency of legal sanction against taking of wood, is common to both cases. Advertisements in the local press were probably as much designed to encourage neighbouring land-owners to take action against offenders as to intimidate would-be criminals. In the case of the dispute in Southwick and Farlington over Peter Taylor's woods, there is also a remarkable feature of a benevolent member of the gentry taking up the cause of wood rights and right of common at court. Rarely did the poor wood gatherer find such a champion.

The crime of taking wood seems to have been widespread in Hampshire in this period. It was reported of Hampshire in June 1773 that 'many people have been committed this week to the Common Bridewell for making it their daily practice to tear hedges; a practice very frequent and pre-judicial to farmers.'[73] A similar situation was apparent in the 1770s in Berkshire where the same pattern of publishing of notices and reporting of offences occurs in the local press.

The practices of wood-stealers in the forest of Alice Holt were so daring and assertive that their reputations were used in a political context. Supporters of one side at a political meeting advertised in 1790 were given criminal associations, when it was said that 'The county is flattered with the expectation of a most respectable attendance of wood stealers and poachers from the Holt Fc⁻ st . . . at the meeting

on the 14th.'[74] The reputation of the inhabitants of the Holt
forest for wood stealing was founded on some dramatic
occurrences. Gilbert White of Selborne wrote that:

> A very large fall of timber, consisting of about one thou-
> sand oaks, has been cut this spring (viz. 1784) in the Holt
> forest; one-fifth of which, it is said, belongs to the grantee,
> Lord Stawel. He lays claims also to the lop and top: but
> the poor of the parishes of Binsted and Frinsham, Bentley
> and Kingsley, assert that it belongs to them; and, assembl-
> ing in a riotous manner, have actually taken it all away.
> One man, who keeps a team, has carried home, for his
> share, forty stacks of wood. Forty-five of these people his
> Lordship has served with actions.[75]

Lord Stawell complained to the Treasury in December 1783
'that the people of Frensham, under a pretended right, took
away not only the stack wood but also the whole of the tops
of the trees of the preceding fall.'[76] Of the actions against the
offenders, the 6th Report of the Land Revenue Commissioners states that in all 'upwards of Forty Actions against
the poor people of the adjoining parishes, for taking away
Parts of Wood; and that they all entered appearances, but
suffered judgement to go by default'.[77] It further records
that the same case of right to wood was tried in 1741 and
found against the inhabitants of Frensham.[78] As to the quantity of wood taken, the Report records that 'the Offal Wood,
after having been made into Faggots, and a Day appointed
for the Sale of it, was openly carried off by the People of
Frensham, to the Number of 6,365 Faggots, in One Day and
Night'.[79]

The same feature of the community solidarity was detect-
able amongst the inhabitants of Frensham. The Surveyor
General's Deputy was absent when

> the Country people began carrying away the wood; and
> that when he returned it was almost all gone; that he
> detected two men loading a waggon with part of it and
> got a warrant for apprehending them; but that the Tything
> man of Frensham, where the offenders live, has never
> executed it, though repeatedly pressed to do it, and

offered Assistance by him, that on his applying to the
Keepers, and enquiring whose teams had been employed
in taking away the wood, they told him they knew nothing
of it; and he could get no information from them against
the Offenders.[80]

The claim to take offal wood after a general fall of timber
had long been maintained in the Frensham area, despite a
judgement against the right in 1741. The inhabitants did not
step over the line into casual taking of wood after specific
timber felling. The Report makes this clear: 'no attempt is
ever made to take Offal wood of Trees felled by Lord
Stawell's order, and that hardly a Faggot is ever missing.'[81]

The right to claim offal wood after the general felling of
timber was a widely held right amongst rural labourers and
forest dwellers. However, by the early-nineteenth century
it had been mostly extinguished. Thomas Smart was ques-
tioned on this point by the Select Committee established to
enquire into the rate of agricultural wages in 1824. The
following exchange indicates a major shift in attitude away
from custom.

Do you cut down much timber? – I do sometimes.
Upon these occasions, you have a right always to as large
a faggot as you can carry home? – No; they will not allow
us any now.
Then you have it in pay, do not you? – No.[82]

The action of the inhabitants of Frensham in 1783 was a last
dramatic assertion of certain long-held customary rights to
wood. By 1824 legal opinion and the practice of landowners
had moved away from the defence or indeed the acknowledgement of such rights.

The latter half of the eighteenth century saw a concerted
effort in parts of Hampshire to preserve these rights, but
despite these efforts the altered opinion prevailed. It is
recorded that 'Philip Loveland, James Coleson, Richard
Binfield and Thomas Quinall, for stealing a large quantity of
oak-timber from Holt forest, the property of his Majesty'
were sent to Winchester Assizes in 1794,[83] whilst in 1790,
'This week was committed to our gaol, William Wooldridge

229

for lopping, defacing and spoiling some oak timber, in the Holt forest.'[84]

By the 1820s prosecutions by summary jurisdiction were frequent but trivial compared with the major conflicts of forest communities previously.[85] The bitterness which remained at the steady denial of the right can be seen in a tale recorded in the mid-nineteenth century in Wiltshire. The Wiltshire antiquary, F. Carrington, in a short note on stocks in Wiltshire recorded that 'Before 1830 the stocks at Ogbourne St. George were opposite the Rectory yard gates, and about 1780 Mrs. Charlotte Mills recollected a woman named Mary Smith being charged by Capt. Rudman of the Woodlands (Mildenhall) with taking wood from his hedge – a man named Hollick swore against her that she took the wood from a hedge in what is now one of Mrs. Banning's meadows. She was taken to Swindon and brought back almost frozen with cold – her clothes were taken off at Peck Cottage and she was whipped at these stocks . . .'[86] Mrs Mills related this account to Carrington in 1852, some seventy years after the event, yet the bitter memory of it still remained in the community. The Rudman family were also active in convicting woodstealers from Bishopstone in Wiltshire during the 1740s.[87]

Some inhabitants of Wiltshire retained the belief that wood could be gathered by right for fuel, and that only a nominal punishment could be inflicted. In 1806 at the Hilary Sessions in Salisbury, one John Aust was indicted 'for cropping and spoiling timber trees in the night time, and was liable for transportation for seven years'. However, the prosecution begged for a lenient sentence as 'he wished merely to undeceive the lower order of people, who fancied that for such offences only a small fine could be inflicted'. Aust was imprisoned for six months.[88] The warning does not seem to have been received, for in 1812 one John Gay was transported for seven years for 'cutting down and destroying a maiden oak tree'.[89]

The taking of wood was a long and persistent custom throughout the eighteenth and early-nineteenth centuries among Hampshire woodland communites and the poor in general in other areas, and was rooted in the context of late-medieval and early-modern manorial custom, sometimes crystallised in writtern charter and thereby recorded. As legal sanctions steadily changed to accommodate new attitudes to property and to the relationship between landowners and tenants or local inhabitants and also new attitudes to the cultivation and management of timber plantation, so this customary claim came under attack and, despite several rearguard actions, was extinguished. Around Fonthill and Great Ridge Woods in Wiltshire, the poor had been accustomed to taking wood, but by the end of the nineteenth century this right was extinguished. W.H. Hudson noted that 'when the wood began to be more strictly preserved for sporting purposes, the rabbits were allowed to increase excessively and during the hard winters they attacked the hazel trees, gnawing off the bark, until . . . [they were] well nigh extirpated. By and by pheasants as well as rabbits were strictly preserved and the firewood gatherers were excluded altogether.'[90]

John Clare was aware that the change in attitude towards gatherers of wood was part of an overall transition from the ordering of relationships in what might be called customary society (that is, where there was a balance between the claims and rights of the lesser members of the community, and the duties and responsibilities of the leading members in reciprocal relationship) to a new form of social order, in which the prime importance was placed upon contract, the cash nexus and where responsiveness to market forces played the major role. In this transition, the denial of the right to take wood for fuel was really the last vestige of these claims and rights. In his poem 'The Parish: A Satire' he wrote of the 'last refuge – which is now denied' of the poor in gathering fuel.

> Born with the changes time and chance doth bring,
> A shadow reigns, yclept a woodland king,
> Enthroned mid thorns and briers, a clownish wight,
> My Lord's chief woodman in his title's height.
> The bugbear devil of the boys is he,
> Who once for swine picked acorns 'neath the tree,
> And starving terror of the village brood
> Who gleaned their scraps of fuel from the wood;
> When parish charity was vainly tried

'Twas their last refuge – which is now denied.
Small hurt was done by such intrusions there,
Claiming the rotten as their harmless share,
Which might be thought in reason's candid eye
As sent by providence for such supply;
But Turks imperial of the woodland bough
Forbid their trespass in such trifles now,
Threatening the dithering wretch that hence proceeds
With jail and whipping for his shameless deeds,
Well pleased to bid their feeble hopes decay,
Driving them empty from the woods away,
Cheating scant comfort of its pilfered blaze,
That doubtless warmed him in his beggar days.
Thus knaves in office love to show their power
And unoffending helplessness devour,
Sure on the weak to give their fury vent
Where there's no strength injustice to resent;
As dogs let loose on harmless flocks at night,
Such feel no mercy where they fear no bite.[91]

A small triumph was achieved at Great Wishford, St Briavels, and probably elsewhere. Wishford preserved its rights to gather wood by continuing to practise the annual ceremony of dancing to Salisbury and affirming its rights in the shout, before the altar, of 'Grovely, Grovely and all Grovely'. By transferring the ceremony to the more officially approved Oak Apple Day, 29 May, the rights were preserved, albeit in a truncated form. There were times when the lords of the manor, the Pembrokes, nearly succeeded in extinguishing them but in 1894 the Oak Apple Club was founded to protect and promote them. Even today the inhabitants gather fuel all the year round and on Oak Apple Day process round the village carrying a banner, very much like a trade union banner, proudly proclaiming, 'Grovely, Grovely, Grovely and all Grovely – Unity is Strength.'[92]

The following events occurred later in the nineteenth century at the Beaminster Petty Sessions:

George Rowe and John Lane, labourers of Thorncombe, the former a married man, were summoned for stealing some pieces of timber valued at 1s. 6d. on the 8th of

February at Thorncombe, the property of Captain Bragge, who retired from the Bench during the hearing of the case – P.C. Pike stated that on the 8th of February he saw the two defendents with a cross cut saw sawing a tree which had been blown down and was lying in a field belonging to Captain Bragge. They cut off two pieces, one of which he produced.

- the Chairman: 'Do you know what they were going to do with it?'
- P.C. Pike: 'Burn it, sir, I believe; they said so.'
- the Chairman: 'Because if they were going to use it for any other purpose it would make the case more serious.'

Rowe admitted the offence and said he acted through want. He had four small children, and had been working all the winter for 10 shillings a week on which the whole family had to live. Both defendents pleaded guilty and were each fined 10s. including costs; 14 days allowed for payment.[93]

Notes

1   John Evelyn, *Sylva: or a Discourse on Forest-Trees and the Propagation of Timber in His Majesties Dominions* (London, 1670), p. 206.
2   See J.S. Cockburn (ed.), *Crime in England, 1550-1800* (London, 1977), see particularly essays by A.D.J. Macfarlane, M.J. Ingram, R.W. Malcolmson, P.B. Munshe.
3   See Douglas Hay *et al.*, *Albion's Fatal Tree: Crime and Society in Eighteenth Century England* (London, 1975).
4   See E.P. Thompson, *Whigs and Hunters: The origins of the Black Act* (London, 1975).
5   Hay, *Albion's Fatal Tree*, pp. 119-66, 'Sussex Smugglers', Cal Winslow.
6   *The Annual Hampshire Repository*, vol. I, 1799-1800, p. 9.
7   For an examination of the bandit as hero and, in particular, Robin Hood, see E.J. Hobsbawm, *Social Bandits* (London, 1972), pp. 41-56. See also J.G. Rule 'Social Crime in the Rural South in the Eighteenth and Early Nineteenth Centuries'. *Southern History*, vol. I, 1979, pp. 140-2.
8   William Marshall, *The Review and Abstract of the County Reports*

to the Board of Agriculture, vol. V: *Southern and Peninsular Departments* (York, 1818), p. 317, quoting: Charles Vancouver, *Report to the Board of Agriculture on Hampshire* (1808), p. 389.

9   *The Sum of the Ancient Customs belonging to Wishford and Barford out of the Forest of Grovely*, printed by Reverend E.H. Steele in a pamphlet entitled: *The History of Oak Apple Day in Wishford Magna* (Salisbury, 1951), p. 9.

10 Ibid.

11 Ibid., p. 10.

12 Ibid., p. 13.

13 *Notes and Queries*, 3rd series (vol. xii), p. 42.

14 *Oxfordshire Archaeological Society Reports for 1903* (Oxford, 1903), p. 31.

15 The custom at St Briavels is kept up to this day, as is the custom at Great Wishford. See chapter 1 for details.

16 *The History of Oak Apple Day in Wishford Magna*, p. 15.

17 *Sylva*, pp. 206-7.

18 Northbrook's *Treatise Against Dicing* (1577) quoted in John Brand's *Observations on Popular Antiquities* (London, 1813), vol. I, p. 194.

19 Thomas Hall, *Funebriae Florae, the Downfall of May Games* (1660), quoted in Brand, *Observations*, vol. I, p. 200.

20 E.M. Leather, *The Folk-lore of Herefordshire* (London, 1912), p. 18.

21 *Transactions of the Woolhope Naturalists Field Club*, vol. I, (1924), p. 82.

22 See the examples on Oak Apple Day quoted in chapter 3.

23 Marx, *Works*, Vol. I, pp. 233-4. See also J. Ditton, 'Perks, Pilferage and the Fiddle: The Historical Structure of Invisible Wages', *Theory and Society*, vol. 4, pp. 39-71.

24 Sir Frederick Eden, *The State of the Poor* (London, 1797), vol. III, p. 797.

25 For riots against enclosure of Royal Forests see *Calendar of State Papers Domestic. 1631-33*. For Braydon riots see p. 67 and p. 74.

26 See Records of Star Chamber Cases Trin. II. Charles I 1633 PRO Sta.Cha. 9: 'A case of riotous destroying of Inclosures in the forest of Braydon.'

27 15.Chas. II C. 2: 'An Act for the Punishment of unlawful cutting or stealing or spoiling of wood and underwood and destroyers of young trees.'

28 Parliamentary Papers Report from the Select Committee on the Game Laws 1845, Pt. I. Qus. 448-54.

29 Hampshire Record Office. 'Minutes of Proceedings of Quarter Sessions QMP/2. Easter Sessions 1784 F.226. For a full discussion of the Black Act see E.P. Thompson, *Whigs and Hunters*.

30 15. Chas.II. C. 2.

31 6.Geo.III.C.48. 'An Act for the better preservation of Timber Trees and of woods and underwoods; and for the further preservation of Roots, Shrubs and Plants.'

32 Cockburn, *Crime in England*, p. 128.
33 6.Geo.III. C.48, f. 1.
34 Ibid.
35 13.Geo.III. C.33.
36 9.Geo.III. C.41.
37 6.Geo.III. C.36.
38 *Hampshire County Magazine*, October 1787, No. XXII, vol. I. p. 341.
39 *Hampshire Chronicle*, 13 August 1792.
40 Ibid.
41 See Winchester College Muniments (WCM) F6667.
42 Winchester College Minute Book. F.33. Entry for 3 December 1794.
43 WCM F6667.
44 *The Annual Hampshire Repository*, vol. I, 1799–1800, p. 98.
45 WCM Bursar's Account Book 1787–99. *Custos Necessariorum Cum Domis*. 1st Qut. 'Expenses of 17s. 8d. two men who gave information, relative to some wood stealers at Eling.'
46 WCM F6667.
47 Ibid.
48 Ibid.
49 Ibid.
50 Ibid.
51 Ibid.
52 Ibid.
53 *Hampshire Chronicle*, 21 January 1793.
54 WCM 6291 a–c.
55 *Annual Hampshire Repository*, vol. I, p. 98.
56 Ibid.
57 Ibid.
58 Ibid.
59 *Annual Hampshire Repository*, vol. I, pp. 98–9.
60 Ibid.
61 Ibid.
62 William Cobbett, *The Woodlands* (London, 1825), Preface, Item 5.
63 WCM 6671. An Act was passed in 1810 for the enclosure of the Manors of Eling and Fowley.
64 An Appendix of statistical information of the parish of Eling attached to *Statements Relative to the Pauperism of Kirriemuir, Forfarshire, from 1814 to 1825*, by Reverend Thomas Easton (Forfar, 1825), pp. 181–2.
65 *Hampshire Chronicle*, 18 March 1776.
66 Ibid.
67 Ibid.
68 Ibid.
69 Ibid.
70 *Hampshire Chronicle*, 30 September 1776.
71 *Hampshire Chronicle*, 7 October 1776.
72 *Hampshire Chronicle*, 27 April 1778.

73   *Hampshire Chronicle*, 14 June 1773.
74   *Hampshire Chronicle*, 11 January 1790.
75   Gilbert White, *The Natural History of Selborne* (Everyman Edn., London, 1912), p. 27.
76   *Journals of the House of Commons*, XLV 1790. *6th Report of the Land Revenue Commissioners.* Appendix No. 17, p. 126.
77   Ibid.
78   Ibid. Appendix 18, p. 126.
79   Ibid. Appendix 19, p. 126.
80   Ibid.
81   Ibid.
82   *Report from the Select Committee on the Rate of Agricultural Wages*, 1824, vol. VI, p. 456. Thomas Smart had been employed at Eversholt, Bedfordshire for 20 years. He had been married for 28 years and had 13 children. He also informed the Select Committee that he received no additional wages during the harvest period, except his food for that month. This fact illustrates that the custom of paying additional wages during harvest, the traditional farm labourer' perquisite, was not practised in that part of Bedfordshire. One form of perquisite was called a Bavin which was a faggot tied with two bands and was a hedge-cutter's perquisite. See A.E. Baker, *Glossary of Northamptonshire Words and Phrases* (London, 1854), p. 36.
83   *Hampshire Chronicle*, 2 June 1794. It should be noted that no bills were found against the accused which might show that the custom was still potent. (See *H.C.*, 4 August 1794.)
84   Ibid., 22 March 1790.
85   See the account of wood-stealing at Greens Norton in 1790 in the unpublished Ph.D. thesis for University of Warwick (1977) by Dr Jeanette M. Hay, née Neeson: 'Common Right and Enclosure: Northamptonshire 1720–1800', pp. 62–70.
86   Devizes Museum. Headquarters of the Wiltshire Archaeological and Natural History Society. Manuscript note books of F.A. Carrington, Ref: 39, Folio 89.
87   See the Summary Conviction Records for Wood Theft. Wiltshire Record Office.
88   *County of Wiltshire. Fisherton Gaol. Statistics of Crime, from 1801–1850.* Compiled by the Governor of the County Gaol, William Dowding (Salisbury, 1855), 1806 Hilary Sessions (c).
89   Ibid. 1812 Hilary Sessions (b).
90   W.H. Hudson, *A Shepherd's Life* (London, 1910; reprinted 1981), pp. 158–9.
91   John Clare, *Selected Poems*, ed. J.W. Tibble and Anne Tibble (London, 1976), p. 166.
92   The shout raised by the villagers in Salisbury Cathedral, and during the pre-dawn perambulation of Great Wishford prior to the visit to Grovely Forest, and the words depicted on the Club banner, give 'Grovely' three times whereas the Charter only specifies twice. This has probably resulted from a combining of

the cry relative to Great Wishford with that of Barford St Martin where the Charter specifies three shouts of Grovely. See R.W. Bushaway, 'Grovely, Grovely, Grovely, and All Grovely: Custom, Crime and Conflict in the English Woodland during the Eighteenth and Nineteenth Centuries', *History Today*, May 1981.

93 *Bridport News*, 11 March 1881. Rowe and Lane used a saw to cut off the wood and this made their conviction inevitable. However, the tree had blown down and was clearly no longer growing timber. Such acts of providence were regarded by villagers as customary windfalls in the same way that coastal dwellers regarded wreck as having no right of property. Fallen timber was the flotsam and jetsam of the countryside. Legal practice sought to define all wood as property.

7 The Control of Custom

Mayday is sometimes all that is lovely and genial, when the children and their flowers are all that their ideal should be . . . In the South . . . it has often dwindled to small children wandering about with an untidy bunch of king-cups and cuckoo flowers at the end of a stick, quavering shrilly out:—

> 'April's gone
> May's come,
> Come and see our garland;'

and halfpence being thrown out till the stock of them and of patience was exhausted, and the whole affair discouraged.

We have found the best way in our parts to be to sanction the whole school going together under some efficient guardian with one general money-box, the proceeds of which, when divided, have always proved more satisfactory than those of individual effort; or, at one parish, all is spent in a general tea, which, of course, gives delight. We also encourage the best garlands with a special prize, and this promotes the keeping of them beautiful. Last year a child named Violet had a small garland, a circlet entirely made of the snake violet from the copse. After it had made its rounds, it was set upon her brother's grave.

Charlotte Yonge[1]

Charlotte Yonge, the novelist, died in the same year as Queen Victoria. She was seventy-eight and had lived all her life in Hampshire. Her comments on the ceremonies associated with Mayday illustrate the transformation of popular customs in general. Her account encapsulates much of the attitude of the Victorian middle class towards popular customary activity and has an aspect of sentimentality verging on the morbid which would have been sympathetically received by her readership. One of her works, first published in 1892, consisted of a monthly record, mainly of events in the natural calendar, of Otterbourne. But it also provided her with opportunities for some reflection on social conditions. She comments, after a lengthy description of changing fashions among the poor, that her life had seen a general 'improvement in the welfare of the poor'. January, however, was still regarded as 'the worst month . . . for work, especially for the brickmakers, who are numerous'.[2] It is interesting to note the similarity between her attitude, particularly with regard to references to the poor, and that of a previous Hampshire writer on the natural calendar - Gilbert White. In both the writing of White and Yonge the poor intrude and disturb the picture of natural life in the countryside.

In Yonge's account, the ceremonies of Mayday were deliberately transformed to accord more with prevailing Victorian taste and ideas of social behaviour. The Ruskinesque image of little schoolchildren or young girls carrying delicate May garlands under the kindly supervision of an adult was a popular one, well known in Victorian art.[3] This image bore little relationship to the earlier more robust customs which had been consistently suppressed and discouraged, but had its origins in the moral perceptions of the Victorian middle class.

The attack on popular customs in the nineteenth century was not a new phenomenon. William Howitt could write in 1840 that 'The Country had passed through deep baptisms and processes of fermentation which have worked out the lighter external characters, and totally reorganised the moral as well as the political constitution of the Kingdom.'[4] Howitt saw the general trend towards 'improvement' both in social and political terms, as the main cause in the decline of popular festivals and festivities. 'What a revolution of taste', he wrote, 'has taken place in the English people . . . The times, and the spirit of the times, are changed: - we are become a sober people. England is no longer merry England, but busy England; England full of wealth and poverty - extravagance and care. There has been no small lamentation over this change; and many of our writers have laboured hard to bring us once more to adopt this state of things. They might as well attempt to bring back jousts and tourneys, popery, and government without representation.'[5] Howitt thought that the causes of the reaction in English society against popular customs were 'Mighty and many'.[6] He did not accept, as had been argued by Sir Edward Bulwer,[7] that Methodism was the principal reason for this change. For Howitt the transformation had begun with the Reformation when 'The people saw they had been treated as children; but they now awoke to the passions and conscious power of men.'[8] This discovery led on to puritanism when 'singing gave way to preaching and listening; dancing, to running anxiously to know the fate of sufferers, and the doctrines of fresh-springing teachers.'[9] The attempt at the Restoration to revive merry England inevitably failed. 'Charles II, indeed, could revive licentiousness, but he could not bring back the holiday guise of "the old profession".'[10] For Howitt, 'the more our humble classes come to taste of the pleasures of books and intellect, and the deep fireside affections which grow out of the growth of heart and mind, the less charms will the outward forms of rejoicing have for them.'[11]

The American writer, Washington Irving, wrote of Christmas festivals in more sentimental terms in 1820: 'The squire went on to lament the deplorable decay of the games and amusements which were once prevalent . . . among the lower orders, and countenanced by the higher; when the old halls of the castles and manor-houses were thrown open at daylight; when the tables were covered with brawn, and beef, and humming ale; when the harp and the carol resounded all day long, and when rich and poor were alike welcome to enter and make merry.'[12] It is not important for the study of nineteenth-century custom whether this image was an historically accurate one, but it is an essential image in the romantic attitude towards custom which was popular with many who sought to restore the simplicity of those customs, and the relationship between rich and poor which was supposed to have generated them. Irving continued, rather unhistorically: 'The nation . . . is altered; we have almost lost our simple true-hearted peasantry. They have broken asunder from the higher classes, and seem to think their interests are separate. They have become too knowing, and begin to read newspapers, listen to ale house politicians, and talk of reform.'[13] He offered the following remedy, in the words of his squire-host, 'I think one mode to keep them in good-humour in these hard times would be for the nobility and gentry to pass more time on their estates, mingle more among the country people, and set the merry old English games going again.'[14] Irving's squire believed that the old sports of 'Merry England' bound labourer and lord together and asserted that 'They made the times merrier, and kinder and better'.[15] Yet the squire's social experiment in restoring open house at Christmas met with less than total success. Irving wrote:

> he had once attempted to put his doctrine in practice, and a few years before had kept open house during the holidays in the old style. The country people, however, did not understand how to play their parts in the scene of hospitality; many uncouth circumstances occurred; the manor was overrun by all the vagrants of the country, and more beggars drawn into the neighbourhood in one week than the parish officers could get rid of in a year. Since then he had contented himself with inviting the decent part of the neighbouring peasantry to call at the hall on Christmas day, and with distributing beef, and bread, and ale, among the poor, that they might make merry in their own dwellings.[16]

This account of the aim and ultimate failure of the squire's experiment is important for an understanding of the prevailing attitude to custom in nineteenth-century England. A sense of role, or at least, the adoption of a passive one by the labouring poor in the face of the benevolence of the rural elite, was a main feature of the middle-class attitude to popular customs. The failure to restore the deferential image of supposed former customs and the resort to mere charity in which the poor were kept at a distance, at home, underlies much of the Victorian attitude to popular custom. The attack on popular customs arose not merely from a negative motive of suppression but also from a positive attempt to construct or recreate an image of rural society in which relations between the classes took the comforting form of deference and paternalism rather than the 'new' forms of antagonism and conflict. The fact that this image was un-historical was not important. Suppression of the vulgar and offensive elements of custom was seen as improving and as necessary if the sanctity of power and property was to be safeguarded. The purging and remodelling of popular customs during the Victorian period was the central feature of this image.

A similar process can already be seen in the late-eighteenth century. John Byng wrote in 1784 that he 'attended to a troop of Morrice dancers headed by the buffoon; but to me, their mummery appear'd tedious, and as little enjoyed by the performers, as the spectators: the genius of the nation does not take this turn'.[17] Malcolmson has described the attack particularly upon popular recreations during the eighteenth and early-nineteenth centuries.[18] Popular custom, however, retained remarkable resilience and it was not until the mid-nineteenth century that successful attempts to suppress or remodel many of the large set-piece customary occasions were effective.

One of the most important ways in which popular custom was assailed was by the increasing denial of access to customary locations and venues. Enclosure, as has been seen, affected the very components of a particular place and could, as with Rogation week perambulations, cause dislocations to the form and even undermine the annual custom itself. Denial of access could be effective when enforced either by the local clergyman or, later in the nineteenth century, by the police. Alfred Williams thought of Wiltshire and Berkshire village life in the later Victorian period when he wrote,

> The villagers blame the police regulations for the extinction of the old festivities, by prohibiting all concourse in the streets and open spaces, and driving the feasters and revellers into far-off fields and obscure corners, they brought about the death of the old fairs and amusements. In many cases the village clergy took a leading part in smashing up the old games, without increasing their congregations, however; it is common knowledge that the churches in country places are barer and emptier than ever before.[19]

The custom of the bread and cheese scambling at St Briavels in the Forest of Dean was transformed in this way. Up to

1857 the scrambling took place within the body of the church, but after that date, it was first transferred to the churchyard and then to the road adjacent to the churchyard. The rough treatment of the clergyman cited earlier doubtless caused the modification of the ceremony.[20]

In Shropshire, at Ashford Carbonel a sustained attempt was made by the local lord of the manor to prevent the use of the village green for the annual May sports on Oak Apple day. Charlotte Burne chronicled this use of litigation:

> So far back as 1846 the Lord of the manor brought an action against the villagers for trespass and damage done on this occasion, but they so fully established their right to the use of the green on two days of the year, that he abandoned the action and paid the costs. In 1864 his successor commenced proceedings on the same account, but he also found it best voluntarily to withdraw from the case, and to admit the rights of the villagers. Yet a third attempt was made in 1874, this time by a Lady of the manor, who on the 16th December of that year sued some of the parishioners in the County Court at Ludlow for trespass and damage. The Judge decided that there was a valid custom authorising the inhabitants to erect a May-pole on the plaintiff's land, and to dance about the same, and otherwise to enjoy any lawful and innocent recreation, and he gave judgement for the defendants with costs: a decision which was hailed with loud cheers by an eager company of Ashford folk who were waiting outside the Guildhall. The plaintiff, not satisfied, appealed to the Court of Exchequer in November 1875, but her appeal was dismissed.[21]

This remarkable series of events illustrates that the most determined and sustained opposition could fail, even when the instruments of threat included the intimidating mechanism of litigation. Charlotte Burne went on to observe:

> The inhabitants . . . take care to exercise their right to the use of the green, both on the 29th of May and the other "lawful" day – Whit Monday, when the whole village turns out to dance there. They also light a bonfire there on the

5th of November . . . and on the marriage of one of the former questioners of their rights, a sheep was roasted, and fireworks were displayed there.[22]

It is perhaps significant that two of the three calendar occasions mentioned in Burne's account were dates which reflected the pattern of state services. The successful defence of the villagers' rights against litigation arose to some extent from a change in attitude on the part of some of the middle class brought about by the foundation, by Lord Eversley, in 1865 of the Commons Preservation Society. In some cases, judgements were found in favour of groups of local people for specific seasonal access to greens – for example, in the case of Mounsey against Ismay in 1863, confirming the rights of the freemen and citizens of Carlisle to hold horse-races over the close of Kingsmoor on Ascension day.[23] Denial of access to customary venues in the rural community was matched by parallel developments in towns. One of the most interesting examples of such denial was that of the suppression of the activities of Leicester's Whipping Toms, cited earlier. An Act of Parliament – the Leicester Improvement Act – which was given the Royal Assent on 18 June 1846 contained a clause specifically prohibiting the annual pass of arms established by the Whipping Toms. It is worth quoting this clause at length.

> Whereas a certain custom or practice called 'Whipping Toms' has for many years existed in a public place called the Newarke, in the said borough, on Shrove Tuesday, which has caused large numbers of people to assemble there, who, by the sport there carried on, occasion great noise and inconvenience, not only to persons residing in the Newarke, but to the inhabitants of the said borough generally, by preventing persons not engaged in the said sports from passing along the said place without subjecting themselves to the payment of money, which is demanded of them to escape being whipped: Be it therefore enacted, That from and after the passing of this Act the said custom or practice called Whipping Toms shall be and the same is hereby declared to be unlawful and in case any person or persons shall on Shrove Tuesday in any year after the

passing of this Act, play at Whipping Toms, Shindy, football, or any other game on any part of the . . . Newarke, or stand, or be in the said place with any whip, stick, or other instrument for the purpose of playing thereat, he or they shall forfeit or pay for every such offence any sum not exceeding the sum of five pounds, to be recovered in like manner as other penalties created by this Act; and it shall be lawful for any police constable or peace officer of the said borough without any warrant whatsoever to seize and apprehend any person offending as aforesaid, and forthwith to convey him before any justice of the peace, in order to his conviction for the said offence.[24]

The mere prohibition of the custom was not enough. On Shrove Tuesday 1847 a great number of labourers, with the Whipping Toms, assembled in the Newarke. After a struggle, the Newarke was cleared by the police and the main protagonists were arrested. It is noteworthy that a correspondent to William Hone wrote of the same custom as it took place in the 1820s as 'a scene of gaiety and humour to which the young look forward with considerable animation' and as 'a scene of considerable mirth'.[25] Some twenty years had seen moral attitudes transform Whipping Toms from harmless but boisterous youths to offensive and violent offenders against the law. The defence of custom had been consciously destroyed by special legislation so that the 'improvement' of Leicester – both physical and moral – could proceed untrammelled.

This transformation can be dated reasonably precisely to the middle decades of the nineteenth century. In a period of some twenty years attempts were made to suppress several of the larger, set-piece customary occasions. The bull-running at Stamford was put down in 1840.[26] Ashbourne's Shrovetide football was opposed in 1821, 1858 and 1860–2, after which agreement was reached that the annual game could continue only if it was removed from the market place to a location outside the town itself.[27] Shrovetide football was successfully suppressed altogether at Derby in 1847.[28] Unsuccessful attempts were made to oppose the Bonfire Boys at Lewes in 1841, 1846 and 1847.[29] In Oxfordshire, at Woodeaton the Good Friday custom of distributing loaves to each household

was extinguished by the trustee in 1854.[30] The elaborate
garland procession at Charlton-on-Otmoor was abandoned
after 1863[31] and the lamb ale at Kirtlington – a Whit Monday
custom involving morris dancing and the election of a kind of
May Queen known as the Lady of the Lamb – was suppressed
in 1858.[32] Captain Dover's Cotswold Games, held annually
on Dover's Hill in Gloucestershire, was celebrated for the last
time in Whit week of 1852, after enclosures of the surrounding fields left the area of land fenced in.[33] This cessation
would not have dismayed some of the inhabitants of Weston
Sub Edge who favoured the disappearance of the old open
fields and with them the Cotswold Games. One later writer
recorded of the Games that

> On the whole, the folk of Campden and the Wolds were
> wise in keeping the Industrial Revolution at arm's length.
> They must have seen it at its worst. To have the scum and
> refuse of the nearest great factory towns shot annually
> into Campden for a week's camping in tents on Dover's
> Hill, two or three thousand at a time, with unlimited beer
> from unlimited booths and hooligans of the type of Tantia-
> topee; to have Kingcomb Lane a whistling Pandemonium
> of roughs and the pleasant valleys of Saintbury and Weston
> tramped by armed bands of Birmingham yahoos was not a
> thing to be desired.[34]

The disruption of Arcadia by urban barbarians must have
created a moral panic equivalent to that caused by modern
Bank Holiday visitations to seaside towns by the variety of
present-day youth factions. The Cotswold games transcended
the specifically local festival and had become an annual
attraction for a wide region.

A similar objection was made about the St Briavels bread
and cheese dole which attracted 'the roughs of the forest . . .
to come over', and which caused the transformation of the
custom, removing the distribution, in 1857, from the church
to the churchyard and subsequently to the road adjacent to
the Church.[35]

The last 'scouring of the White Horse' of Uffington occurred in 1857. The festivities which had accompanied the
cleaning of the chalk figure every seven years included the

usual country sports and attracted large numbers of people. In 1892 the horse was scoured again but without the festivities. A member of the Berkshire, Buckinghamshire and Oxfordshire Archaeological Society wrote that 'The historic "White Horse" . . . has recently undergone another scouring, by order of Lady Craven. The lover of ancient customs would have been glad to see the revival of the ancient rural festival which formerly accompanied the scouring, but in these days of enlightenment such a revival would probably be impossible.'[36] Alfred Williams could write, in the early-twentieth century, that 'The scouring of the White Horse, which used to be the occasion of much festivity and mirth, proceeds on different lines nowadays . . . whatever cleansing and renovation is needed now is carried out privately by the workmen of the estate . . .'[37]

It is significant that the middle decades of the nineteenth century also saw the abolition of the state services of the Church of England. With the exception of the Accession service, the last celebration of the state services took place in 1858. In 1859, by royal warrant, the services used on the day of the commemoration of the execution of Charles I, the restoration of Charles II, and the gunpowder plot were abolished. The reasons for this included the increasing sense among churchmen that the services were not of a religious nature at all and that, in the case of the gunpowder plot, the state service was objectionable to Roman Catholics.[38] For popular customs, the abolition of the state services was a further undermining of their legitimacy.

The opposition of key individuals was also a crucial factor in the destruction of the customary calendar. In particular the role of local clergymen in opposing popular customs or in withdrawing their support conditioned, in an immediate way, certain customary activities, significantly those which had occurred within the ecclesiastical calendar or which had previously required the sanction of the church. George Eliot could write of a reforming clergyman:

> until it can be proved that hatred is a better thing for a soul than love, I must believe that Mr Irwine's influence in his parish was a more wholesome one than that of the zealous Mr Ryde, who came there twenty years afterwards,

when Mr Irwine had been gathered to his fathers. It is true, My Ryde insisted strongly on the doctrines of the Reformation, visited his Flock a great deal in their own homes, and was severe in rebuking the aberrations of the flesh – put a stop, indeed, to the Christmas rounds of the church singers, as promoting drunkeness, and too light a handling of sacred things. But I gathered from Adam Bede, to whom I talked of these matters in his old age, that few clergymen could be less successful in winning the hearts of their parishioners than Mr Ryde.[39]

As Eliot's hero Adam Bede pointed out, suppression of the church singers – something of which Woodforde would not have conceived in an earlier period – went hand in hand with a whole pattern of new attitudes. Mr Ryde 'was sourish-tempered, and was for beating down prices with the people as worked for him; and his preaching wouldn't go down well with that sauce. And he wanted to be like my lord judge i' the parish, punishing folks for doing wrong; and he scolded 'em from the pulpit as if he'd been a Ranter and yet he couldn't abide the Dissenters'.[40]

The attitude of the local clergyman to the labouring poor had an economic importance as well in the maintenance of customary rights. Alexander Somerville pointed out in the 1840s that attendance at church was the condition attached to the continuation of certain customary dues. ' "But, good friends",' he wrote ' "you surely do not always come out of the church with such bitter feelings towards the preacher? Why do you go at all?" "Why do we go?" said the woman. "We must, if we do not want to lose everything, work and all, we must." I learned later that they had certain little privileges of fire-wood and potato land (which they paid for!) on condition of going to church.'[41]

Customary activities associated with the ecclesiastical calendar were increasingly opposed in the nineteenth century. Cecil Torr's grandfather wrote in 1847 that 'The church singers by their inveteracy have rather disturbed the neighbourhood both Friday night and last night. (They used to bring the church bass-viol and violin and flute) I order them not to come near, but unfortunately I am surrounded by a road, and they will pass near me! which the dogs notice.'[42] Yet, despite his opposition to the church singers, he continued the custom of providing his labourers with a Christmas dinner. 'The men were here yesterday: (Christmas day) goose and plum pudding as usual. Bob had the key of the cider cellar and was butler; so, depend on it, there was no lack of cider. However they all left in good order.'[43]

Occasionally the direct intervention of a local clergyman had the effect of extinguishing a particular local custom. For example, the Venerable Henry Moore, vicar of Eccleshall (Staffordshire) suppressed the local bull-baiting in the 1830s. One commentator recorded:

> He rushed into the bull ring in his cassock and gown, seized the huge mall, which they had used to knock in the stake, loosed the bull, with the words, 'I am going to put a stop to this cruelty,' and then had to look to himself. He was surrounded by a crowd of roughs, who tore his gown off his back, and otherwise maltreated him until he was rescued by more sensible parishioners. This was the last bull-fight at Eccleshall. And Mr Moore followed up his action on the next day – Sunday. Seeing one or two of the ringleaders in Church, he told them plainly of their conduct and cruelty from the pulpit.[44]

In other instances, the form of intervention was less vulnerable to direct personal attack. At Didsbury, Lancashire, according to one writer, the annual rush cart ceremony in early August 'was continued until the Rev. W. Kidd came to Didsbury as incumbent when it was discontinued on account of the objections urged by that and other gentlemen in the parish.'[45] The custom had been previously described, in 1825, as 'always well regulated' and an event at which 'the display of youths of both sexes, vieing with each other in dress and fashion, as well as cheerful and blooming faces, is not exceeded by any similar event – and the gaieties of each day are succeeded by the evening parties fantastically tripping through the innocent relaxation of countrydances, wakes etc.'[46] Clearly, the Rev W. Kidd did not regard Didsbury wakes, which was held over a three-day period, as 'innocent relaxation' or as 'always well regulated'. For him, to be well regulated, the wakes needed to be extinguished.

A century earlier, when a West Country clergyman had sought to control the excesses of a local parish wake he had been charged before the Episcopal Consistorial Court with neglect of duty by his own churchwardens. The Rev. Samuel May, in 1765, had attempted to regulate Revel Sunday in his parish and to remove the 'fightings, bloodshed, drunkenness and riot' which regularly accompanied the service on that day. He was found guilty by the Consistorial court and was ordered to pay costs.[47] In this case, custom supported the activities of the local parishioners and the opposition of the local clergyman could not prevail. At Didsbury, the position was reversed. Custom had been undermined. A correspondent to William Hone could refer to an account of a rush-burning in the 1830s in which the reform of behaviour had already been accomplished: 'The vain custom of excessive drinking, dancing etc, having been laid aside, the inhabitants [of Warton] and strangers, spend that day in duly attending the service of the church, and making good cheer within the rules of sobriety in private houses.'[48] The regulation of behaviour at the annual rush-bearing was not known at the end of the eighteenth century as Samuel Bamford's famous account of Middleton Wakes testifies.[49] After Bamford's childhood, the church had merely withdrawn support, no longer permitting the rushes to be delivered to the church and to be strewn on the floor.[50]

Direct opposition to some popular customs was not always successful, even when initiated by the local clergyman. At Hallaton, in Leicestershire, the annual 'bottle kicking' – a kind of football – is played annually to the present day. This sport takes place on Easter Monday and was supported by rents from a piece of land known as 'Hare-Crop Leys'. In 1790 when the parish clergyman attempted to use for more benevolent purposes the funds which supported the custom, and from which hare pies were provided as well as beer for the 'bottles', he was met with strong opposition from his parishioners.[51] It was said that some of them chalked a warning on his walls, 'No pie, no parson, and a job for the glazier'.[52] Much later, in 1878, a further attempt to redirect the funds was made and this was again defeated. A correspondent to the *Leicester Journal* in 1892, wrote: 'parish meetings were held, to consider the desirability of taking the money and appropriating it to sports of other kinds, and more in character with the tastes of the age; many of the inhabitants, however, wishing to retain the old custom, the proposal fell through.'[53]

The intervention of the police or other agents of the local authorities was a frequent means used in the suppression of customary events. This became more common with the establishment of a rural police force after Chadwick's Report of 1839. At Whittlesey, in Cambridgeshire, the annual appearance of 'straw bears' on the Tuesday after Plough Monday was put down by local police intervention.

An account of 1909 recorded that 'two years ago [1907] a zealous inspector of police had forbidden "straw-bears" as a form of cadging, and my informant said that he thought in many places they had been stopped by the police. He also said that at Whittlesey the police had prevented the people on Plough Monday from taking round the plough, as they always did when I was a boy. It seems a great pity that primitive customs should be suppressed by Bumbledom.'[54] As has been seen elsewhere, the operations of the adherents of Plough Monday were attacked earlier in the nineteenth century as the form of behaviour embodied such strong elements of conflict. In 1821, Plough Monday customary activity was condemned, as one writer noted: 'It gave me great pleasure at the last Quarter Sessions at Kirton to hear from the Chairman that the magistrates have determined to visit with exemplary severity the misconduct of persons who appear as Morris-dancers, or Plough Bullocks, or under other names of a similar character'.[55]

The police could not always be sure of success, especially when large numbers of people were involved. Folk football at Nuneaton continued into the later decades of the nineteenth century, In 1881 Everard Home Coleman wrote:

The ancient custom of playing at football in the public streets was observed at Nuneaton on the afternoon of March 1st. During the morning a number of labourers canvassed the town for subscriptions and between one and two o'clock the ball was started, hundreds of roughs assembling and kicking it through the streets. The police attempted to stop the game, but were somewhat roughly handled.[56]

Shrovetide street football had been a source of concern for town authorities at an early date. In 1799, the Home Secretary received correspondence about an affray which had broken out at Kingston as a result of the playing of Shrove Tuesday football.[57] As well as embodying obvious violent elements – it was not unknown in the medieval and early modern period for deaths to occur[58] – football often showed solidarity among the labouring poor. At West Haddon, Northamptonshire, in 1765, a football game was used as a cover for an anti-enclosure riot.[59] At Atherstone in Warwickshire, where Shrovetide football still takes place, links with the poorest and most disadvantaged members of the community were made during the course of play, when the ball was kicked into the precincts of the workhouse, so that the inmates could participate, albeit briefly and within the confines of the yard.[60] The police continue to play a crucial role in limiting the range and length of time of the Atherstone game and, at the conclusion of the play, intervene to bring a stop to the event.[61]

The attempts to extinguish the Lewes bonfire custom of 5 November were amongst the most sustained. As has been seen already, the Guy Fawkes night celebrations in the Sussex town had attracted considerable opposition during the late-eighteenth century. In 1841, police action resulted in the prohibition of the more alarming fire displays – tar-barrels and fire balls.[62] An attempt to move the custom from the streets of Lewes to a location elsewhere was strongly opposed in 1846. The magistrates made a concerted effort to suppress the commemoration in 1847. In one account, written some time after the event, it was recorded that 'At mid-day a hundred men of the A Division of the Metropolitan Police came into Lewes, and, at dusk, were formed up in front of the County Hall . . . Eight o'clock came, and the crowd had greatly increased . . . Lord Chester promptly read the Riot Act . . . only a few of the more timid attempted to depart, and . . . the police were commanded to charge the multitude. By these means the streets were cleared, but in the melee many Metropolitan constables were seriously hurt.' In 1853, the Bonfire Boys established an organisation based on local societies, to promote and defend the custom.[63]

Simple withdrawal of economic support lay at the root of the control of some nineteenth-century popular customs. In other cases, local financial support was lacking in the first place. Alfred Williams, writing about village brass bands, commented: 'There is a brass band in the village [Uffington] the members of which are farm workmen – ploughmen and foggers – and the conducter is carter at a farm under the downs. These hold their practices at the school in the evenings, but call themselves "The Kingstone Lisle Band", because, as the old carter says: "Ther's nob'dy yer to support a band, the fawks got nothin' to gie, tha be too poor; us want gentry to kip us again".'[64]

The withdrawal of support for charitable customs and calendar doles was also marked during the nineteenth century. The activities of the Charity Commissioners in the early decades of that century served to bring into question any charitable distribution or dole for which, although there might be evidence of customary legitimacy, no documentary evidence could be discovered. This attitude was particularly strengthened in cases where a history of conflict over a certain customary right could be discovered.

This process can be observed in the experience of the inhabitants of Drayton Beauchamp, in Buckinghamshire. It was customary in the village for the labouring poor to go 'a-stephening' on Boxing Day. This practice was well-established by the end of the eighteenth century. The poor visited the rectory on 26 December and claimed an annual right to partake of as much bread and cheese and ale as they chose, at the rector's expense. According to local tradition, one rector of the late-eighteenth century, renowned for his meanness, determined to resist the claim. On St Stephen's day he bolted the door and locked the shutters in an attempt to prevent the crowd gaining access to the rectory. Not to be so easily disappointed, they removed some slates from the roof, and broke in to open the door to the rest of the poor waiting outside. The crowd then proceeded to the larder and ransacked it unchecked. In the early-nineteenth century, the

Reverend Basil Wood decided that the custom occasioned too much drunken and riotous behaviour and therefore distributed an annual sum, in lieu of food and drink, in proportion to the number of claimants. By 1827, even this proved too expensive and so he ceased the annual distribution completely. It was reported to the Commissioners that the poor continued to go to the rectory on St Stephen's day but were turned away empty handed. In 1834, consequent upon the Charity Commissioners' enquiry, the legitimacy of the claim was examined. They concluded that 'Nothing is known concerning the origin or duration of this usage, nor was any evidence produced showing any legal obligation on the part of the rector to continue the . . . practice.' As a result of this decision, the custom was totally extinguished.[65] It is possible that 'Stephening' at Drayton Beauchamp merely formed part of the local customary calendar and should be viewed as one of several non-institutional folk charities, such as the widespread practice of claiming Christmas boxes on Boxing day, when the poor claimed a customary dole as of right. Yet there is evidence to suggest that this was more than a non-institutional charity.

The parishioners of Clifton Reynes in Buckinghamshire claimed a similar right. The Charity Commissioners reported:

In the Parliamentary Returns of 1786, some land, then let as 12ℓ. per annum, is stated to have been given by Sir Hugh Kite for the poor of this parish. It appears from a book in the custody of the minister, entitled 'Some Account of Clifton Reynes, in the county of Bucks.' dated 1821, which was compiled by a Mr Edward Cooke, late of Amersham, an antiquary, for a history of the county, not yet published, that the rector holds a close of pasture ground called Kite's, which had been formerly given to support a lamp burning in the church of Clifton Reynes, but which was subject to a charge of finding one small loaf, a piece of cheese and a pint of ale to every married person, and half a pint for every unmarried person resident in Clifton, on the feast of St-Stephen, (the rector by immemorial custom retaining the residue for his own use,) when they walked the parish boundaries in Rogation week.[66]

The report continues:

> The Parliamentary Return of 1786 confirms the above
> account. In the month of January a distribution is made
> by the rector to all parishioners of this parish. Each person
> receives a twopenny loaf, a piece of cheese and a pint of
> ale, if married, and half a pint if single. No perambulation
> has taken place for above 20 years. A note in the Parlia-
> mentary Return states the custom to be to treat inhabit-
> ants, sick and poor, on procession to settle the boundaries
> of parishes. Kite's close is arable and contains about 16
> acres. It is let to Thomas Lineham as yearly tenant, at a
> rent of 12ℓ. per annum. The cost of finding the above
> provision is about 6ℓ.[67]

From the above account, it is clear that half the annual rent
was not put to the use of the poor but was kept by the parish
rector for his own use. This custom, not altogether dissimilar
to that of Drayton Beauchamp, was well enough defined in
legal terms to be admitted by the Commissioners. It would
seem that, even if Drayton's custom had a similar foundation,
the behaviour of the parishioners or the activities of a past
rector had militated against its continuance, the disputes
which occurred overshadowing the legitimacy of the claim to
the extent that no memory of the origins could be produced
sufficient to satisfy the Commissioners.

It was not uncommon for cases of deliberate abuse or
negligence on the part of trustees, in many charities often the
local clergyman, to come to the attention of the Commissioners. For example, at Castlethorpe in Buckinghamshire,
the Commissioners noted with regard to the Poor's Allotment
that 'nothing it is believed has been received by the poor in
respect of this charity since 1826, as extensive repairs of the
church have been effected since that period'.[68] In this case,
recorded in 1834, the charity provided for the maintenance
of the poor and of the church fabric. The local clergyman
had clearly favoured church restoration. The mode of distribution, and the accuracy of the record kept, was, in many
cases, the responsibility of the local clergyman. In some
cases, possibly including Drayton Beauchamp, legitimate
rights to charity had either deliberately or inadvertently

255

been abrogated.

In some cases the Charity Commissioners themselves mis-applied charities. At Bovey, according to Torr, 'Two fields . . . are called the Portreve's Parkes: a Tracey gave them to this Bovey (Bovey Tracey) as endowment for a banquet at the beating of the bounds. But the Charity Commissioners have flouted the pious donor's wishes, and the rents are now applied to praiseworthy prosaic purposes. Till these Commissioners came the bounders all rode horses decked with ribbons and flowers, and it was called the mayor's riding. And now we all trudge round on foot, and are reduced to ginger-beer and buns.'[69] Abuse can be charted in other instances. In one Norfolk parish (Pentney), for example, in the last decades of the nineteenth century, the local customary charities had almost disappeared. One inhabitant recalled:

> The parish where I was born had a great lot of Common land enclosed. The money for the rents of these Commons was supposed to go to the Parishioners in the shape of coals at Christmas time, but every year it kept getting lower and lower. It happened one day that a friend of mine came across the History of the charities of Norfolk in a very old book. I had a look at it and found by that book there were a lot of things to do with the village lands and monies that the People did not know about or had forgot. As I have said the People of the seventies and the Fore part of the eighties were very ignorant, and the Upper Classes led them where they liked – In that way a lot of the old rights and customs had died out.[70]

Upon further investigation he learnt that a memory of these charities was preserved in the parish: 'some would say "I have heard my father talk about them things." '[71] He requested that the local clergyman should hold a vestry meeting at night and not at eleven o'clock in the morning as was usual so that all the parishioners could attend. He stated at the outset of the meeting that the parishioners 'wanted to know where those lost charities were gone to and what had become of the money'.[72] The local clergyman and gentleman farmers had brought along a lawyer who argued that these customary charities had been lost in the past through default and could

not now be restored. Three separate charities were referred
to, all of which involved distributions or other benefits to the
poor. The villager concluded in his account that 'the lawyer
blustered and threatened and all that, and said he would have
the Poor Law Commissioners down and that if they did come
the parish would have to pay them. Be that as it may, the
next year when the time came round, the Dole coal come to
a ton, and the blankets and all the other things were given to
the very old people in the village as had been meant by those
as had left the money.'[73] He also recalled that extensive
repairs were carried out to the local Alms Houses. After this
meeting, he 'got a letter one day to tell me that they would
get me a free passage to Canada if I would like to go. But I
was not to be driven out of my country by any of them'.[74]
If it is accepted that this account is authentic, and there is
no reason to doubt it, then it is a remarkable record of how
a series of local customary rights were saved from extinction
through the spirited action of one independent-minded
parishioner.

Many of the ritual calendar doles were also opposed. In
some cases, such independent behaviour was looked upon
with displeasure by the local farmers and proprietors. The
Christmas visits of local mummers were not well supported
by the end of the nineteenth century and many of the bands
had disappeared. Mummers plays, offering as they did an
opportunity for horseplay and general affronts to social
status, were discouraged. Cecil Goddard recalled of his Wiltshire childhood that 'Mummers gradually ceased to come
round at Christmas. It was one of the delights to see the
saracen run through with a sword of ash-wood and fall flat on
his back on the stone floor of the vicarage kitchen.'[75] Their
performance was not always greeted sympathetically. One
account of a mummers play at Calne, Wiltshire, in 1885
noted that 'the play ended by an appeal for gifts (with at
that time a scornful allusion to old farmer Woodward who
was so stingy)'.[76] This kind of behaviour was increasingly
opposed.

In towns the collection of Christmas boxes by tradesmen
and others was discouraged during the nineteenth century.
At Southampton in 1825 it was observed that 'Although
Christmas boxes are on the wane in this vicinity yet the

257

donations to the poor from the neighbouring gentry have this week been very numerous and liberal.'[77] Charity, upon condition, and to the deserving poor was given as the donor was able to discriminate. In the same year, it was recorded that, at Bremhill, on Christmas Day 'the Rev. W.L. Bowles gave a dinner of old English fare to 400 of his parishioners. Doubtless, these parishioners were well-chosen and could be described as 'deserving'. Also, one Stephen Mills 'made a liberal Christmas benefaction to the poor. He had ordered fifteen fat sheep to be distributed amongst the poor of his immediate neighbourhood; and five fat sheep have been given by Mrs Mills to the poor of East Street in this city [Salisbury.]' Topping up of local benefit club distributions was common. At Wylie, in Wiltshire, 'a distribution was made at the Parsonage House . . . of different articles, according to the choice and much to the satisfaction of the industrious penny-subscribers to the club of that parish, suggested and greatly assisted by the benevolence of the Right. Hon. Earl of Pembroke.'[78] Customary charitable collections which were beyond the control of local dignitaries were suppressed. At Bridport in 1880, a notice was published that 'In consequence of the increased competition in Trade the Grocers of Bridport and neighbourhood have unanimously agreed to discontinue the practice of giving Christmas Boxes.'[79] At Trowbridge, in 1925, a similar, though longer prohibition from the local tradesmen was published. The notice argued that 'The practice appearing to be an increasing and injurious evil to the Trade, without being a subject of much value to the receiver', it was resolved 'respectfully to give notice . . . that they will in future discontinue the custom of giving Christmas Boxes in any form whatever.' In order to prevent abuse, an agreement was made between the grocers to levy five pounds for any infringement.[80] Most charitable doles were distributed only among the deserving poor, that is, those 'poor' who had not become chargeable to the parish rate during the year, and who were regular attenders at church. William Cobbett was critical of the major Hampshire landowner, for providing charity with conditions. He wrote that Sir Thomas Baring:

and also Lady Baring are very charitable; that they are very
kind and compassionate to their poor neighbours; but that
they tack a sort of condition to this charity; that they
insist upon the objects of it adopting their notions with
regard to religion; or, at least, that where the people are
not what they deem pious, they are not objects of their
benevolence . . . Amongst the labouring people, the first
thing you have to look after is, common honesty, speaking
the truth, and refraining from thieving; and to secure
these, the labourer must have his belly-full and be free
from fear; and this belly-full must come to him from out
of his wages, and not from benevolence of any description
. . . I think Sir Thomas Baring would do better . . . by
using the influence which he must naturally have in the
neighbourhood, to prevent a diminution in the wages of
labour.[81]

The collection of folk charities did not allow those who
donated to influence the recipient. Therefore, in the interests
of social control, such customary collections were suppressed
either directly or by the withdrawal of support.

In many cases, the dates chosen for the distribution of
formal charities reflected the customary calendar. At Chiche-
ley, Buckinghamshire, Mansill's gift, a rent-charge of £2.12s
was disbursed to the poor. The Charity Commissioners noted
that 'It is regularly paid to the vicar by instalments of 20s
and 30s, on Good Friday and St. Thomas's Day in every
year, and by him distributed, in shares of 1s each, to poor
persons selected by him. The objects chosen are chiefly
widows and widowers of good character belonging to the
parish and in the receipt of parish relief.'[82] There was confusion, in some instances, between formal charitable distributions and folk charities as in the following example from
Piddle-Hinton, Dorset. 'There is an ancient custom for the
rector to give away; on old Christmas day, annually a pound
of bread, a pint of ale and a mince pie, to every poor person
in the parish. This distribution is regularly made by the
present rector to upwards of 300 people.'[83] Whether this
was a folk charity or an institutionalised charity, the terms
of which had been forgotten, cannot be deduced. It is probable that the custom's relationship to an important date

in the community's calendar contributed, by way of legitimation, to its maintenance.

Opposition to a particular custom sometimes led to its transformation rather than to its extinction. In the example of Whit feasts or wakes this was particularly discernible. The activities of Whit parish revels, involving rough rustic sports, were challenged at an early date by Puritanism in the seventeenth century and Methodism in the eighteenth. Yet, as Howitt observed, Whitsuntide was 'the only ancient religious festival that has become a popular one since the Reformation, through the addition of a modern circumstance. Clubs, or friendly societies, have substituted for the old church ceremonies, a strong motive to asemble in the early days of this week as their anniversary.'[84] At Whit, or sometimes on Easter Monday, local village friendly societies paraded round the village, carrying banners. These parades gained in popularity during the nineteenth century. In the Wiltshire village of Pewsey, one inhabitant described the Whit Monday club day in the following terms: 'At Whitsuntide the friendly clubs were in their glory. On Whit-Monday the old club, with its dark red and purple ribbons, and the pretty old flags, had the first turn; and on Whit-Tuesday the new club had its innings. This was an innovation and its formation had given rise to much bitterness and illwill. The members of this club wore blue and white ribbon rosettes, and had the gayest purple flags.'[85] The Whit-Monday club walking provided a suitable occasion for display and local rivalry – as in this case where two clubs existed. Borrowing elements from other, older customary activities, such as parish perambulations and the older Whitsuntide feasts, the club day was often described as the most important event in the customary calendar during the nineteenth century.[86] Although not specifically involving the local gentry, the club day required their passive support, as Mrs Haughton made clear when describing the enmity which existed between the two Pewsey clubs. 'However, we of course had nothing to do with all that. We were considered to have fulfilled our part, if we attended the service specially given for them, and made their own by a sermon appropriate to the occasion, and were ready to receive the club when in the course of the afternoon we were honoured by a visit from it, attended by its band.'[87] These visits, based upon models of earlier perambulation and largess collection customs, embodied elements of social cohesion. They were attended with much pomp and ceremony. Mrs Haughton continued: 'the great event of the day to us as children, was when the band, preceded by the standard-bearers, and followed by all the members of the club bearing long wands, with the colours of the club tied to the top, entered the garden, and arranged themselves . . . before the house door.' The band then played many tunes, culminating with 'God save the Queen' and, 'After a few kind words of thanks to them for coming, they all marched round the ring in the same order they had entered, and we heard the band till the evening, as the club visited the farmers and chief people of the village.'[88] The Reverend Skinner took the playing of the national anthem as a direct affront. He wrote in 1829: 'The Camerton Club marched today, in number about 1,400. They played "God Save the King" as they passed the Parsonage.'[89] Clearly not in favour of the activities of the club day, he noted, on a visit to Weston whilst the club day was taking place, that the village had 'nothing at all to recommend it as to external appearance, and the noise and rioting of the club by no means added to its agreeableness just now'.[90] The preaching of a Club Day sermon by the local clergyman was a common feature of the custom for which he expected payment from club funds.[91]

Why should the activities of the Whit-Monday club day supplant older festivities? Partially because, as Richard Jefferies noted, it was sponsored by the local farmers who were in favour of the thrifty self-help of benefit clubs. He wrote that 'The club and fete threaten, indeed, to supplant the feast altogether – the friendly society having been taken under the patronage of the higher ranks of residents.'[92] It was this patronage, and its indirect support for the excesses committed on some club days, which was attacked by critics of the benefit clubs. 'The sharing-out club', wrote Reverend J.Y. Stratton in 1870, 'is the offspring of the beerhouse and the union, and is nourished and maintained by those who, in the long run, whether landowners or labourers, have small cause for congratulation.'[93] Stratton cited an estimate, which he thought too high, of 100,000 as the number of benefit clubs in the country.[94] He recorded, with disapproval, the activities of club members on the club day: 'On Whit-Monday or Easter Monday', he wrote:

> the village is enlivened by flags and banners, and the sign of the Black Bear [the motif of the club he cited] is entwined with garlands, and my specimens, good, bad, and indifferent, may be seen mustering in front of the inn in their Sunday clothes, with sashes and scarves, behind the band which is to 'play them' to church. The strong box is carried by the treasurer and two or three wands and baubles dignified by the outlandish name of 'regalia' are distributed into the custody of the stewards, and away they go to the church, where the vicar says the prayers, and preaches an appropriate sermon . . . In asmuch as the public act of worship is often times regarded by the managers and members merely as a means of consolidating and strengthening the position of the club, caution is needed in opening the church for special service and sermon. And not only by the prostitution of divine service, but by the attendance of the clergyman of the parish, and other influential parishioners at the dinner, and by their subscriptions, support is too commonly afforded which is in no way merited.

He opposed friendly societies which were not organised along sound financial lines. He concluded that 'where moral and pecuniary aid are given to a pauperising sharing-out club, evil is done, however excellent the intentions of those who bestow it.'[95] In Stratton's criticisms can be discovered the social functions of the club walk to the labouring poor. It provided a substitute for older customary festivals which was, in many cases, legitimated both by church and local landowners and farmers. The occasion afforded an opportunity for public display and public merriment, which reaffirmed an image of the corporate community based upon the commensal features of food and drink, contributed to by the upper ranks of village society. As early as 1797, Eden noted of the rules of one village friendly society, Stapleton in Gloucestershire, that 'of 46 articles, 15 or 16 relate to eating and drinking. The order of the annual feast is set down with as much precision as the ordinances of a royal household.'96 A sense of the ceremonial importance of the annual club day can be gained from these articles:

> 30. That all and every member of this Society shall attend at the house where the society is held, on the morning of the feast day, in due time, to walk in procession to hear divine service, except sickness, lameness, or being at a distance of 20 miles, on the forfeiture of 1s or be excluded.

> 31. If any member refuses to follow the procession to hear divine service, hides himself, or stays behind, not keeping his rank when commanded by the stewards, he shall forfeit 1s for every such offence, or be excluded.

> 32. If any member behaves himself disorderly going to church or returning from the same, to any member of members of another society, by pushing his stick at them, cursing or guiling at them, or challenging them to fight, or do strike any or either of them, he shall forfeit the sum of 2s 6d or be excluded.[97]

The procession, the use of willow wands and garlands, the wearing of best clothes and the general feasting were all elements of the older Whitsuntide custom. Thomas Hardy used a 'club walking' – in this case a women's club – as the occasion for the introduction of Tess Durbeyfield in his famous novel. He wrote that 'In addition to the distinction of a white frock, every woman and girl carried in her right hand a peeled willow wand, and in her left a bunch of white flowers. The peeling of the former, and the selection of the latter, had been an operation of personal care.'[98] William Howitt, conscious also of the older Whitsuntide elements in the club feast, wrote, in romantic form, of other motives behind the custom: 'Well then may they come together on one certain day or days throughout the country, to hold a feast of fellowship and mutual congratulation in a common hope. Their wealthier neighbours have encouraged them in this bond of union and mutual help, and have become honorary members of their clubs. It is a friendly and Christian act.'[99]

Attempts to control some customs led to their transformation. Whitsun ales were translated, in the nineteenth century, into club walkings. Yet behaviour at the club feast day, and imprudent control of the financial aspects of some benefit clubs, in turn, led to opposition from the more respectable members of the village community. Charlotte Yonge could write of the club day – an occasion already passing by 1896:

> of the ecstasy it used to be to see the Whit-Monday procession of the village club when . . . the club "walked" as it was technically called. Each member carried a blue staff tipped with red, and had a blue ribbon round his tall hat, and almost all wore the old white round frock. The big drum was beaten lustily at their head . . . all the rabble rout of the village stepped after them, and it was certainly a picturesque specimen of genuine village sports, perhaps the more so because the procession was, at the best, straggling and knock-kneed and often unsteady . . . And oh! the odour of the church – a mixture of beery and tobaccoey human nature together with that of the fading young greenery of infant beech and large boughs with which, even in these days, Whitsuntide decoration was kept up.

She concluded that it 'was a melancholy affair after all. The investment was anything but a safe one. The meetings for payment were at the public-house, and involved cups of beer each time.'[100] Attempts were made, she wrote, to encourage the labourers to purchase government securities as a more reliable form of investment. But these attempts had not been successful because government securities did not hold the attraction of the club walking. 'At the present time', she added (i.e. 1897), 'the prudent are divided between the Foresters, who . . . keep their great day with green banners and ribbons, in great numbers generally at the county town, and the county friendly society, whose carefully calculated tables they have become better able to appreciate, and which affords them a holiday, band, procession, and feast, much more decorous and civilised than their grandfathers would have relished.'[101]

One form of social control was the conscious attempt to

remodel and revive some forms of customary behaviour to comply with a middle-class image of respectability and to promote middle-class values. This was particularly marked after the middle of the nineteenth century. Simple repression was replaced with more subtle reformation. Bourgeois culture annexed and moulded much of the older customary framework for its own ends.

The older style harvest homes or sheep-shearing suppers had almost disappeared by the last three decades of the nineteenth century. Earlier in the century, commentators had already noted their decline. William Barnes wrote that the 'Harvest-home, formerly celebrated with great mirth but now a declining usage, was a feast given by the farmer, at the end of the harvest.'[102] By the 1870s this process was almost complete. J.S. Udal, writing of Barnes's Dorset, in 1873 spoke of an 'old-fashioned' harvest home as something of note. He also suggested that a transformation had taken place regarding the end of harvest celebrations.

> It was my good fortune [he informed his readers], to be present in September last at one of those old-fashioned gatherings in the West of Dorset – a harvest-home, and I thought that perhaps an account of such a quaint and time-honoured custom might not be unacceptable . . . especially as these congenial meetings are becoming scarcer year by year, and ere long bid fair to rank amongst the things that have been. Small sums of money are now, in many places, given to the men, women and boys, instead of the usual supper, a practice that I am sorry to say seems to be on the increase, and which I here offer my voice to protest against . . . At the time of such a general holiday in the parish, the labourers of one farm do not seem willing to disperse quietly to their own homes and husband the few shillings they may have received as 'largess' whilst their fellows are enjoying themselves on another farm, but rather to keep up a harvest-home of their own in the village ale-house, though . . . not of so orderly a character as that of the bona fide supper, and which . . . they themselves much prefer.[103]

It could be written of this period that 'Such was formerly the method of conducting the harvest-feast, and in some instances it is still conducted much in the same manner, but there is a growing tendency in the present day, to abolish this method and substitute in its place a general harvest-feast for the whole parish, to which all the farmers are expected to contribute, and which their labourers may freely attend.'[104] These parish harvest thanksgivings were usually conducted under the auspices of the local clergyman and involved attendance at a special religious service. One critic of this form of harvest home wrote that 'It provides no particular means for attaching the labourers to their respective masters . . . The hospitality of the old-fashioned harvest-supper . . . was a bond of union between the farmer and his work-people of inestimable value.'[105] He concluded that the harvest thanksgiving was of value in itself but should not be regarded as a social substitute for the old harvest home.

It is easy to gain an impression of the new form of harvest home which was instituted in many places after the middle of the nineteenth century. Respectable and morally sound, accounts of these festivals were readily afforded space in the paragraphs of local newspapers. One such was celebrated in 1890 at the parishes of Popham and Woodmancote, Hampshire. The report began that the 'harvest in gathering was celebrated here with great heartiness, and in a very thorough and pleasant manner'. The festival began with a special service for the combined parishes at four o'clock at Popham church, the preacher being the Dean of Winchester. The report described the church as being 'very beautifully decorated with an abundance of lovely flowers, fruit, etc by the Misses Pain, Saul, Allen, and Godwin, the cottagers having so liberally offered of their best that three large hampers of fruit and vegetables were afterwards sent to the Royal Hampshire County Hospital at Winchester.' The report stated that the *customary* harvest hymns were sung with Mrs Edith Godwin providing the accompaniment on the harmonium. The Dean preached a sermon on the text (Ruth,ii,4): 'And behold, Boaz came from Bethlehem, and said unto the reapers, the Lord be with you. And they answered him, the Lord bless thee.' The newspaper account observed:

The church was crowded to excess. After the service the congregation adjourned to the vicarage grounds, by invitation of the vicar, the Rev. G N Godwin, until tea was ready, which was served in the schoolroom. This part of the proceedings was largely attended, a very small charge being made for adults and childred admitted free, through the kindness of the vicar. When the tables had been cleared, a magic lantern lecture on 'Pictures of our Country' was given by the vicar, illustrated by capital views, which, it need hardly be said, were much enjoyed. Altogether, the whole festival was a great success.[106]

The Reverend Godwin was keen on such controlled revivals and similar occasions took place on the dedication of a new fence and gates for the church, and at the conclusion of the hay harvest.[107] The practice spread by example, and similar activities were reported at East Boldre where 'The decorations of this church at the harvest festival were very beautiful and effective. There are 143 houses in the parish, and from nearly or quite 50 of these came offerings of fruit, flowers and vegetables, a pleasant proof of union and goodwill.' A sermon was also preached on the text of 'Giving thanks always for all things' (Ephesians, v, 20). The Rev. W. Perrin pointed out in his sermon 'the duty of thankfulness under the most trying circumstances, and urging his hearers to show their gratitude for their beautifully restored church by attending the services more regularly, more especially for Holy Communion'.[108] The reformation of the local customary calendar at Woodmancote and Popham was completed with generous distribution of food to the workmen and their families at Christmas. During the same period 'Surgeon-Major Lane, who rents the shooting over the Manor farm, Woodmancote, has lately made a liberal distribution of rabbits to the men employed upon the farm. Mr King, of the Manor Farm, gave all his workmen a large piece of beef at Christmas, as did Mr Charles Pain, of West Farm, Popham.'[109] These Christmas distributions were not carried out in response to a demand for the fulfilment of customary right, but as conscious processes which aimed to establish a paternal social hierarchy in which deference was required from the labouring poor. In itself this was not new, but in the context of an entirely reformed local calendar it was novel. Merry England was also deferential England in the opinion of Victorian farmers, landowners and rural clergymen.

The point of transformation from the customary harvest home, claimed as part of the harvest contract, to the harvest festival well depicted in the cited accounts of Popham and Woodmancote, can be identified reasonably precisely. One commentator believed that the origin of the harvest thanksgiving was to be found in the West Country:

> The West Country is undoubtedly entitled to the credit of having instituted the harvest thanksgiving service, now [1904] almost universal in Protestant places of worship. Sixty years ago . . . the Rev. George Denison, the vicar of East Brent, Somerset, held special services to celebrate the ingathering of the fruits of the earth, and in the same year [1843] . . . the Rev. R.S. Hawker, vicar of Morwenstowe, Cornwall, began similar services. Dean Alford's 'Come, ye thankful people, come,' without which no harvest festival is now complete, was first printed in 1844, and as the Dean was a Somerset man, it is very probable that he wrote the hymn for the service at East Brent.

The writer continued by citing Royal legitimation for the custom of decorating churches with flowers and fruit which became widespread after the general thanksgiving ordered by Victoria in council in 1854.[110]

It is not altogether unlikely that the harvest thanksgiving service did originate at a precise time and location as the writer suggested. Other similarly restructured harvest festivals took place during the same year.[111] The East Brent festival took on gargantuan proportions as can be seen from the following description in a letter dated 15 September 1883 from Archdeacon Denison:

> Harvest Home great success . . . the people indefatigable as soon as huge tents had been got up in rain set to work. Vicarage and village to decorate; great work of high art; all complete by mid-day, Tuesday. From early morning Tuesday up to today, Saturday weather perfect . . . large company. Took £43 at gate; subscriptions £68; £113 in

all; will pay all expenses and leave some balance. Wonderful Punch, steam merry-go-round, fortune telling, various other amusements; teetotal drinks only; football etc; 1,000 people in tent Tuesday night, 500 Wednesday night; had food over on Tuesday enough for poor parishioners' second meal Wednesday. I think our new plan has saved us £50 or more, and left all more contented than they used to be. Very fine music, dressing in best taste, manners and general demeanour perfect; no doubt an admirable institution; should be witnessed to be comprehended. Dancing from seven to eleven Tuesday night, to twelve Wednesday night; then I told them they were to go. They cheered and thanked, and in ten minutes tent was cleared, and all went away quietly. I am told the merry-go-round man made £20, costing me nothing; Punch cost £1.1s and did not send round plate.[112]

This account is in marked contrast to those of the more unruly customary set-pieces which had continued until mid-century, such as Captain Dover's Cotswold games. Denison reported good behaviour and no alcohol. The form of the harvest thanksgiving at East Brent was repeated in many parishes throughout England, but particularly in the southern counties. It was rare for these proceedings to be on as large a scale as those which Denison described, but the motive and method were the same.

One description of the decoration of the church for the occasion at Farley Hungerford, near Bath, in the 1870s is very elaborate and illustrates that the action of leading parish members was important.

The chancel arch was wreathed with leaves, which terminated in bouquets at the capitals, and on the front of the pulpit was a device of barley, berries and flowers. The piscina, which quite recently has been uncovered at the south-east corner of the nave, afforded space . . . for another bouquet, and altogether the general effect well befitted the occasion of the harvest festival. I cannot forbear to add, that this labour was carried out by Lady Houlton, who lives in a charming cottage near.[113]

The writer proceeded to describe the thanksgiving service which included the singing of 'the grand harvest hymn "We plough the fields and scatter".'[114] The sermon included topical references to 'that scourge, that great agricultural plague which was passing like a flame of fire through the length and breadth of the land', which the clergyman took to be 'a judgement of God for the cruelty of man to what we call the brute creation.'[115] At Cherhill, Wiltshire, a continuous record of harvest thanksgiving suppers in the late-nineteenth century can be recovered, which was terminated by the sale of the principal estate in 1918. A similar pattern of activities, beginning with a church service and ending with dancing during the evening, can be found.[116]

Such reformed harvest homes were not always introduced successfully. At Rownhams, near Southampton, a reformed harvest home was first introduced in September 1863. The following year an invitation to the parishioners was published in the *Parochial Chronicle*: 'Another Harvest is over; once more the crops sent to support and cheer us through the coming year have been for the most part safely carried, and again I invite you to join me in God's House, in giving thanks and praise to Him for His manifold mercies.'[117] Having set out the reasons for thank offerings at the service, the local clergyman, R.F. Wilson, explained that it was also appropriate that feasting should take place:

> But in the Bible, and indeed in the customs of all nations, occasions of common joy and public thanksgiving are usually coupled with Feasting, and therefore I am very glad to be able (through the kind liberality of various members of our congregation) again this year to invite all the labouring population of our parish (excepting those for whom Harvest suppers have been provided separately by their own masters) to a dinner . . . The rest of the day will be kept as a Holiday and I venture to hope and believe that we shall all remember that we begin the day with a Religious Service, and therefore shall be very careful that our subsequent conduct is in accordance with that beginning.[118]

After lengthy details of the church decoration and service,

the account depicts a scene which would have gladdened the heart of Washington Irving or William Howitt. The entrance to the tent was decorated with the motto 'Peace and Plenty' done in the ears of wheat. Mr Wilson, it was recorded, 'told the men that he would trust the beer to their honour, and leave it to their own discretion to take care that they behaved themselves as sober Christian men.'[119] The evening was concluded, after much festivity, with fire-balloons.

In 1865, the Harvest thanksgiving was again held without any incident. However, by 1867 some disorderliness had begun to take place. The Reverend Wilson wrote:

> there is one matter connected with the day's proceedings which was not quite satisfactory . . . The case is this: when a company is asked to an entertainment, those who entertain desire to see all who are asked; but the presence of guests who have not been asked, is a perplexing and disturbing thing . . . The tent is not a Public-house, for any to come to who choose. If it were, we should expect those who come to pay the reckoning. Nor is it intended when a man and his wife are asked by name, that they should bring two or three children besides. This is not fair by those who make provision for the feast, and I mention it, because I wish you to know that it was not our fault if the provisions ran short . . . I believe there were thirty or more at the table who had no invitation . . . we don't want unbidden guests; and if such will thrust themselves in, they must not be surprised if they are thrust out.[120]

In 1868, a thanksgiving service was held in the church but without any festivities afterwards. The Reverend Wilson gave the reasons for this as a withdrawal of support by local farmers and the previous year's disorderliness. He wrote that 'there are now only two of our farmers who wish to join in the Parish entertainment. The others seem to prefer having private suppers for their own men.'[121] Of the disorderliness he recorded that 'after our party broke up, some (I trust not of our own people) adjourned to the Public-house, and kept up a late carouse there. It is hard to get at the truth . . . but your clergyman ought not to be forward in promoting amusement in which there is risk of this sort.'[122] After 1868, the service was maintained but the feast was not revived. The failure of Rownham's labouring poor 'to play their parts', in Washington Irving's terms, is clear. Respectful behaviour was reserved only for the more sober activities of the service. As with Irving's squire, deference did not extend beyond face-to-face contact. At the squire's revival 'two or three of the younger peasants, as they were raising their tankards to their mouths, when the squire's back was turned, making something of a grimace, and giving each other a wink; but the moment they caught my eye they pulled grave faces, and were exceedingly demure'.[123]

More generally, the remodelled custom triumphed. The Reverend Baring-Gould could write in 1889: 'The harvest home is no more. We have instead harvest festivals, tea and cake at sixpence a head in the school-room, and a choral service and a sermon in the church . . . There are no more shearing feasts; what remain are shorn of all their festive character. Instead, we have cottage garden produce shows. The old village "revels" linger on in the most emaciated and expiring semblance of the old feast. The old ballad-seller no longer appears in the fair.'[124] In the words of one of Baring-Gould's singer-informants, Roger Luxton: 'in old times us used to be welcome in every farm-house at all shearing and haysel and harvest feasts; but, bless' Y' now the farmers' d'aters all learn the pianny, and zing nort but twittery sort of pieces that have nether music nor sense in them; and they don't care to hear us, and any decent sort of music. And there be now no more shearing and haysel and harvest feasts. All them things be given up.'[125] Conscious remodelling of the harvest home so that new forms of behaviour were established was seen as proof of general moral improvement. Charlotte Yonge believed, however, that such good intentions could not force the acceptance of these new forms:

> Old-fashioned farmers still give their harvest supper; but the new generation, without mutual hereditary interests between them and the labourers, disregard it. A general harvest feast for the entire parish has been tried; but to make it a success, there should be a thorough element of geniality and enjoyment in the entertainers. If they only do the thing as a duty, it will fall flat, and the company

will look with regret to the ruder pleasures, unrestrained by the gentry.

She noted of the thanksiving service: 'It is a modern invention, but is thoroughly enjoyed by the people, if they are encouraged to make their offerings in kind for the sick in hospitals.'[126]

A process similar to the development of harvest homes can be seen with other central calendar customs. The 1860s saw a revival by the clergy in some areas of the ceremony of parochial perambulations to instill into the labouring poor the message of God, the Provider, and to strengthen social relationships within the parish. Indeed Chambers could refer to the 'Christianising' process at work upon the custom of perambulating the parish.[127] The late-Victorian age was the era for Ruskinesque May-day ceremonies which involved may queens, poles and flowers. Plough Monday festivities disappeared and Plough Sunday services for blessing the plough were established. The refining process was endorsed by William Howitt:

> let them root out cruelty and rudeness and drunkeness, as they have done already in a great degree – for where now are bull-baitings, bear-baitings, dog-fights, and cock-fights, which twenty years ago were the invariable accompaniments and great attractions of these wakes? Let Christian knowledge root out these things, and thus perfect this one white season of the cottager's year – making it entirely an occasion for cultivating the best affections and knitting together family ties.[128]

In the reform of these calendar customs elements of contrived social orderliness were emphasised and disruptive elements were submerged. Remodelled popular customs attained respectability and were afforded a regular place in the social calendar of the more sober members of the community. Earlier in the century a note of regret had already been sounded. One writer noted, on the customs of St Clement's Day in Worcestershire: 'Much has been said of improvements, and the happy state of the present over times past; but on striking the balance, it may be found that the poor have lost much of their solid comfort, for the little improvement they have obtained.'[129] The popular customary calendar had been annexed by the Victorian middle class, purged of its disagreeable features and restored as a respectable medium for the expression of social order within the village community in which concepts of 'Merry England' actually represented a new form of deference. The sense of community solidarity and popular right which had, in the minds of the labouring poor, illuminated much of the popular customary calendar had been replaced by a sense of duty and respect to the village hierarchy. This annexation was not always successfully achieved and an unofficial culture still remained, albeit less publicly displayed.

The disappearance of Christmas singers perambulating the villages of Hampshire by the end of the nineteenth century was charted by Charlotte Yonge. She wrote:

> The shrill thin voices of the children were only ignorantly irreverent but there were parties of boisterous lads or idle men and ignorant, more profane, and sometimes half-tipsy, and on the way to be entirely so. The practice had to be reformed. Picturesqueness is apt not to bear close inspection, and propriety and reverence must be enforced even through primness and a little hard-heartedness. So now the children of a fit age are taught well-chosen carols, and go round under the surveillance of the master and mistress, and the money-box is divided at the end . . . and the children, who do not remember the old days of license, greatly delight in their rounds.

The older villagers were encouraged to join the local church choir.[130] This pattern was repeated in many parishes during the last half of the nineteenth century and the custom, in Yonge's words, was 'reformed'. 'Picturesqueness' gave way to respectable behaviour.

Notes

1   Charlotte M. Yonge, *An Old Woman's Outlook in a Hampshire Village* (London, 1896), pp. 90–1.
2   Ibid., p. 5.
3   See particularly the painting: 'Rushbearing' at Grasmere by Frank Bramely, R.A., or the more famous 'May Morning on Magdalen Tower, Oxford' by William Holman Hunt. See also the painting of 'The May day procession of Queen Eva' by Anna Richards which depicts the Ruskin-inspired festival at Whitelands College, London.
4   William Howitt, *The Rural Life of England* (London, 1841), p. 352.
5   Ibid., p. 351.
6   Ibid., p. 352.
7   Edward George Bulwer, later first Baron Lytton, novelist, playwright and statesman. Bulwer is best remembered as the author of *The Last of the Barons* published in 1847 but in his work *England and the English* published in London in 1833 he cited Methodism as the main cause for the decline in popular festivals.
8   Howitt, *The Rural Life of England*, p. 353.
9   Ibid., p. 354.
10   Ibid., p. 355.
11   Ibid., p. 356.
12   Washington Irving, *The Sketch Book of Geoffrey Crayon Gent* (first published 1920; Cassell Edition, n.d.), p. 240.
13   Ibid.
14   Ibid.
15   Ibid.
16   Ibid., p. 241.
17   F. Harvey-Darton, *English Fabric: A study of Village Life* (London, n.d., probably 1935), p. 205 which quotes *The Torrington Diaries* ed. C.B. Andrews, (London, 1934), vol. I, pp. 124–5.
18   R.W. Malcolmson, *Popular Recreations in English Society, 1700-1850* (Cambridge, 1973), chapters 6 and 7.
19   Alfred Williams, *Villages of the White Horse* (London, 1918), p. 214.
20   E. Sidney Hartland, 'The Whitsuntide Rite at St. Briavels', *Transactions of the Bristol and Gloucestershire Archaeological Society*, 1893–4, vol. 18, p. 83.
21   Charlotte S. Burne, *Shropshire Folklore* (London, 1883; reprinted 1973), p. 366.
22   Ibid., p. 367.
23   Lord Eversley, *Commons, Forests and Footpaths* (London, 1910), p. 282.
24   Quoted in Edwin S. Hartland (ed.), *County Folklore* (London, 1885), vol. I, p. 115.
25   William Hone, *Year Book* (London, 1864), p. 270.
26   See Malcolmson, *Popular Recreations*, pp. 130–3.
27   See Adrian Henstock (ed.), *Early Victorian Country Town: A*

portrait of Ashbourne in the mid 19th century (Ashbourne, 1978), pp. 63-6.

28 Ibid., p. 63.

29 Arthur Beckett, 'Lewes Gunpowder Plot Celebrations', *The Sussex County Magazine*, vol. II, 1928, pp. 487-90.

30 Rev. R.C. Prior, 'Dedications of churches, with some notes of village feasts and old customs in the Deaneries of Islip and Bicester', *Oxfordshire Archaeological Society Reports*, 1903, p. 27.

31 Ibid., p. 23.

32 See Percy Manning, 'Some Oxfordshire Seasonal Festivals: with notes on Morris-dancing in Oxfordshire', *Folklore*, vol. VIII, 1887, pp. 313-16.

33 See Christopher Whitfield, *Robert Dover and the Cotswold Games* (Evesham, 1962), p. 80.

34 C.R. Ashbee, *The Last Records of a Cotswold Community* (Weston, 1904), p. xxiii.

35 E. Sidney Hartland, 'The Whitsuntide Rite at St. Briavels', p. 83.

36 *The Berkshire, Buckinghamshire, Oxfordshire Archaeological Journal*, vol. II, July 1892, p. 174.

37 Alfred Williams, *Villages of the White Horse*, p. 273.

38 See Owen Chadwick, *The Victorian Church Part I* (London, 1971), p. 491.

39 George Eliot, *Adam Bede* (London, 1900), p. 153.

40 Ibid., pp. 153-4.

41 Alexander Somerville, 'One who has whistled at the plough', in the *Morning Chronicle* quoted in F. Engels *The Condition of the Working-Class in England* (1973), p. 305.

42 Cecil Torr, *Small Talk at Wreyland* (London, 1979), vol. II, p. 23. Letter dated 26 December 1847.

43 Ibid., vol. II, p. 10. Letter dated 26 December 1858.

44 Weston E. Vernon Yonge, *Some Bye-Paths of Staffordshire* (Market Drayton, 1911), pp. 104-5.

45 Alfred Burton, *Rush-Bearing* (Manchester, 1891), p. 55. See also E. France and T.F. Woodall, *A New History of Didsbury* (Didsbury, 1976), p. 58, where this event is described as not having taken place before 1870.

46 Hone, *Year Book*, p. 479, quoting *The Stockport Advertiser* for 5 August 1825.

47 For a full account see Arthur Warne, *Church and Society in Eighteenth-century Devon* (Newton Abbot, 1969), pp. 68-9.

48 Hone, *Year Book*, p. 554. The account quoted is from T.D. Whitaker, *A History of Richmondshire in the North Riding of the County of York* (London, 1823), and is contained in a letter to Hone dated 4 May 1831.

49 Samuel Bamford, *Early Days* (London, 1849), pp. 146-55.

50 Ibid., p. 154. He recalled earlier times when the church bells were rung to herald the arrival of the rush cart in the village. He wrote 'but as the rushes are now seldom left at the church,

so neither is the ringing so strictly performed as it was wont to be.'

51 See *Notes and Queries*, Second series, vol. XI, 1915, pp. 320, 407.

52 *Leicestershire Journal*, 22 April 1892. Letter from Mr Thomas Spencer quoted in *County Folklore*, vol. I, p. 79.

53 Ibid.

54 *Folklore*, vol. XX, 1909, p. 202, contribution on 'straw-bear Tuesday' from G.C. Moore Smith.

55 Alex Helm, *The English Mummer's Play* (London, 1980), p. 17. which quotes a correspondent to the *Lincoln, Rutland and Stamford Mercury*, 26 January 1821. The effect of the visits of Plough Bullocks was a dramatic one. As late as 1927 the theme of such a Plough Monday visit was used by the writer, David Garnett. See David Garnett, *Go she must!* (first published 1927; Penguin edition 1939), chapter II, pp. 20–32, called 'Plough Monday', contains a vivid impression of a visit from the Plough Boys. I am grateful to Dr W.R. Jones for drawing this to my attention.

56 *Notes and Queries*, 6th series, vol. III, 1881, p. 207. See also the account in George Morley, *Shakespeare's Greenwood: The Customs of the Country* (London, 1900), pp. 102–3.

57 See PRO HO 42/46 quoted in full in Roy Palmer, *A Touch on the Times* (London, 1974), pp. 126–8.

58 See Norbert Ellis and Eric Dunning, 'Folk football in Medieval and Early Modern Britain' in Eric Dunning, *The Sociology of Sport: A selection of Readings* (London, 1971), pp. 118–9. For the eighteenth century see Burton, *Rush-Bearing*, p. 71 which relates an account of a player being killed in 1745 at Rochdale.

59 See J.W. Anscomb, 'An Eighteenth Century Inclosure and Foot Ball play at West Haddon', *Northamptonshire Past and Present: Journal of the Northamptonshire Record Society*, vol. IV, 1968–9, pp. 175–8. This occurrence was also reported in *The Gentleman's Magazine*, vol. 35, 1975, p. 391: 'The same day a number of people assembled at West Haddon in Northamptonshire, under pretence of football playing; but in an instant formed themselves into a tumultous mob, and pulled up the fences of the new inclosure there, and laid the whole field open. Several of the rioters have since been apprehended, and committed to prison.'

60 Frank N. Punchard, *Survivals of folk football (Great Britain)* (Birmingham, 1928), p. 12: 'During the playing of the ball along the streets it is kicked over the workhouse wall for the inmates to have a few kicks.'

61 As recently as 1980, the local Chief Inspector had to request that players cease play at 5 p.m., as the previous year the Police had spent thirty minutes attempting to break up the concluding scrum. See *Coventry Telegraph*, 13 February 1980.

62 See Beckett, 'Lewes Gunpowder Plot Celebrations', p. 487.

63 See Arthur Beckett, *The Spirit of the Downs* (first published

1909; reprinted London, 1949), pp. 178–80.

64 Williams, *Villages of the White Horse*, p. 279.
65 See the account in R. Chambers (ed.), *The Book of Days* (London, 1888), vol. II, p. 763. See also 27th Report of Charity Comissioners 1834, vol. 21, pp. 83–4.
66 27th Report of Charity Commissioners 1834, vol. 21, p. 133.
67 Ibid., p. 134.
68 Ibid., p. 133.
69 Torr, *Small Talk*, vol. III, p. 15.
70 Lilias Rider Haggard (ed.), *I Walked the Night* (London, 1936), pp. 108–9.
71 Ibid.
72 Iibd.
73 Ibid., p. 110.
74 Ibid., p. 111.
75 'Wiltshire and General: Folklore and Tales. Notes on Beacons, Gibbets, Holy Wells', collected by Cecil V. Goddard, F69, Wiltshire Archaeological and Natural History Society Headquarters, Devizes, Wiltshire.
76 Ibid., f. 89.
77 *Salisbury and Winchester Journal*, 3 January 1825.
78 Ibid. All these accounts appear in the pages of the same edition.
79 *The Bridport News*, 2 January 1880.
80 See Garlick Collection, Trowbridge museum. Notice published at Trowbridge on 12 December 1825 and printed by E. Sweet.
81 William Cobbett, *Rural Rides* (London, Everyman edn., 1912; reprinted 1973), pp. 104–5.
82 Charity Commissioners 27th Report 1834, vol. 21, p. 133.
83 Charity Commissioners 29th Report 1835, vol. 21, p. 108.
84 Howitt, *The Rural Life of England*, p. 375.
85 Mrs Haughton, *In a Wiltshire Valley* (London, 1879), p. 41.
86 Ibid.
87 Ibid., p. 42.
88 Ibid., pp. 42–3.
89 Reverend Skinner, *Journal of a Somersetshire Rector*, ed. Howard Coombs and Reverend A.N. Bax (London, 1930), p. 222. Entry for Thursday, 11 June 1829.
90 Ibid., p. 284. Entry for Monday, 23 July 1832.
91 See Weston E. Vernon Yonge, *Some Bye-Paths*, pp. 114–5.
92 Jefferies *Wild Life*, pp. 109–10.
93 Reverend J.Y. Stratton, 'Farm labourers, their Friendly Societies, and the Poor Law', *Journal of the Royal Agricultural Society of England*, vol. VI, 1870, p. 103. Stratton also refers to the clubs as 'Brummagen Clubs', see p. 99.
94 Ibid., p. 99.
95 Ibid., p. 102.
96 Sir Frederick Eden, *The State of the Poor* (3 vols., 1797), vol. II, p. 210.
97 Ibid., pp. 214–15.

98   Thomas Hardy, *Tess of the d'Urbervilles* (London, 1974), p. 41.
99   Howitt, *The Rural Life*, p. 376.
100 Yonge, *An Old Woman's Outlook*, pp. 97-9.
101 Ibid., p. 100. See also Alun Howkins, 'The Taming of Whitsun in nineteenth century Oxfordshire' in Eileen and Stephen Yeo (eds.), *Popular Culture and Class Conflict 1590-1914: Explorations in the history of labour and leisure* (London, 1981). See also Alun Howkin's earlier work: *Whitsun in 19th century Oxfordshire* (Oxford, 1973), Ruskin College History Workshop Pamphlets, No. 8.
102 Hone, *Year Book*, p. 586.
103 J.S. Udal, 'A Dorsetshire Harvest Home', *Notes and Queries*, 4th series, vol. XII, 1873, p. 491.
104 R. Chambers (ed.), *The Book of Days* (London, 1888), vol. II, p. 380.
105 Ibid.
106 This account can be found in the Hampshire Newspaper Cuttings in the Cope Collection, University of Southampton Library. Cuttings 1883-91 Godwin press cuttings, vol. I, ff 34-5. The report is probably clipped from the *Hampshire Chronicle*.
107 Ibid.
108 Ibid., f. 40.
109 Ibid., f. 41. See also report f. 35.
110 *Somerset County Herald*, September 1904, quoted in W.G. Willis Watson (ed.), *Calendar of Customs* (1920), pp. 340-1.
111 See Willis Watson, *Calendar of Customs*, pp. 341-3.
112 Letter quoted in ibid., pp. 336-7.
113 *The Church Rambler* (London, 1876), pp. 56-7.
114 Ibid., p. 58.
115 Ibid., pp. 59-60.
116 J.H. Blackford, *The Manor and Village of Cherhill: A Wiltshire village from early times to the present day* (1941), p. 259.
117 R.F. Wilson, *Short Notes of Seven Years' Work in a Country Parish* (Oxford and London, 1872), p. 77.
118 Ibid., pp. 78-9.
119 Ibid., p. 82.
120 Ibid., pp. 91-2.
121 Ibid., pp. 94-5.
122 Ibid., p. 95.
123 Washington Irving, *The Sketch Book*, p. 242.
124 S. Baring-Gould, *Old County Life* (London, 1913), p. 177.
125 Ibid., p. 175.
126 Yonge, *An Old Woman's Outlook*, pp. 198-9.
127 Chambers, *The Book of Days*, vol. I, p. 584.
128 Howitt, *The Rural Life of England*, p. 415.
129 Hone, *Everyday Book*, vol. II, p. 789.
130 Yonge, *An Old Woman's Outlook*, pp. 283-4.

APPENDIX 1

The Development of Folklore Studies in England

From Popular Antiquities to Folklore

1586   William Camden (1551-1623): *Britannia* (1st Latin edition), translated and expanded by Edmund Gibson (1695) and Richard Gough (1789).

1598   John Stow (1525-1605): *A Survey of London. Contayning the Originall, Antiquity, Increase, Moderne Estate, and Description of our Citie*.

1607   William Camden, *Remaines of a Greater Worke, concerning Britaine*.

1670s-1680s   Robert Plot, *The Natural History of Oxfordshire* (1677), and *The Natural History of Staffordshire* (1686).

1696   John Aubrey (1626-97): *Miscellanies*. Also published *Natural History and Antiquities of Wiltshire* and *Natural History and Antiquities of Surrey*.

1725   Henry Bourne (1694-1733): *Antiquitates Vulgares: or, The Antiquities of the Common People. Giving an Account of several of their opinions and ceremonies. With proper reflections upon each of them: shewing which may be retain'd and which ought to be laid aside*.

1777   John Brand (1744-1806): *Observations on Popular Antiquities* (an expanded and revised edition of Bourne's *Antiquitates Vulgares*).

1785   Francis Grose (1731-91): *A Classical Dictionary of the Vulgar Tongue*. Also editor and founder of the *Antiquarian Repository: a Miscellany, intended to preserve and illustrate several valuable Remains of Old Times*, vol. I (1775).

1801   Joseph Strutt (1749-1802): *Glig-Gamena Angel-Deod, or the Sports and Pastimes of the*

People of England: including the Rural and Domestic Recreations, May-Games, Mummeries, Pageants, Processions, and Pompous Spectacles, from the earliest period to the present time . . . ('The Father of English Antiquaries', he said of himself: 'My love for my national antiquities is greater than I can express.')

1813   Sir Henry Ellis, *Observations on Popular Antiquities: chiefly illustrating the origin of our Vulgar Customs, Ceremonies and Superstitions.* (Definitive expanded and revised edition of Bourne/Brand.)

Late 18th and early 19th century   Golden age of 'Tours', 'Travels' and 'Descriptions'. This trend began with Daniel Defoe's *A Tour Through the Whole Island of Great Britain* (1724-6). Continued with Gilbert White's *The Natural History and Antiquities of Selborne* (1789); Thomas Pennant's *A Tour in Scotland* (1769); Benjamin Heath Malkin's *The Scenery, Antiquities and Biography of South Wales* (1804).

1825-27   William Hone (1780-1842): bookseller and radical. *Every-Day Book or Everlasting Calendar of Popular Amusements, Sports, Pastimes, Ceremonies, Manners, Customs, and Events.*

1827   William Hone, *The Table-Book.*

1831-32   William Hone, *The Year Book.*

1844   James Halliwell (1820-89): *Popular Rhymes and Nursery Tales.*

1846   Thomas Wright (1810-77): essays on *Subjects connected with the Literature, Popular Superstitions and History of England in the Middle Ages.*

James Halliwell, *The Nursery Rhymes of England.*

William Thoms (1803-85): letter printed in the *Athenaeum* (22 August 1846); coined the term 'folklore'.

1849   Thoms founded *Notes and Queries.*

1859	Thoms's *Choice Notes from 'Notes and Queries': Folklore*.
1863–64	Robert Chambers (1802–71): *The Book of Days*.
1878	Founding of The Folklore Society by 'The Great Team' – Andrew Lang, George Lawrence Gomme, Alfred Nutt, Edwin Hartland, Edward Clodd, William Clouston.
	'Scientific' collection of folk material. Important county studies. Among the most significant are: Charlotte Burne, *Shropshire Folklore* (1883); William Henderson, *Notes on the Folk-lore of the Northern Counties of England and the Borders* (1879 Folklore reprint): Robert Hunt, *Popular Romances of the West of England* (1865): Sydney Addy, *Household Tales with other Traditional Remains Collected: the Counties of York, Lincoln, Derby and Nottingham*; John Udal, *Dorsetshire Folklore* (1922).
1890	George Gomme, *Handbook of Folklore*. Sir James Frazer, *The Golden Bough*.

APPENDIX 2
The Ritual of the Year

A Checklist of Festival Dates

December

24	Christmas Eve
25	Christmas Day
26	St Stephen's or Boxing Day
31	New Year's Eve

January

1	New Year's Day
6	Twelfth Day
closest Sunday to Epiphany	Plough Sunday
Monday after Epiphany	Plough Monday
20	St Agnes's Eve
25	St Paul's Day

February

2	Candlemas
14	St Valentine's Day
Tuesday before Lent	Shrove Tuesday
1st day in Lent	Ash Wednesday
4th Sunday in Lent	Midlent or Mothering Sunday

March

25	Annunciation or Lady Day

April

1	All Fool's Day
Sunday before Easter	Palm Sunday
Friday before Easter	Good Friday
	Easter Sunday
Monday following Easter	Easter Monday
23	St George's Day
30	May Eve or Mischief Night

May

1	May Day
29	Oak Apple Day

2nd Sunday after Easter, & Monday & Tuesday following	Hocktide
5th Sunday after Easter	Rogation Sunday
7th Sunday after Easter	Whit Sunday
Monday following	Whit Monday

June

24	Midsummer Day and St John the Baptist's Day
Rural holidays	⎡ Hay Harvest ⎢ Corn Harvest ⎨ Sheep-shearing ⎢ Apple harvest ⎣ Hop-picking

September

29	Michaelmas Day

October

31	All Hallows' Eve (Hallowe'en)

November

1	All Saints' Day ⎤
2	All Souls' Day ⎥
5	Guy Fawkes Night ⎥ 'Doleing Days'
23	St Clement's Day ⎥
25	St Catherine's Day ⎥
30	St Andrew's Day ⎦

December

6	St Nicholas's Day ⎤ 'Doleing Days'
21	St Thomas's Day ⎦

General Index

Index of Places

ST. PAUL'S SCHOOL LIBRARY
LONSDALE ROAD, SW13 9JT